Professionalism
and Community

To Erica, who always challenges adults to think about
what is right and good in education
(and whose name was misspelled in a recent dedication—
she deserves another shot)
and
Taylor, one great kid, whose brief career in school
has provided his mother with additional fascinating
insights into the world of learning.

Professionalism
and Community

Perspectives on Reforming Urban Schools

Karen Seashore Louis
Sharon D. Kruse
and Associates

CORWIN PRESS, INC.
A Sage Publications Company
Thousand Oaks, California

371
.104
L888p

For information address:

Corwin Press, Inc.
A Sage Publications Company
2455 Teller Road
Thousand Oaks, California 91320

SAGE Publications Ltd.
6 Bonhill Street
London EC2A 4PU
United Kingdom

SAGE Publications India Pvt. Ltd.
M-32 Market
Greater Kailash I
New Delhi 110 048 India

Printed in the United States of America

Library of Congress Cataloging-in-Publication Data

Louis, Karen Seashore.
    Professionalism and community : perspectives on reforming urban schools / authors, Karen Seashore Louis, Sharon D. Kruse.
        p. cm.
    Includes bibliographical references and index.
    ISBN 0-8039-6252-5 (cloth : acid-free paper). — ISBN 0-8039-6253-3 (pbk. : acid-free paper)
        1. Teachers and community—United States. 2. Education, urban—United States—Case studies. 3. Educational change—United States—Case studies. I. Kruse, Sharon D. II. Title.
LC227.L68 1995
371.1'04—dc20   94-46409

This book is printed on acid-free paper.

95 96 97 98 99 10 9 8 7 6 5 4 3 2 1

Production Editor: Susan McElroy   Typesetter: Christina Hill

Contents

About the Contributors

Karen Seashore Louis is currently Professor of Educational Policy and Administration and Associate Dean for Academic Affairs in the College of Education at the University of Minnesota. Her research and teaching interests focus on educational reform, knowledge use in schools and universities, and schools as workplaces. Recent publications include "Beyond Managed Change: Rethinking How Schools Improve," *Reforming the Urban High School* (with Matthew B. Miles), and *Reshaping the Principalship: Lessons for Restructuring Schools* (coedited with Joseph Murphy).

Sharon D. Kruse has recently completed her Ph.D. at the University of Minnesota in the Department of Educational Policy and Administration, where she is currently studying school reform issues and teachers' reflective processes. Sharon received her M.Ed. from Seattle Pacific University and her B.A. from Western Washington University. Her practical experience includes 10 years in elementary and middle-school classrooms.

Anthony S. Bryk is the Director of the Center for School Improvement and the Consortium on Chicago School Research and a Professor of Education at the University of Chicago. Among his current interests are the social organization of schools and their effects, and understanding how the cultural and moral aspects of school life can lead to school improvement.

Jeremy Hopkins is currently teaching fourth grade at Sheridan Arts Magnet School in Minneapolis, Minnesota. He completed his undergraduate work at London University and received his M.A. from the University of Minnesota.

Jean A. King is an Associate Professor in the Department of Educational Policy and Administration in the College of Education at the University of Minnesota. She directs the Evaluation Studies Program and serves as co-coordinator of the Professional Practice School for the college. Her research interests include action research, participatory evaluation, and outcome-based education.

M. Peg Lonnquist recently completed her Ph.D. at the University of Minnesota. Her research focuses on socially responsible women leaders in nonprofit organizations experimenting with innovative organizational designs. She received her B.S. and M.S. degrees from the University of Wisconsin.

Mary Anne Raywid is a Professor of Administration and Policy Studies at Hofstra University in Hempstead, New York. Most of her current work is in the areas of school organization and the politics of education. For the past 2 decades she has focused on school reform and restructuring—in the several roles of researcher, developer, consultant, author, evaluator, and critic.

Sharon Rollow is the Director of Research at the Center for School Improvement at the University of Chicago. She received a B.A. and an M.A.T. from Stanford University and an M.A. from the University of Chicago. Her research is concerned with urban school politics and school restructuring.

Daniel A. Weiss received a master's degree in public policy from the University of Chicago. He is currently a doctoral student in Educational Policy and Administration at the University of Minnesota. He is the executive director of Amizade, Ltd., a nonprofit organization dedicated to promoting volunteerism and providing community service around the world.

Introduction

Matt Miles, a friend and colleague, recently passed along a book that belonged to his grandfather, a pioneer in progressive education in New York State at the turn of the century. The book must be one of the first that sets out principles of "school management," and, as such, is something of a curiosity. However, as we read the book, written by Arnold Tomkins in 1895, it struck us that many of the issues that we have debated in our work are raised in this little volume. We are humbled that some of our most profound conclusions were invented 100 years ago:

> Professional spirit, in general, is the feeling of urgency produced by an ideal, in order that the ideal may realize itself. It is the craving for the ideal to such an extent that its realization is both the motive and the reward for the labor required to realize it. . . . (p. 48) The ideal teacher is not one who has reached perfection, but one at the upper limit of the profession pushing vigorously for better things. (p. 93)
>
> The teacher comes into unity with the pupil through the elaborate machinery of the school organization . . . and this requires, that along with his own sense of immediate unity with the life of the pupil, there be sensitiveness to the unity of the whole organism which conditions his success in the act of instruction. . . . (p. 64) If the student is not realizing

himself daily, we look at once to the teacher, primarily; and then to the conditions under which he labors. (p. 101)

The organization of the school must be kept mobile to its inner life. To one who is accustomed to wind up the machine and to trust it to run itself for fixed periods, this constantly shifting shape of things will seem unsafe and troublesome. And troublesome it is; for no fixed plan can be followed; no two schools are alike; and the same school is shifting, requiring constant attention and nimble judgement on the part of the [school leader]. (p. 124)

Thank you, Mr. Tomkins, and Matt.

PART ONE

PROBLEMS AND CONCEPTS

1

Professionalism and Community

What Is It and Why Is It

Important in Urban Schools?

KAREN SEASHORE LOUIS
SHARON D. KRUSE
ANTHONY S. BRYK

$\mathbf{M}$ost people assume that teachers' work occurs almost exclusively within the confines of a single room, interacting with pupils. The classroom is the dominant setting for teachers' daily life and the focus of their energies and concerns, but it is not the only context for their work (McLaughlin, 1992). At a minimum, the school's organization and the other faculty members and administrators in it will offer reasons for smiles or frustrations. At a maximum, as we also know from studies of school effects, the organization's interpersonal and structural conditions will affect the impact that teachers have on their students (see, e.g., Lee, Dedrick, & Smith, 1991; Rosenholz, 1989).

But in spite of the emphasis of some recent studies on teachers' work outside the classroom, most policy discussions relating to educational reform emphasize the interaction between teachers and students within the classroom.[1] Teachers' effectiveness must, of course, be judged by what they do when they are involved in direct contact with students, but they are also members of an adult work world that, whether studied or not, affects what goes on in classrooms. In many restructuring and traditional schools, however, administrators and policymakers virtually ignore the broader context of teachers' work (Louis & King, 1993).

Our research is based on the assumption that what teachers do when they are not in their classrooms may be critical to school restructuring and helps them to do their essential work better. In this book we propose a framework for thinking about teachers' work that focuses on two key aspects related to current pressures for educational reform. We call this framework *professional community* to emphasize our belief that unless teachers are provided with more supporting and engaging work environments, they cannot be expected to concentrate on increasing their abilities to reach and teach today's students more effectively. We are not the first to point to this need, as will be apparent when we outline the particulars of our framework in Chapter 2. However, we have tried to bring existing ideas together so that they are consistent with the well-established assumption that the school, rather than the individual or a small group, is the critical unit of change (Van Velzen et al., 1985).

Urban Education as a Special Context for Teaching

The conditions in some of our schools are so bad, and the physical and social environments in which these schools are located are so frightful, that we may have to cross off some . . . as expendable. (Halpin, 1966, quoted in Englert, 1993, p. 3)

Our work focuses on creating professional community in urban schools. We believe that the issue of professional community is applicable to all schools, and that the findings presented in later chapters can easily be extended to many other contexts. We choose to emphasize working conditions in large cities because the problems and failures of our educational system are nowhere more apparent.

Also, as exemplified in the quotation above, the deficiencies of urban education are a source of considerable ambivalence and even downright hostility for both pundits and policymakers, who don't see simple solutions to the intersecting problems that characterize our cities, of which education is only one.

But poor, minority, or first-generation immigrant students are increasingly concentrated in urban areas, and to ignore these schools is to ignore the needs of our most vulnerable students and teachers. As a nation, we are deeply engaged in programs of reform, and there is increasing concern about the lack of progress in meeting the educational needs of the students who are most at risk of failing to achieve. Previous policies for improving urban schools have often been linked to simple financial or structural reforms, ranging from subsidies for schools with poorer students, magnet schools, schools of choice, or the introduction of special structured curriculum/testing programs. Rarely have we looked seriously at incremental, human resource or social capital-based strategies for improving urban settings. This book, in contrast, focuses not on the characteristics of urban schools that may make them less effective for children (see Cibulka, Reed & Wong, 1992; Englert, 1993), but on those that affect teachers' motivation and ability to teach all students who appear at the classroom door. We hasten to point out that these conditions—disengaged students, social problems that impinge on classroom teaching, and public apathy about local schools—are increasingly characteristic of even affluent suburbia.

Field reports suggest that urban schools are frequently bureaucratic, politicized, and isolated from the most up-to-date information about educational innovations that may improve the educational opportunities for disadvantaged children. This isolation, in turn, makes them less able to adopt and implement innovations (Natriello, Pallas, & McDill, 1990), and it clearly makes them less inviting places for teachers to work. In our view, finding a staff that has the energy and skill to teach today's urban students is not a matter either of matching students and teachers, or of improving the skills of individual educators. Rather, it is a matter of creating schools where all teachers are learners together with their colleagues—or, in the currently fashionable parlance, of creating schools that are learning organizations. Before we begin to enumerate the features of urban schools that make them vital places for professional growth, we must first briefly outline the reasons why they are often difficult settings for adult work and professional development. These include socioeconomic, political, and organizational conditions that, though not unique, converge to make urban schools both vulnerable and demanding places for teachers.

Socioeconomic Conditions

The social and economic characteristics of urban communities have significant implications for teachers' work. Urban schools may be overwhelmed by the problems that their students bring to work, making it more difficult for them to successfully engage with normal dilemmas of pedagogy. For example, Louis, Rosenblum, and Molitor (1981) found that the larger the proportion of disadvantaged students in a school, the lower were the school's capacities to engage in an effective problem-solving process. Schools also receive less support in the educational process where most parents are disadvantaged and the immediate communities are low in easily accessible resources (Pallas, Natriello, & McDill, 1989). The assumption, based on theories of social capital, is that lower-income communities have fewer human resources to supplement the work of schools.[2] For example, in more affluent communities there may be intersecting networks that include parents and members of the business community, both of whom have an interest in a healthy school system; these networks may be absent in many of our poorer urban communities. This premise is supported by Garner and Raudenbush (1991), who show that children in low-income communities perform more poorly on achievement tests than peers from similar families who live in higher socioeconomic status (SES) communities. This double disadvantage—poor students and poor communities—puts a particular strain on teachers, who are often from different socioeconomic backgrounds than their students, yet who must organize a pedagogy that will engage and connect the classroom to the students' own experience.

Neighborhood wealth has an additional impact on teachers because the limited resources of the community may also affect access to resources outside the community. For example, urban schools are harder to reform because many of them are weakly linked to the natural professional networks through which ideas are diffused. During the mid-1980s only a tiny fraction of urban schools were basing any major change efforts on the then-popular "effective schools" literature (Louis & Miles, 1990), which suggests that they were not well connected to the many change agents who were promoting these principles at the time. Many major schools of education have recently developed "professional practice" relationships with local schools, but few of these are in major urban districts. Internal human resources may also be limited due to the socioeconomic setting: Rollow and Bryk (Chapter 5) note that the Chicago Public School System is staffed largely by teachers who went through that system, received their teacher training locally, and have taught in no other district. Although this is, in part, because urban systems like to "hire their own," it is also very likely due to the general preference of teachers from more affluent and cosmopolitan backgrounds for other teaching venues. Though the Chicago case may be extreme, it is not the only case in which the inbred character of urban schools diminishes easy access to new ideas.[3]

Political Conditions

All schools exist in a political environment because the goals and means of educating our young are contested everywhere. In urban settings, however, interest group politics mix with educational politics in a more volatile way than in smaller towns (Peterson, 1985; Reese, 1986), and this also affects teachers' work. As Louis (1991) notes, many urban settings display fragmented values concerning education and, in particular, are more likely to exhibit distance or even antagonism between the professional values of teachers and the concerns of parents and community members. Although this can make them exciting places to work, it may also provoke highly politicized local school board elections and responses by unions that are viewed in the community as self-serving. The classic case is the New York controversy over "Ocean Hill-Brownsville," which, 25 years ago, pitted community control advocates against members of the nascent American Federation of Teachers.

Recent restructuring efforts in major cities have almost uniformly revealed deep-seated differences between proponents of parental control over schooling and professional judgments. There is more likely to be antagonism between professional educators and parents, and there are more parent and community groups that form distinctive perspectives on what should happen to schools. Although unions are often scapegoated in the press, there is some evidence that union militancy is often a response to bureaucratization and political pressure, and that many urban unions are eager to collaborate in school reform, but may feel excluded (Hill, Wise, & Shapiro, 1989; McDonnell & Pascal, 1979).

Urban communities are often ethnically and racially heterogeneous, so the community may also be deeply divided. When this diversity is present in a school, it can negatively affect decentralized school improvement efforts (Bryk, Easton, Kerbow, Rollow, & Sebring, 1993). Under these conditions, many urban districts evidence the attributes of a *policy vacuum*—an absence of clear, organized constituencies, a clear understanding of policy issues and choices, consistency in policy initiatives, and coordination between overlapping or complementary policies (Corwin & Louis, 1982). Policy vacuums lead to instability in educational policy, which also undermines school and teacher efforts for reform (Louis & Miles, 1990).

Fragmented and politicized environments make the development of a community among adults more difficult, in part because all outsiders may be viewed as potential sources of problems for the school. In addition, the absence of serious discussion within the broader educational community about the need for a different approach to pedagogy for poor, disadvantaged, urban youths inhibits debate inside the school. Learning among adults requires recognition and open debate about change conditions by key constituencies as a prerequisite for professional growth and improvement.

Organizational Conditions

In addition to socioeconomic and political circumstances, many organizational conditions need to be addressed before urban schools can be effective. The Carnegie Foundation (1988), for example, pointed to the need for school-based management, clear accountability standards, and intervention procedures when schools are not meeting their objectives. Factors such as school size, teachers' working conditions, and centralized and nonparticipatory decision-making structures may also affect the inclination of teachers to focus their efforts on reform and student learning.

Urban school districts are, almost by definition, large, and urban schools are larger than average (although they are not, especially at the high school level, the largest in the United States). Recent efforts to look at the combined effects of district and school size, which are associated, suggest that big is more bureaucratic, and also bad for children—at least where students are of lower socioeconomic status (Wahlberg, 1989). For teachers, however, there is an added problem: Larger schools in lower SES communities tend to develop a lesser sense of community among teachers than do other schools (Bryk & Driscoll, 1988), and sense of community is also associated with student achievement (Lee & Smith, 1993).

Creating a professional community focused on the common problems of teaching demands a great deal of the faculty, and we would thus hope that the best candidates would step up to the challenges. Yet urban schools have more difficulty than others in recruiting and retaining the most talented teachers (Englert, 1993, p. 38). This is perhaps not surprising when we note that teachers' working conditions in urban schools are often less conducive to energetic involvement in knowledge use and reform than are conditions in newer and/or smaller districts. Urban teachers are less involved in policy decisions, are treated with less respect by administrators, have fewer opportunities to engage in significant work with one another, and are generally subjected to unprofessional working conditions (Corcoran, Walker, & White, 1988). Teacher turnover may be either too high (where seniority rights encourage "bumping" of less senior teachers from desirable schools) or too low (in schools with poor reputations) to support effective social construction of knowledge for reform. Each of these features is related to teachers' sense of efficacy and commitment to their work—and inversely related to negative attitudes about the students that they teach (Rosenblum, Louis, & Rossmiller, 1994).

In addition, the nature of work in urban schools is hurried, focused on the short term, and subject to the interruption shared by teaching in other contexts. No matter what we would like them to be, few teachers and administrators are easily able to be reflective prac-

titioners who eagerly seek complex information to improve their
work. Rather, they are often harassed and looking for information
that will solve today's problem today. And in this regard they get
little assistance, because urban schools typically lack basic information that would encourage reflection and experimentation (Louis, in
press). In addition, urban districts rarely have information management systems that allow them to gain access to usable data, much
less information and ideas that are less familiar (Cibulka, 1992, p. 37).

Summary

The discussion above has emphasized some social, cultural, political, and organizational characteristics of urban schools that make
them difficult settings for teachers. We suggest that although an emphasis on professional community would be beneficial to all schools,
it is particularly pressing for urban schools, where other resources
supportive of school reform are limited. In Chapter 2 we will present
a detailed discussion of school features that signify the presence or
absence of professional community. Before we do this, however, we
need to map the larger terrain by defining what we mean by the terms
professional and *community* and by outlining briefly why people who
are interested in the reform of urban schools should care about these
concepts.

Professionalism and Community

Leithwood (1993) argues that professionalization of teachers'
work is at the heart of the current school reform movement. Important efforts are underway to raise entry standards into the profession,
to introduce a national teacher license for more advanced teachers,
and to increase pay and professional development opportunities.
Moving beyond these aspects of professionalism, we concur with the
many scholars who have argued that if education is to improve, we
must focus on schools as well as national professional standards.
Thus, rather than concentrating only on teachers as individual workers, we must also consider the decisions and actions that teachers

take collectively that are directed toward the improvement of their schools' performance.

The sociological writings on professionalism and community remain distinct and offer different premises about the attainment of social goals. The classical literature on professionalism emphasizes that such work is selective, requires high levels of training, and addresses a task of recognized value to society. Virtually any definition of a profession emphasizes the nonroutine character of the work that must be done, namely, that it requires considerable individual judgment in how to apply the expertise of the profession to a given problem. Because of the emphasis on judgment, professions often emphasize a form of social control that requires members of the profession to regulate the conduct of their peers.

The community literature, on the other hand, focuses on the primacy of sustained face-to-face relationships and the activities that support such relationships. In the community literature, social control is established through the norms and values espoused by the community. Social integration within and across subgroups is achieved by aligning important norms and values while simultaneously creating a supportive environment for individual development.

Professionalism

Sociologists have long distinguished between occupations—even high-status occupations such as managers—and professions (Benveniste, 1988; Zald, 1970). This classification corresponds to public opinion: Private-sector executives, for example, are viewed by survey respondents as less prestigious than doctors or lawyers, although on average they earn as much. Academic credentials are a fundamental basis of prestige: The earliest universities were founded to train doctors, lawyers, and priests—the only occupations that required more than minimal literacy in the Middle Ages. In general, the higher the academic degree required to be in a particular position, the more prestigious that position will be.

However, not all occupations that require much formal education are viewed by either sociologists or the public as professionals. Physical therapists and teachers, for example, increasingly have master's degrees to either enter or remain in the profession, yet both are seen as "semi-professions," for reasons that will be discussed later.

The educational reform literature is studded with exhortations to increase the professionalism of teachers (Darling-Hammond, 1987; Darling-Hammond & Goodwin, 1993; Forsyth & Danisiewicz, 1985; Rowan, 1994). Among the key distinctions between highly educated work groups and "real professions" outlined in the sociological literature are the following:

A Technical Knowledge Base. Professions share a body of abstract knowledge that takes time to acquire and cannot easily be shared with or assessed by lay persons. Moreover, the determination of what knowledge is important is decided by members of the profession itself rather than by people outside the profession.

Control Over Entry to the Profession and Conditions of Work. The profession itself decides when the individual is sufficiently knowledgeable and/or possesses the personal qualities to enter or practice the profession. Although licenses are granted by the state, the boards that grant such licenses are composed of practitioners in the field, and any examinations or criteria for entrance are decided by the profession. Even professionals who are employed in bureaucracies retain considerable control over their work environment, either through direct involvement in management (as in a law firm), or because their supervisors are members of the same profession (the medical director of a hospital is always a physician).

A Strong Client Orientation. The traditional professions—law, medicine, and the clergy—have often been viewed as altruistic callings. At the center of each profession is an abstract but highly valued social aim, such as promoting justice, curing the sick, and attending to the spiritual well-being of the community. Professions have a strong code of ethics that emphasize client needs over personal interests. Doctors, for example, are expected to treat patients with communicable diseases; lawyers are required to do a certain amount of pro bono work. All clients are expected to be treated as equally deserving of professional attention, irrespective of their ability to pay. Clearly, many members of professions do not live up to these standards, but when they do not, they may be open to public criticism. In extreme cases, where professional practice norms are violated, they may be prevented from practicing.

Empowerment Is Not Enough

One response to the perceived low status of teachers in urban and other school settings is to argue that if they had more control over policy and practice in school settings, as doctors and lawyers do in their settings, they too could begin to achieve a more professional status, display their technical knowledge base, and enact the altruistic passion for the development of the young that led many to their careers. This empowerment of teachers would then result in better teaching and learning as teachers gained control over curriculum and school organization (Fullan, 1992). In many districts, teachers are being given increased responsibility for making important curricular and policy decisions in the schools, and there is evidence to suggest that this increases teachers' sense of professionalism and efficacy (Louis, Marks, & Kruse, 1994).

Why do we emphasize professional community when the idea of teacher empowerment is so central to the current school reform movement? Our answer is simple: The available data suggest that school-based decision making and teacher empowerment is an important but insufficient stimulus for developing teachers' performance as professionals. Instead, studies of teacher empowerment often find that there is false participation, which either augments principal control (Malen, Ogawa, & Kranz, 1991) or fails to focus on the essential issues of classroom work (Ford, 1991). In addition, teachers may resist the extra administrative work (Cohn, Kottkamp, McCloskey, & Provenzo, 1987; Johnson, 1990), or they may really want something different from the formal involvement in decisions, because their definition of what it means to operate professionally does not focus on power and control (Louis & Smith, 1992). We do not argue that empowerment is wrong or unnecessary, but rather than it has proven insufficient to change teachers' relationships to their work in many settings. We contend that for empowerment to work to the advantage of students and teachers, a shared commitment to a fundamental change of teaching practice must emerge. For this to happen, we argue, requires the addition of a focus on community.

Community

Where professional community is an element of the definition of professionalism, it is often synonymous with promoting strong national professional associations whose role is to uphold the above privileges and responsibilities. The community literature, in contrast, presents an image that emphasizes personal connection.

The contrast between community and forms of organization based on expertise is not new. Early sociologists distinguished between forms of social organization based on *Gesellschaft*, in which interdependency is based on division of labor, and *Gemeinschaft*, where social organization is based on common expectations and standards for all (Tönnies, 1957). In the former situation, groups remain cohesive because people's individual talents are available to all, and individuals are valued because of the unique contributions that they make to the group. In the latter, cohesiveness is achieved through personal intimacy and recurring interactions among people who are alike, and membership is based on the whole person, rather than on specialized contributions.

The call for community has become a popular theme in contemporary political and social philosophy (Bellah et al., 1985, 1991; Etzioni, 1991, 1993; MacIntyre, 1981; Sandel, 1988; Young, 1986, 1990). The educational literature has accumulated rapidly as well (Bryk & Driscoll, 1988; Bryk, Lee, & Holland, 1993; Bull, Fruehling, & Chattergy, 1992; Newmann & Rutter, 1987; Raywid, 1988, 1993; Sergiovanni, 1994; Strike, 1993). In the literature on work (as distinct from professions), some have argued that occupational communities located in a specific workplace can foster work commitment and satisfaction (Van Maanen & Barley, 1984). Clearly, the notion that we should balance our emphasis on individualism and individual achievement with equal consideration of the common good has struck a resonant cord among many academic and nonacademic writers. Calls from the White House for increased national and public responsibility for health care, the elderly, the impoverished, and welfare reform all have a communitarian message. President Clinton appealed to this ethic in his 1994 State of the Union Address, stating:

> Let us give our children a future. Let us take away their guns
> and give them books. Let us overcome their despair and re-
> place it with hope. Let us by our example teach them to obey
> the law, respect our neighbors and cherish our values. Let us
> weave these sturdy threads into a new American community
> that can once more stand strong against the forces of despair
> and evil, because [then] everybody has a chance to walk into
> a better tomorrow. (*The Congressional Record*, January 25,
> 1994, p. 13)

Present in these words is the theme of a common value base providing a framework for shared, collective, ethical decision making. His
words resonate with the notion that community can be formed by a
diverse group of people around basic shared purposes and dreams.

Yet the concern for community, whether it is embodied in our
nation-state, in neighborhoods, or between teachers and students in
school, is not a new idea. Over time, the notion of community has
been used to describe a common legal interest, the emotional ties one
holds with intimates and sometimes share with strangers (for example, the loyalties fans have for a favorite team, or members of a
fraternity hold for their brothers), and as a partnership "not only
between the living, but between those who are living, those who are
dead and those who are to be born" (Edmond Burke, in Avineri &
De-Shalit, 1992).

The new emphasis on community is, at its essence, an attempt to
move beyond the articulation of individual rights and prerogatives
that has dominated contemporary liberal philosophy. The focus on
community argues that excessive individualism results in many
Americans experiencing isolation, exclusion, and polarization
(Bellah et al., 1985; Dworkin, 1989; Etzioni, 1991, 1993; Minow, 1990).
A convergence around a "politics of common good" (Sandel, 1988)
rather than the politics of rights (Dworkin, 1977, 1989) has emerged.

As many argue, ideas about community have much to say to
schools and teachers. Society has traditionally seen teachers as individual workers rather than as a group (except at the time of contract
negotiations), and this has helped to isolate teachers in classrooms.
In response, teachers have traditionally viewed their work this way
(Lortie, 1975) and have used collective action through unions to
increase individual prerogatives and perquisites, rather than to

advance collective interests in changing their work settings. This isolation and the emphasis on individual rights in the micro-setting of
the classroom have reinforced teacher isolation, lack of connection,
and, given the relatively high rates of job dissatisfaction expressed in
surveys, a sense of meaninglessness and ambiguity in their work. In
urban districts, where the actual isolation in the school may be coupled with the socioeconomic, political, and organizational conditions
outlined above, it is hardly surprising that many teachers express a
sense of anomie, which contrasts strongly with the generally optimis-
tic and altruistic sentiments expressed by beginning teachers.

Teacher isolation and lack of connection to the world outside the
school become even more problematic when society demands improved performance. Community is necessary to address the debili-
tating conditions that we have outlined above; individuals, no matter
how determined, cannot change them, as Tomkins (1895) points out.
Philosophers and social analysts have commented on the meaning of
community in the broader society, but what do we mean by the notion of community in a school or other occupational setting? Specifically, in a school characterized as a community, three key features
operate (Bryk & Driscoll, 1988; Bryk, Lee, & Holland, 1993):

- A common set of activities that provides many occasions for
  face-to-face interactions, and the potential for common understandings, values, and expectations for behavior to evolve
  (Van Maanen & Barley, 1984);
- Specific organizational structures that promote this, such as
  time and expectations that people will gather and talk, small,
  stable networks of teachers, etc. (Schein, 1985); and
- A core of shared values about what students should learn,
  about how faculty and students should behave, and about the
  shared aims to maintain and promote the community. Central
  to a school community is an ethic of interpersonal caring that
  permeates the life of teachers, students, and administrators
  (Beck, 1992; Firestone & Rosenblum, 1988; Noddings, 1984).

If the community of teachers is a necessary focus of school restructuring, it is one that is poorly understood. There are many studies examining specific aspects of professional community, which we

will review in Chapter 2, but only one major study (by the Context for Secondary School Teaching at Stanford) has been conducted using this concept. This latter groundbreaking work focuses on "typical" comprehensive high school settings (McLaughlin, 1992). The findings from this research focus on the variety of contexts, from departments to subject-matter networks outside of school, from which teachers can draw support for their professional growth and development (McLaughlin, in press; Siskin, in press). This stream of research is exciting, but still limited both by the sample and by the nature of the questions asked. Our study, which was initiated at the same time as that of McLaughlin and her colleagues, is also limited, but it adds to the Context Center's by addressing a different type of professional community: one that is firmly embedded in the school, and uses school-wide involvement in reform as the basis for teachers' commitment and interaction. Together, these unique but overlapping studies will help to reframe the way we think about teachers' work.

The Longitudinal Study of Restructuring Schools

Our examination of professional community emerged from a longitudinal study of schools that are well along in the process of restructuring. The study, which is part of the Office of Educational Research and Improvement's Center for the Organization and Restructuring of Schools, focuses on how restructuring affected teachers' work over a 3-year period.

Design

Our study design called for examining schools serving school populations that are statistically most likely to be at risk of performing poorly in school: those located in our inner cities. It was conceived as a loosely organized collaborative effort among researchers who were interested in developing a theoretical basis for understanding the intersection between school reform and teachers' work. Three themes motivated the study: (a) understanding the nature and development of professional communities within restructuring schools; (b) examining the degree to which restructuring creates different power bases and political environments within schools; and (c) examining whether restructuring schools have the potential to become *self-designing* or *learning* organizations. The first of these is the focus of this volume. The overall goal of the study is to integrate the three theoretical framework perspectives, but only after a thorough analysis of the data, taking each perspective separately.

We began a search for schools using several criteria. The schools were selected because they had been involved in a major restructuring effort for several years (we wished to avoid a study of "early implementation" problems), and they had to be accessible to the researchers who were participating in the study so that they could be visited on a regular basis. Previous studies of teacher collegiality or professionalism have often concentrated on only one level in the educational system, and we decided, in the interest of more generalizeable conclusions, to include elementary, middle, and high schools. A final criterion for selection was that we wished to examine schools with a variety of initial stimuli for restructuring, and to introduce some variation in the surrounding social and political contexts of the schools.

We finally sampled two alternative high schools in New York City, where the initial impetus for restructuring was a district policy providing settings of choice; two elementary schools in Chicago, where restructuring was driven by a political agenda of changing the power structure of education; and two urban middle schools, both of which had been initiated because of a curricular and instructional vision of a small number of individuals.[4]

Data Collection

Each of these settings involved data collection by one to three field-workers who were either advanced graduate students or faculty members, each of whom spent between 30 and 45 days at the site over the 3-year period. Researchers conducted interviews with teachers (in all schools except two larger schools, this included the universe of teachers and professional staff); with the administrators, with members of the site council, where relevant; and other important actors outside the school, such as district administrators, external evaluators, experts who were brought in to help, and so on.

Classroom observations of multiple teachers were also part of the required data collection procedures, as was attendance at any meeting that occurred during the time that the researcher was on-site.

Although data collection targets were specified, procedures varied slightly between the sites due to differences in the relationship between the researcher and the school, distance of the researcher from the site, and school characteristics. Because we hoped to capitalize on proximity to increase both the frequency of data collection and the opportunity for the "moment of learning," we did not use formal interview or observation guides. Instead, we followed the research strategy pursued by Louis and Miles (1990), and jointly designed a set of topics for which data needed to be gathered (see Appendix A). Each case study is based on the field notes collected over the period of study. Efforts to protect data quality included use of multiple informants and observations, site team familiarity with the *context* that allowed them to interpret and ask additional questions, triangulation of multiple data sources, and most important, collegial challenge, which was a fundamental component of data analysis.

Maintaining Data Quality: Collegial Challenge

Regular meetings allowed exchange of data, interpretation, and theoretical development among team members. All written materials have been shared for critical review, questioning, and emendation. We used staff meetings for three purposes: first, to generate theory based on emerging data; second, for within-case analysis; and third, to improve data quality and interpretation. At quarterly retreats, all project staff were required to present results from their schools relating to one of the three main study questions. Other staff members, who had not visited the schools, challenged the site visitor's interpretation, asking for evidence, and posing alternative interpretations. Based on these discussions, site visitors were often asked to collect additional observational data, to interview other actors, or to reinterview faculty to clarify what was "known." Some individual cases that result from this effort will be published separately. In addition, our reports have been regularly reviewed by individuals outside the project, including members of the schools in the study, the advisory board of the Center for Organization and Restructuring of Schools, other principal investigators in the Center, and outside reviewers, who also raised questions about preliminary findings, data, and methods.

Data Analysis

Each field-worker produced a working case study organized around the agreed-upon topics. These case studies were a *working database*, rather than a publishable document, and were therefore to incorporate extensive documentation, including quotes, documents, minutes from meetings, and so on.[5]

A second strategy for data analysis was directed at preserving the *integrity* of each site's story, but leading toward a cross-case interpretation. This volume represents one such effort. Here, each of five site visitors/teams was asked to prepare a case study representing a within-case analysis of a specific topic, professional community.[6] These cases were shared with at least one key informant at each site to ensure their fundamental accuracy. The cross-site analysis team then used both data displays and causal maps (Miles & Huberman, 1984) to present data from each school and, where particular matters had not been addressed, asked for revisions to deal with the missing topic. The original case writers had the opportunity to react to the data displays to assess whether the cross-site team's interpretation of their school was accurate. Finally, the cross-site analysis text was prepared.

In some senses, therefore, this study represents an intersection between a comparative case study design (Miles & Huberman, 1984; Yin, 1984), and a secondary analysis of case study data, as conducted by Louis and Miles (1990). The cross-case analysis is not based on personal observation and field notes of the authors; indeed, the authors of this chapter and the cross-case analysis have conducted only limited fieldwork in the schools discussed in this volume. In doing the cross-case analysis, the researchers relied not only on the case material presented in this document, but also on the informal comments, reactions, and discussions from retreat meetings. The final versions of Chapters 1, 2, 8, and 9 were circulated to all project staff for comments.

What Can the Reader Anticipate?

The organization of this volume reflects the methodology described above. The introductory section of this book continues in Chapter 2, by laying out in more detail the way in which we have come to think about the dimensions of professional community in schools. This framework, we should hasten to add, is the product of many hours of collegial discussions among the various authors who have contributed to this book, and has been tested against the tough audiences of colleagues and practitioners.

In Part II we present the fruit of our collaborative research—five case studies of urban schools that in various ways have been deeply affected by the restructuring and reform movement. The major point of these cases is that achieving a viable professional community and its benefits in urban schools is possible, but involves both personal struggle and administrative commitment. Of the schools that we studied, two are "successes" in that they have managed, under difficult circumstances, to build a real school-wide professional community focused on the improvement of students' learning. An interesting feature of the two success stories presented in Chapters 3 and 4 is that one is a small, alternative high school, and the other is a more typical comprehensive high school. Two additional cases (Chapters 5 and 6) illuminate some reasons why professional community is fragile in urban settings. In these schools we see evidence of many factors that should have led to the development of vital places where teachers exchange ideas and visions for students, yet in both there is a sense that initial promise may not be fulfilled. It is not always easy to learn from insufficiency, but the last case, presented in Chapter 7, is significant because we find that professional community failed to develop in a new, experimental middle school in spite of an array of structures and resources intended by policymakers and administrators to foster it, and there are some rather clear reasons why the aspirations were not met. We can learn from this case not merely that achieving professional community is hard work but also some of the avoidable pitfalls. In Part III we reflect on the cases to provide further development of the framework presented in Chapter 2, and the practical and policy dilemmas outlined above. Chapters 8 and 9 are based on data presented in the case studies, although they are enriched by the experiences of all of the authors in other urban schools, and also the larger research effort emerging from the Center for the Organization and Restructuring of Schools. Chapter 8 synthesizes what we have learned about how teachers enact professional community, and Chapter 9 focuses on what administrators can do to promote it.

Notes

1. We acknowledge that there are a number of authors who have investigated teachers' work life in schools in the recent past. Rather than cite them all in this introduction, we refer the reader to Chapter 2, where we will review recent research that bears on our work.

2. This is also an argument that applies to rural schools. See Coleman and Hoffer, 1987.

3. The exception, of course, is the superintendency, where national recruitment is the norm.

4. In order to preserve our focus on underserved and at-risk populations, while providing an internal test of our work, we also chose a small rural high school and middle school, both located in the same Midwestern community, where reform was externally initiated by a consultant who was seeking to promote "global education." The latter school will not, however, be featured in this volume. In addition, two schools were "relocated" to preserve their anonymity. Although this limits our description of the school context in the case studies, it does not change any of the conclusions.

5. Because the number of sites was small, we have not yet attempted to use the reductive data displays recommended by Miles and Huberman (1984), nor have we used formal within-case causal networks.

6. Two of the case studies—Thomas Paine and Dewey—were written later than the other three. In this case the authors had access to the first three cases, in addition to drafts of the cross-case analysis. This may, of course, have biased the authors' work, but the decision to add these cases after the fact occurred because all staff members believed their inclusion would enhance the discussion of professional community.

2

An Emerging Framework
for Analyzing School-Based
Professional Community

SHARON D. KRUSE
KAREN SEASHORE LOUIS
ANTHONY S. BRYK

Most teachers enter the profession because they identify with its intrinsic satisfaction, namely the opportunity to work with and affect the lives of young children. They confront work settings, however, that lack external rewards, whether these are salary, quality working conditions, or prestige (Apple, 1985; Darling-Hammond, 1984; Lortie, 1975; Warren, 1989). Teaching is also characterized by other persistent work-related problems, such as isolation, time constraints, a limited knowledge base, and scarce resources (Louis & Smith, 1992). These conditions create uncertainty in teachers about their practice that, in turn, militates against the development of an enduring intrinsic reward system (Grimmett & Crehan, 1992). Consequently, many excellent teachers leave the profession, choose to enter administrative positions, or burn out but remain in the classroom. In this chapter we will lay out the research base supporting our argument that school-based professional communities can help develop lasting intrinsic rewards for teachers by moderating both professional uncertainty and isolation. By doing so, they will improve the quality of schools and workplaces, and their effectiveness in teaching and learning.

Like most literature reviews, this chapter is somewhat dense. Figure 2.1 provides an overview of the topics that will be treated in the chapter. In addition, a brief summary of the key definitions that emerged from our review is presented in Appendix B.

School-Based Professional Community: How Can It Benefit Urban Schools?

Creating strong professional communities holds several potential advantages for schools. Among the positive outcomes that writers on professionalism and community have asserted are the growth of increased responsibility for performance (including instructional expertise), increased personal commitment to work, the replacement of bureaucratic, rule-based controls over teacher behavior with values that promoted self-regulation, and the promotion of a climate of inquiry and innovation that leads to greater organizational learning and effectiveness. The hypothesized outcomes of increased professional community can be categorized under three broad headings: (a) an increased sense of efficacy relating to work that results in increased motivation in the classroom; (b) an increased sense of satisfaction with the personal dignity of work; and (c) greater collective responsibility for student learning. Although these are conceptually distinct, they are also related, as will be apparent in our discussion.

Increased Efficacy

Teachers' sense of affiliation with each other and with the school, and their sense of mutual support and individual responsibility for the effectiveness of instruction, is increased by collaborative work

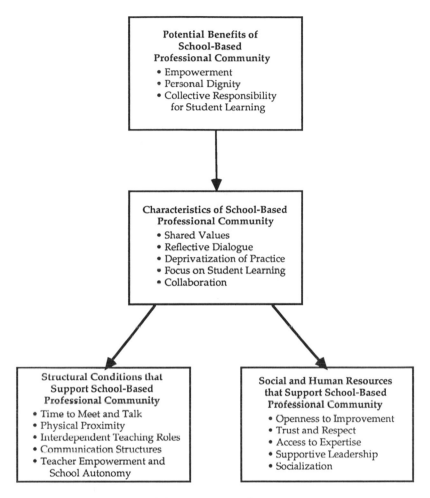

Figure 2.1. Overview of the Topics in Chapter 2

with peers (Louis, 1992a). Emergent professional communities increase opportunities to improve classroom practice by expanding the
number and quality of feedback mechanisms available to teachers.
In general, teachers will only seek out and accept serious reviews of
their work when there are more open and supportive relationships
among staff. Thus, the importance of frequent reactions to perfor-

mance from peers and supportive school leaders is a consequence of its strong relationship to sense of efficacy among teachers (Louis & Smith, 1992); and sense of efficacy is, in turn, related to personal commitment to teaching and students (Louis, 1991a)

Professional community can reinforce a collective sense of efficacy as well as that of individuals. Teachers can work to get through their own day—or they can perform daily tasks with the intention of contributing to the organization's objectives. The latter organizational behavior can be considered prosocial, because it is focused on the collective implications of the school's mission rather than on meeting individual needs. Teachers themselves suggest that potential benefits of a prosocial orientation to teaching include more effective job performance; improved communication and coordination between individuals and subgroups; improved job satisfaction and morale; improved satisfaction of parents, students, and faculty with the organization; and improved organizational efficiency (Brief & Motowidlo, 1986).

Satisfaction Emerging From Personal Dignity

One issue that frequently arises in talking about teachers' work is the discouragement that many of them feel when they believe that their best efforts are neither respected nor valued by peers, supervisors, or the public. In Chapter 1 we suggested that empowerment is not an adequate tool to eliminate this problem. However, when it is combined with other strategies for improving teachers' work, it appears to contribute to teachers' sense of responsibility for student learning (Lee & Smith, 1993) and also their sense of efficacy (Louis, Marks, & Kruse, 1994). We hypothesize that this occurs because some strategies for increasing teacher influence validate teachers' perception of their own value as social agents. Newmann (1991b), for example, suggests that giving teachers more individual autonomy, discretion, and control in conducting their work will encourage a greater sense of ownership of and responsibility for quality in student learning. Johnson (1990) suggests that teachers obtain the greatest satisfaction from empowerment that focuses on teachers and classrooms; and that involvement in policy setting that is not directly related to their own work is viewed as a distraction.

Collective Responsibility for Student Learning

Any professional is, by definition, expected to be responsible for the quality of his or her own work. Good teachers, for example, typically view themselves as accountable for their students' learning, even when there are no external systems that would hold them up to some performance standard. This private sense of accountability is, however, an ineffective means of maintaining organizational performance (Mitchell, 1993). In addition, however, we suggest that publicly acknowledged *collective responsibility* for performance is an important outcome of increasing professional community in schools.

Furthermore, developing effective school-level accountability systems depends on professional community. At minimum, limited professional community may allow teachers to agree on standards for assessing their individual performance. At a more advanced level, when they work as a unit, members of a school may take on the joint responsibility for considering and monitoring the effectiveness of the school. This may involve setting informal or formal standards for performance related to instruction, pedagogy, and student learning, as well as the willingness to confront and/or mediate poor performance of teachers in the school. The collective responsibility for performance may manifest itself in increased assistance between teachers in instruction, volunteering for additional assignments, and putting forth extra effort in creating opportunities for student learning (Little, 1990).

Responsibility and accountability are closely linked. Collective obligation for performance suggests that all teachers should contribute to the achievement of all students in the school. Moreover, the pedagogical growth and development of all teachers are considered a community-wide responsibility, and organizational structures such as peer coaching and time for conversation about practice are viewed as central to the continued growth of the school community. Collective responsibility also means strong participation in governance tasks, and the regularized use of self-evaluation strategies to assess the quality of the organization's programs and practices (Darling-Hammond & Snyder, 1992).

Just as there is a link between efficacy and dignity, there is also a link between individual accountability and dignity found through meaningful participation in school-wide decisions about teaching and learning. Teachers' engagement with the school community can stimulate more concerted efforts to resolve the problems associated with student development and, in turn, reinforce a shared sense of purpose. Without this base, the development of standards for judging teaching performance will be largely mechanical and lacking in insight, or may even be rejected by faculty members.

Collective responsibility also suggests a shift in the way in which schools think about controlling teacher behavior. Rules, regulations, and division of labor have traditionally been the means to control life in schools, and these are usually developed and applied by the state or district. Unions often reinforce rather than contest bureaucratic regulations because they are a means of protecting their members against arbitrary action (Perrow, 1972). Collective responsibility, on the other hand, reinforces policies that promote decentralization and debureaucratization of schools. Successfully transformed or restructured schools substitute professional norms, values, and beliefs for these traditional external control structures. Where they can be developed, internalized social control mechanisms are far stronger than more bureaucratic controls or fiscal incentives (Abbott, 1991; Angle & Perry, 1983; Bucher & Stelling, 1969; Forsyth & Danisiewicz, 1985). Coherent values and norms also allow professional discussions that encourage growth and improvement (Litwak, 1961).

Characteristics of School-Based Professional Community

Professional school communities share five core characteristics: shared values, reflective dialogue, deprivatization of practice, focus on student learning, and collaboration. We will define each of these below, and show how current discussions of school reform portray them.

Shared Norms and Values

Shared norms and values are the fundamental bedrock upon which all other aspects of professional community are built. We asserted above that professional communities are based on moral authority derived from the central social importance of teaching and socializing children. But this moral authority is fragile, and hardly akin to other broadly shared assumptions of American society, such as the sanctity of the lawyer-client relationship, or even the right to medical care. Without entering the debate about the relative importance of medical care versus education, the lack of social agreement around educational goals means that teachers and school administrators need to reinforce their own understandings about children, learning, teaching and teacher's roles, the nature of human needs, activity, and relationships (Schein, 1985) and also the school's extended role in the broader community and society (Giroux, 1988).

Without a core of shared beliefs about institutional purposes, practices, and desired behavior, the other elements of professional community that we will describe below cannot emerge. Even if teachers want to form more tightly connected social and professional connections, the absence of a core of shared values will instead produce misunderstanding and conflicts and may also lead to interpersonal mistrust. This does not mean that teachers need full consensus about all aspects of their work, which erects an impossible standard against which to measure professional community. However, a delimited core of value positions in the school permits teachers to begin the task of developing a moral community that ultimately allows them to become advocates for teaching and learning.

This may start with very concrete behavior. For example, when teachers explain their specific actions, they often appeal to their values concerning children, but fail to either make these values explicit or follow through on the implications of their values. Thus, mandating after-school study sessions for failing students suggests that teachers value student achievement and performance. This action also implies a belief that teachers are responsible for providing additional help for failing students and conditions that support additional student efforts. If an explicitly shared value base exists that reflects these assumptions, it is also easier to discuss how they must be woven throughout other school policies in ways that support student learning. In this specific instance, teachers must also agree about a variety of other value-based policies, such as providing some credit for late work, for such time to be considered productive.

Reflective Dialogue

Growth of the school-based professional community is marked by conversations that hold practice, pedagogy, and student learning under scrutiny (Clift, Houston, & Pugach, 1990; Liebowitz, 1991; Little, 1990; Osterman, 1990, 1993). Rich and recurring discourse promotes high standards of practice, and both generate and reinforce core beliefs, norms, and values of the community. In other words, talk is the bridge between educational values and improved practice in schools.

Reflective practice denotes a self-awareness about what one does and, according to Schön (1983), is a condition toward which all professionals should strive. By engaging in reflection, teachers become students of their craft as they puzzle through the assumptions basic to quality practice. Although typically identified with self-analysis and critique, in organized settings reflection becomes a joint responsibility as teachers' work toward a better understanding of their own learning and abilities. School-wide commitment to reflection further implies a joint interest, which in turn suggests the value of public conversations that advance reflection.

Public conversation concerning practice within the school needs to focus on four topics: academic content, the intelligent use of generic teaching strategies, the development of students, and the social conditions of schooling and issues of equity and justice (Zeichner & Tabachnick, 1991). In an effectively functioning "traditional" setting, teachers may prefer to delegate responsibility for school organization to administrators. This is not unreasonable because, in general, reflection is more likely to result from talk that starts with classroom work, and later moves out toward school organization, than by beginning with school organization as the focus of discussion and reform (Crandall, Eiseman, & Louis, 1986). However, these discussions necessarily take on a broader focus when teachers and administrators decide to rethink fundamental issues of teaching that bear directly on the school's routines (for example, the schedule). In restructuring schools, and particularly in urban schools, conversations must also turn to the school organization itself, because this is viewed as problematic and connected with the main topics of concern to the community of teachers. Conversations therefore demand that teachers expand their thinking beyond those areas that are familiar parts of their repertoire and daily experience.

Reflective dialogue enlarges the teachers' world in other ways as well. It reduces isolation by asking teachers and administrators to genuinely "walk in each other's shoes" during intensive interaction. This empathetic collaboration leads to deepened understandings of the processes and products of teaching. In the end, reflection becomes a form of both individual activity and social interaction, carried on among all members of the school community to create joint understandings related to students, learning, and pedagogical practice.

Deprivatization of Practice

Teachers within professional communities practice their craft openly. Teachers can share and trade off the roles of mentor, adviser, or specialist when providing aid and assistance to peers (Lieberman, Saxl, & Miles, 1988; Little, 1990). Within these relationships teachers work to define and develop their own practice in public, deprivatized ways. Peer coaching relationships, based both in the mutual solving of problems through discussion and in classroom observation, have been accepted by many schools as a method to improve both classroom practice and collegial relationships.[1] Moreover, bringing real teaching problems to the table and engaging in mutual observations provide a richer context for discussions of practice because such action is specific and event focused, and thus encourages new forms of conversation among teachers. It allows teachers to be analytic in their planning and thinking and to use observations from others about student effort and achievement that cannot be obtained while in the act of teaching. Through discussion of specifics, teachers grow in their teaching practice by developing skills for describing, analyzing, and executing the instructional act. They also develop a shared common language with which to discuss these tasks; consequently, their instrumental and technical expertise advances.

Previous research has shown that deprivatization, where it is accompanied by frequent feedback about performance, augments the individual teachers' sense of efficacy (Louis, 1991b). There is also a significant social consequence for the community. Teachers deepen their levels of mutual trust and respect, thereby creating greater openness to further improvement within the school. The dialogue around publicly shared practice allows teachers to display their successes, but more important, to learn from their disappointments in a low-risk environment.

Collective Focus on Student Learning

Many programs that purport to improve teaching emphasize techniques, skills, and delivery strategies. Even where teachers are presented with research showing that these techniques affect achievement, they are rarely taught how they can monitor the connections between their use of these practices and learning. Under these conditions, practice remains mechanical and unexamined (Hord, Rutherford, Huling-Austin, & Hall, 1987). In contrast, when teachers begin to place sustained attention to students at the core of school-wide professional community, the emphasis shifts to how pedagogy is linked to the process of student learning, and professional actions increasingly focus on choices that affect students' opportunity to learn and provide substantial student benefit (Abbott, 1991; Darling-Hammond & Snyder, 1992; Darling-Hammond & Goodwin, 1993; Little, 1990). For this to occur, teachers' beliefs and values must wholeheartedly support notions of children as academically capable, and provide learning environments responsive to and supportive of student achievement. Thus, the central focus on student learning creates a sense of moral authority in both private practice and public conversation. Members of the school attend to this as their primary voice of conscience (Green, 1985).

Collaboration

Much has been written about the need to promote greater teacher collegiality and more cooperative work settings as part of restructuring schools. There are several related but conceptually distinct ideas here that merit clarification.

Teacher actions that focus on student learning may be considered cooperative, collegial, or collaborative (Hord et al., 1989). Cooperation represents a very basic level of social interaction among teachers: We say that teachers cooperate when they group students across classes for academic purposes, assist in parent conferences, or help one another with lesson planning. Cooperation, however, does not necessarily entail a shared value base about teaching practice, students, and learning, but focuses on mutual aid in order to get work done more efficiently.

In contrast, collegial relationships are characterized by mutual learning and discussion of classroom practice and student performance. Collegial teachers may share lesson plans around interdisciplinary theme units or work toward common expectations concerning student work and behavior. Time spent together in joint planning sessions focuses less on classroom war stories and more on issues related to future teaching activities, or ways that the school can support improved learning.

The most advanced forms of collegiality evolve further into genuine collaboration, the essence of which is codevelopment. Faculty may call on one another to discuss the mutual development of skills related to the new accomplishments in practice, or to generate knowledge, ideas, or programs that will help advance their expertise or contribute to school performance. Complex and confusing data, including classroom experience, can create shared understandings, as well as enhancing the community in which the members work. This stands in sharp contrast to Hargreaves's (Hargreaves & Dawe, 1990) descriptions of contrived collegiality, where teachers go through the motions of peer coaching or other administratively imposed practices, yet have little real connection with one another around their practice. True collaborative efforts, on the other hand, have not only tangible products but also lead to voluntary commitments among teachers that stimulate "richly substantive discourse" (Little, 1990, p. 522).

There are probably few schools where one cannot find a few instances of collaborative bonds between pairs of teachers. However, central to our idea of school-wide professional community is that collaboration is a generalized attribute of the school. Collaboration among many professionals, including across groups, is critical for the development of school-wide professional communities. It is important, for example, that teachers in the first and fifth grades, in science and math departments, and even administrators and teachers view themselves as part of the same endeavor. Role and department boundaries, which often serve as rigid barriers, become more permeable, although these groupings may remain very meaningful sources of professional engagement. This flexibility helps to shape information, routines, and the transfer of knowledge between grade levels and departments—an important feature of any organization that is adaptable and open to change (Cohen, 1988). Individual skills and knowledge provide the foundation of the school's capacity, but a school's ability to manage complex cycles of innovation depends on the ingrained habits of learning from colleagues both within and across work groups.

What Conditions Support
School-Based Professional Community?

Professional communities are supported by autonomy from a centralized bureaucratic structure, such as site-based management and school-based decision making. In our view, however, the current focus on school-based management has obscured the wide variety of other conditions that help to promote professional communities in schools. In the remaining section of this chapter we will focus on two broad categories: structural conditions, and the characteristics of human resources within and outside the school. Throughout this discussion the identification of specific features of school organization that may promote professional community should not be construed as a checklist. As we will see in the next section of this volume, the different features of school organization identified above interact in complex ways to affect teachers' focus on students, their own professional development, and the development of the school; no feature by itself is adequate.

Structural Conditions

The design of the school as a work setting either nourishes or impedes the formation of a strong professional community. Structural conditions that create interdependent work settings foster interdependence in other parts of the school, creating connections between different aspects of teachers' academic work. Issues of time, size, physical conditions, coordination among teachers, communication and autonomy, and control over membership affect practice. Together these structural conditions can create the needed foundation for professional community to emerge.

Time to Meet and Talk. Louis (1992b) and Raywid (1993) suggest that time is not only necessary to carry out change agendas, but also essential if innovation is to be maintained. A decade ago, Goodlad (1984) claimed that schools could not remain both static and exceptional. He argued that an institutionalized, ongoing self-renewal process is necessary for the maintenance of school effectiveness, and that this, in turn, implies a need for considerable and regular blocks of time devoted to professional learning and school improvement. Teachers need opportunities to consider pedagogy within department or grade level gatherings and in the context of all-school efforts. However, tacking additional voluntary time onto the ends of already tiring school days rarely works; it must be built into the school day and calendar. Consequently, the use of professional time must be understood in two ways. First, teachers must be provided the means to meet on a daily basis to address issues of concern to immediate work groups of faculty—departments, grade levels, or teams. Second, provision must be made for cross-connection among smaller work groups that emerge in the full faculty.

Physical Proximity. Structures that provide opportunities for informal communication can be important in promoting teacher effort on school improvement projects. Teachers need places in which to interact, but physical conditions, especially in large schools, are often a barrier to the exchange of ideas and the establishment of a sense of identity relating to common interests and goals (Louis & Miles, 1990). Creating common work spaces, such as team planning rooms, is one way to provide relief from the classroom isolation and pressured work schedules found in most school buildings. Moreover, when teachers are physically close, occasions for sustained observations and conversations related to teaching and student learning increase. Over the long run, this offers teachers more chances to learn about the effects of their work. Teachers interacting in new roles—mentors, advisers, and specialists concerning classroom practice—create feedback mechanisms to learn.

Interdependent Teaching Roles. Professional communities are marked by reciprocal influence among the teaching staff. A hallmark of mutual leverage is the presence of recurring and predictable situations in which teachers work together on teaching. Team-teaching and integrated lesson design are two examples of formal interdependent teaching roles. Collaborative teaching teams, another common characteristic of restructuring schools, work toward both short-term and long-term goals related to student learning by addressing curricular content, instruction, and other teaching practices. Teachers who work in interdependent settings act as professionals when their interactions support a shared value structure rather than reinforcing artificial boundaries between their roles (Kanter, 1983; Meyer & Rowan, 1983; Miller, 1985). In turn, interdependent teaching develops closer relationships and provides teachers more opportunities for dialogue, feedback, and discussion of specifics of practice—all of which produce a greater certainty about their pedagogical practice (Louis, 1991a).

Communication Structures. Creating school-wide professional community requires structures that encourage exchange of ideas within and across organizational boundaries. Regular meetings, with agendas focused on teaching and learning, provide opportunities to discuss instruction and curriculum, personal and professional growth experiences, and the establishment of discourse communities that encourage the exchange of ideas. Teacher networks within the school may help to foster an environment where talk about pedagogy, school organization, and student learning is common. Communication does not, however, need to be face-to-face to be effective; technological advances such as electronic mail can help teachers whose schedules do not mesh. By linking teachers engaged in similar work or with similar interests, communication networks of every sort promote discussion and reflection.

Teacher Empowerment and School Autonomy. Professional communities are distinguished by high degrees of teacher empowerment and school autonomy. Autonomy to act as individuals frees teachers to decide what is the best practice, given their classroom situation. Individual autonomy alone, however, does not necessarily promote school-wide professionalism or school change. In fact, research suggests that high levels of individual autonomy may have a negative impact on school-wide improvement efforts (Rosenblum & Louis, 1981). We believe that this is because excessive individual autonomy is antithetical to professional community. Rather, in a professional community, teachers become empowered as a group to consider the impact of their collective actions and practice on students, and jointly arrive at decisions to limit individual freedom in order to promote the effectiveness of the group. Thus, teachers in a school-wide community turn away from traditional autonomy, from operating as they wish within their own classroom, to consider the physical and social growth and development of their students as a school-wide issue.

Social and Human Resources

The significance of the human and social dimensions of schools for community has been articulated by Bryk and his colleagues (Bryk & Driscoll, 1988; Bryk, Lee, & Holland, 1993; Bryk, Easton, Kerbow, Rollow, & Sebring, 1993; Bryk & Rollow, 1992). The factors include openness to improvement, trust and respect, access to expertise, supportive leadership, and mechanisms to socialize new members.

Openness to Improvement. Openness to improvement within the school is important to ensure teachers' sense of professional community (Louis, Marks, & Kruse, 1994). Teachers also report that a key to successful school restructuring is support for faculty risk taking (Louis, 1992a), and we would argue that this means that school policies for change should reflect the needs of those willing to carry out innovations.

Trust and Respect. Trust and respect from colleagues inside the school and key members of relevant external communities, such as parents and the district office staff, are necessary conditions for developing commitment (Cohen, 1988; Firestone & Rosenblum, 1988; Louis, 1992b) as well as professional community. Respect refers to honoring the expertise of others, whereas trust refers more to the quality of interpersonal relations. Trust is an essential ingredient of the recipe for collegiality because it helps to induce a sense of loyalty, commitment, and effectiveness necessary for shared decision making and the establishment of collegiality. Without trust among faculty, change efforts may become contrived and without lasting impact (Hargreaves, 1992).

Hargreaves argues that trust involves both predictability and common goals. We would argue that the common goals are most central to trust because they are a reflection of the foundation of shared values. Trust manifests itself as confidence "invested in persons or process" (Hargreaves, p. 22), and may emerge when responsibility is delegated to either people and processes created for school improvement. Trust may be particularly important in a school where practice is changing and is more widely shared, because it permits teachers to overlook many behavior and activities that may not parallel their own. We can trust someone whose actions we do not always agree with if their actions are knowable, and they do not violate our common values and goals.

Access to Expertise. Professional community is based on an intellectual and practical grasp of the knowledge base and skills underlying the field. Normative practices that are not grounded in expertise are often unprofessional, involving an unspoken preference to avoid confronting the poor functioning of the group. In other cases, however, teachers may discuss practice, but persist in affirming the value of poor pedagogy because they lack access to information that would suggest otherwise (Louis, in press). Part of the problem is lack of access to the expertise of peers, and structures need to be devised to increase sharing around issues of practice. Ideally, the sharing of expertise will result in collaboration and the construction of new knowledge as richer and more complex problems are resolved.

The salient point is that the quality of the school, as contrasted with the individual classroom, can only be maintained when individual teachers improve learning for their own students but also make their expertise available to their colleagues. Thus, the practice of teaching becomes understood, generated through development, and enhanced through innovation in schools with strong cognitive and skill bases (Brown & Duguid, 1991). Without continued individual growth in teachers' knowledge and skills, in concert with supportive leadership to mediate existing poor performance, it is unlikely that a collectively rewarding environment can be established (Louis, 1992a).

Supportive Leadership. Leadership, whether provided by school administrators or site-based teams, needs to focus efforts on the core issues of shared purpose, continuous improvement, and structural change (Fullan, 1992; Murphy & Louis, 1994). Leaders are crucial for organizational innovation because they act as a constant source of pressure to think in ways that deviate from the current culture (Miles & Huberman, 1984). In addition, supporting a shared vision acts to create coherence and unity, and establishes a sense of "internal quality" (Vandenberghe & Staessens, 1991).

School leaders stimulate general commitment of participants to organizational effectiveness by creating meaningful interaction among faculty that focuses on a supportive environment and a climate for learning (Angle & Perry, 1983; Caldwell & Spinks, 1992). What leaders say and do expresses what they value for the organization, and the behavioral expectations that they communicate on a daily basis either reinforce or call into question these basic values and assumptions (Staessens, 1991). Principals who focus on classroom practice demonstrate through their actions that pedagogy is important, which, in turn, supports the expectation that conversation around these issues is worthy. In contrast, principals who contact teachers only around matters of administrative, procedural, or organizational concern imply that these areas are of most concern and focus staff efforts on ends that are unrelated to student learning.

Socialization. Socialization refers to the processes for inducting new members of the group. In many schools these are limited to procedures for recruitment; specific mechanisms for induction and purposeful reinforcement of group expectations for members of a school are typically weak. Yet, clear socialization procedures must be present to maintain a sense of community, because this is the main mechanism for helping new members to become part of the group (Van Maanen & Schein, 1979). Where strong organizational norms exist, we are also likely to find processes to socialize new members into the school (Driscoll, 1989). Through their mutual efforts, teachers generate an informal induction process to protect existing routines and perpetuate the school community. Because administrators often pay minimal attention to mentoring new teachers, veteran teachers have become, by default, the "bearers of the vision" (Vandenberghe & Staessens, 1991) that ensures conformity with valued practices. While this may work to ensure coherence and quality in teaching in schools where professional community already exists, where it does not, the result is often the reinforcement of the "egg carton" model of teacher isolation.

Development activities need to focus not only on training in new curriculum practices and instructional techniques but also on the development of the staff as an effectively functioning group. Collective work is the vehicle for clarifying the expected and possible, as well as the prohibited and unthinkable. These interactions therefore become a form of social control, as certain behavior is accepted and some other is discouraged in a daily process aimed at creating a common social reality.

Summary

The framework outlined above is not the only way of thinking about professional communities among teachers. By focusing on the school as the unit from which teachers derive their sense of community, we follow one set of arguments in the literature but ignore another. In particular, the work of McLaughlin and her colleagues (McLaughlin, in press; Siskin, 1991, in press; Talbert, McLaughlin, & Rowan, in press) makes a compelling argument that, for most high school teachers who are located in large schools fragmented by discipline, schedules, and student tracking, factors other than schoolwide community may have a bigger impact on professional commitment.

We agree with the findings of the research cited above that it is the embedded nature of teachers' work that best accounts for professionalism in many schools. For example, teachers who have low-ability students, but who work in highly committed departments, or who have external networks to others in their discipline, may exhibit high professionalism. In contrast, those who do not may fail in spite of the general professionalism of the school. Similarly, teachers in high commitment schools may develop professional communities with colleagues in the school even if their department does not provide a nourishing context.

Though acknowledging the importance of these findings in large high schools, it is not clear that they necessarily delimit the most desirable conditions for school organization. Expertise in subject matter is clearly central to good schools. Internal structures and external connections in support of expertise are central to this notion. However, in our view this is not enough to really "break the mold" of our current educational system, any more than the introduction of increased disciplinary capacity would dramatically alter the efficacy of higher education. While some problems stem from lack of content, expertise, and stimulation, we must be mindful that education occurs not just in individual classrooms or in a subject matter, but throughout a continuum of experiences. As Dewey noted many years ago, to support the educative nature of life experience, the school should be a community in all that this entails (Dewey, 1915). In its absence students' experiences can become fragmented and even anomic, leading both to problems of engaging with the work of school and personal unease with the processes of schooling (Newmann, 1991a). This goes to the adage that educators should focus on teaching children as the foreground, and subject matter as the vehicle.

The key is to find ways to support technical expertise—what professionalism has now largely come to mean in popular terminology—while promoting social structures that create school community between adults and students. The ideas presented in this chapter describe such an enterprise and the structural and social factors that may ease its emergence and sustain subsequent efforts of teachers. Although comprehensive high schools are now commonplace structures, our arguments challenge the wisdom of the "shopping mall high school," not only for students but also for teachers. In this instance, studying how things currently work in existing institutions should not limit our subsequent discussions about what better institutions might look like.

We argue this even more forcefully as we consider middle and primary schools. The education of the whole student, not just academic subject matter, must be the primary driving force. In more general terms, though subject matter disciplines may be primary organizing bases for the university, we caution how much elementary and secondary education should follow this lead.

Having introduced our conception of professional community, we will turn to Part II of this volume, in which we will present case studies of schools that have been striving to become more integrated, supportive, and effective environments for students and teachers.

Notes

1. However, mandated deprivatization, such as peer coaching that is driven by an administrative agenda, has produced little more than contrived collegiality (see Hargreaves & Dawe, 1990).

PART TWO

CASES FROM URBAN SCHOOLS

The next section presents five cases of urban schools that began intensive programs for school reform by the 1989 school year, whether the reform was internally initiated or imposed from outside. All of these schools value the role of individual teachers and subject matter competence in teaching, although they are not equally successful in delivering it; but they vary more widely in the degree to which they have focused on providing an environment that integrates pedagogical competence and a sense of community based on the principles outlined earlier. The schools are presented in order of the degree to which they meet the criteria for professional community outlined in Part I. We hope that the readers will keep our framework in mind as they read through the cases, and will refer back either to this chapter or to Appendix B, which briefly summarizes the argument put forth here. We hope, in addition, that the readers' attention will be drawn to the schools that are less successful as well as those that are more successful. The former are not "bad schools" or "failures" in any sense: Both of the schools arrayed toward the end of our continuum of professional community continue to receive significant public and media attention as important examples of school restructuring—for students.

Our cases have deliberately not followed a common outline. However, because all of the authors have been part of the collaborative program of research, the themes outlined in Part I are incorporated into the individual sagas of each school.

The names of people and schools in the following cases have been changed to protect their identities.

3

Professional Community and
Its Yield at Metro Academy

MARY ANNE RAYWID

Metro Academy is a high school of the New York City style of school-within-a-school, or mini-school. It is an independent program housed within a building that also houses another, entirely separate program, the High School for Social Sciences. The latter is a semi-selective high school with 1,500 students. Altogether, nine of the host school's rooms have been given to the Metro Academy, a program enrolling perhaps 100 10th through 12th graders. Metro is an alternative school, a designation that allows it considerably more freedom from central control than the average city high school. New York City's High Schools Division is widely perceived as one of the most rigid and controlling units within the school system. The Alternative Schools Office, on the other hand, is more likely to be perceived as a source of information and advice, and a buffer from the rest of the educational bureaucracy.

AUTHOR'S NOTE: Portions of this chapter were published in Raywid, M. A. (1994), "A School That Really Works," *The Journal of Negro Education, 63*(1), pp. 93-110. Reprinted with permission.

45

To be admitted, Metro students must visit the school, be interviewed, and fill out an application that includes brief thoughtful essays and general math problems. But the application is not used as a screening device. Metro is not a selective school, and admission is not based upon prior achievement or behavior. Indeed, many students entering from other high schools are quite explicit about seeing Metro as "Last Chance High." Certainly, student abilities, achievement, and performance span a wide range, although most Metro students are minority and, according to staff reports, few are middle-class. What most students explicitly share is a past that has included difficulties in accepting and dealing with school authority. When they enter, very few see themselves as college bound. Yet according to Esther, the staff member primarily responsible for college advisement, 95% of Metro Academy's students enter college after graduation. Essentially, the only graduates who do not are those entering the military.

The Development of Metro

The Metro Academy grew out of an instructional program, an inquiry learning project developed some years ago by its two directors and operated by them in what eventually grew to be 12 New York City high schools. Begun initially as a staff development project for teachers, the program then evolved into a half-day instructional program for students. Eventually, it appeared that both youngsters' needs and staff interests might better be accommodated in a full-time school. Thus, Metro Academy opened in 1985, featuring an inquiry approach to learning. The teachers consisted of interested people the two directors had either met during the staff development project or known earlier. Although some of these people had met one another at summer workshops associated with the demonstration project, they had never worked together and had not really known each other.

Staff members construe the Academy as "the working laboratory for the Inquiry Demonstration Project" (Cook, 1991, p. 149). Partly because of its past, partly due to still continuing activities, and partly due to its experimental and nontraditional orientation, the Metro Academy characterizes itself as a laboratory school. A steady stream

of visitors comes to observe, and several faculty members still offer
in-service courses on the Academy's approach to teachers in other
schools.

Metro Academy reports 16 staff members, but this total is misleading because it includes the two codirectors, full-time teachers,
part-time teachers, and interns. Nine of Metro's teachers are full-
timers. There are only two formal status differentiations, teachers
and codirectors. Until last year there was also an assistant principal
who took care of much of the administrative work, but when he left,
staff decided together to assume his duties and use his salary for
other purposes. Thus there is considerable differentiation as to function among staff now, because teachers share most administrative
tasks, including admissions, keeping track of attendance, handling
student transportation (New York City students get special passes),
and the record-keeping role of registrar. These assignments appear
to have been arrived at by mutual agreement and in consequence of
individual teachers' interests and talents. Thus faculty view them as
permanent assignments, until a reason for changing them surfaces.
(A request for reassignment, or an interest in the function by a new-
comer would stand as such a reason.) Besides the teaching staff, there
is one individual who coordinates the community service program
and has responsibility for helping with college applications, and
there is one secretary who serves the entire faculty. A single former
classroom houses all of Metro's offices, making for a room so
crowded with teachers' desks that navigating the four narrow passage aisles can prove challenging. An adjacent room serves as a gathering place for both students and faculty.

The codirector arrangement is novel on several counts. One of
the two codirectors, Art Coe, functions in effect in the more familiar
role of principal, assuming responsibility for coordinating Metro's
daily operation. Staff look to him for instructions, help, and advice,
and he is also perceived by students as a strong, supportive, and
benevolent though firm father figure. The other codirector, Lynn
Adams, functions primarily in the role of ambassador to and liaison
with the external educational and political community. She is active
in New York City educator circles and assumes a major role in bringing news and also new pedagogical ideas into the Metro Academy.
Although Lynn regularly teaches at least one course (as does Art),

and is almost always present for staff meetings, she spends a lot of time out of the building and is often on the phone when she is there.

Metro's codirectorship arrangement is also novel in that Adams and Coe have been longtime professional collaborators, having devised and pursued a number of projects together. They designed and piloted the Inquiry approach that is the theme of Metro Academy. They are also husband and wife, and the parents of three adolescent daughters.

According to Wisconsin's federally sponsored Center for School Organization and Restructuring, one of the hallmarks of a restructured school is that the experience of being a student—or a teacher— in such a school is quite different from what it is to be a student or a teacher in a traditionally structured school (Newmann, 1991b). One's days are spent differently and the school has a different sort of ambiance, leading both students and teachers to feel differently about being associated with it and about their roles within it. In short, the lived experience of school has been transformed for these students and teachers. This is clearly true of school life at Metro. As students readily report without prompting, it is quite different from their previous school experiences.

Modifying Student Experience

Perhaps the most arresting qualities of restructured student experience at Metro Academy accrue from (a) the literally ceaseless efforts to make school a thought-provoking place; (b) the determined arranging and rearranging of the daily schedule to serve programmatic purposes, rather than vice versa; and (c) the unremitting efforts to provide needed support for students.

Insistence on thought-provoking pedagogy is rooted in the Inquiry Method that is the school's theme and unifying thread. The single word "WHY" dominates the front cover of Metro's brochure. Opening sentences on the following page elaborate:

> That's what the students at the Metro Academy ask each day, in every class, at every opportunity. When they enter the Metro Academy they become members of an academic community seeking understanding in the same way as inquiring

minds have done over the centuries. They ask questions and examine the variety of ways they can be answered.

But one of the most noticeable ways in which the Metro Academy differs from many schools as an institution is that these words are not simply words. Metro means what it says it means, and students get just what they've been told they'll find. Put succinctly, the school mission is not simply the "philosophy" statement prepared by some authority to satisfy some regulation or other: It represents a commitment that suffuses everything the school does.

For instance, the attempt to arouse questioning and thoughtfulness is reflected in the curriculum and the courses offered. Although there are some standard, discipline-based classes like American History, Algebra, Economics, and Chemistry, most are topically articulated instead, and by topics of concern to urban students. Telling Stories, Popular Culture, Puzzles, Evolution, Religion and Society, American Autobiography, Utopia/Dystopia, Animal Rights, and Women Across Cultures are a few of the courses from recent semesters. Moreover, students can expect to encounter at least three types of learning in virtually every course: There is always material they recognize as usable now (e.g., knowledge of the city's subway system or its museums, or landmark buildings); there is also content they can use later, which is more typical school fare; and content is always treated in such a fashion as to increase reflectiveness and thinking ability, as well as to enhance work habits.

The thoughtfulness theme is omnipresent. This is not easy to accomplish with a student population that would probably not comply with the reading and other daily assignments associated with traditional secondary education. It is also very challenging to get students to tackle activities that must be sustained over an extended period. One response on the part of the faculty is to probe different facets of a broad topic on different days, introducing novelty through added complexity as the discussion proceeds. Most classes manage to present an issue students find genuinely challenging. It is always one that can be tackled at a more penetrating level than simply "getting the facts" or "mastering the basics" during a class. Thus, Art's popular course titled Issues one day tackled, "What are the most important values?" and another, "What rights does a parent have and what rights does a kid have?" Marcus's Pop Culture course demanded inferences about popularity and power from data detailing cassette and CD sales by various vocalists and instrumentalists. And Jan's Seminar on Animal Rights explored whether zoos are, in the very nature of the situation, inhumane. On a day when I visited, a Women's Studies class taught by Lynn tackled "Which is more dangerous: pornography or censorship?"

As this suggests, efforts to make students think don't end with the in-class efforts of individual teachers. The entire school is constructed to provoke adolescents to think. For instance, a question based on a prominent current news issue is always posted in the hall outside the office: for example, "Should football be outlawed?" (following the accident of a professional player whose neck was broken) and "Should gays be allowed to serve in the military?" (while the issue was being discussed in the press). The question is mounted on a large sheet of poster paper, where students anonymously pen their responses to the question and to each other. (There is also a sheet of similar size on a nearby board, inviting Graffiti, which serves to keep the question sheet, and other Metro Academy areas, largely graffiti-free.)

Another means of provoking thought is the 3-week project that launches each semester at Metro. This is a carefully worked out cross-disciplinary venture that involves the whole school, working in groups of 8 to 12, to tackle the various dimensions of a broad question. For instance, one recent project theme was "What makes for a good subway system?" For a previous semester it was "What is community?" Prior to that, another theme was "How does architecture affect lifestyles?" Each project is planned in detail, with intensive day-long group activities, some exercises and activities shared by all students and others that are differentiated according to student interests and the talents and focus of individual teachers. Fulfilling project requirements is a demanding and intensive venture occupying the full day of students and teachers working together in school and outside it. After the 3-week project period has ended, the semester's regular classes begin.

Meanwhile, the September project has served as a notable way to induct new staff and students into the life of the Metro Academy. (And the February project has served as a welcome midyear change of pace, bringing variety to the school.) The project yields extended opportunity for teachers to work together in planning a set of experiences equally novel to beginners and old-timers. Moreover, it provides an opportunity for the staff to pursue and model the same sort of inquiry process they want students to internalize. And it enables students, teachers, and the two groups together to work less formally and more closely with one another than class time usually allows.

A new way to stimulate student thinking added this year is special-topic seminars on issues of sure concern to students. The seminars are small classes by design and they make heavy demands on those enrolled. In addition to extensive reading assignments, a paper is due each week. Because Metro has no library of its own, and because it would be unlikely that daily reading assignments requiring library access would be completed, readings are typically photocopied for students. Seminar students receive weekly packets of carefully chosen articles that form the basis for their papers.

Events that began in the Animal Rights Seminar yield further evidence of staff commitment to generating student thinking. Jan, the teacher, was disappointed by students' failure to fulfill his writing assignment that called for *analysis* of the materials in the reading packet. So he made multiple copies of one articulate, otherwise well-written paper that erred by instead *summarizing* one article after another. He brought copies of the papers for all to the staff meeting that afternoon and distributed them at the start, because Art had placed him first on the agenda. Thus, for 45 minutes the staff discussed what an adequate response to the assignment would be, and the challenge of how to teach students to undertake genuine analysis. The discussion ended with an agreement to return to the matter for general staff consideration after Jan and another teacher had a chance to consider some further ideas. *Analysis* is a frequently used term at Metro, and there seemed embarrassment as well as chagrin that the concept at issue—and how to operationalize it—appeared so elusive. At a subsequent meeting, two teachers agreed to bring in selected packets of student papers so that the staff could together advance the effort by exploring which papers provide the best analyses and why.

A statement that hangs on the wall beside Art's desk, having struck a responsive chord, seems to project the sort of ambiance Metro Academy students have come to expect: *I fully realize that I have*

*not succeeded in answering all of your questions. . . . Indeed, I feel I have
not answered any of them completely. The answers I have found only serve
to raise a whole new set of questions, which only lead to more problems, some
of which we weren't even aware were problems. To sum it all up . . . In some
ways I feel we are confused as ever, but I believe we are confused on a higher
level, and about more important things.*

As previously suggested, a second way in which the lives of
Metro students and teachers differ quite extensively from the lives
lived in most other schools is associated with the way in which the
school schedule is viewed. At Metro, the schedule is not the all-
powerful structure to which everything must conform. Instead, it is
designed, and constantly redesigned, to serve the programmatic purposes staff have selected. When it fails to do so, it is the schedule and
not the instructional program that must give way. Although that is
more easily accomplished at the end of a semester, when the schedule
is regularly redesigned anyway, adjustments can be made in mid-
semester. As will be seen, the schedule at Metro is simply not construed as unvarying; by design it contains enough day-to-day
variation that everyone must be reminded of each day's components
and sequence. Thus changes are far more easily introduced than
when the mindset calls for invariant time segments and sequences.

The design and use of the school schedule at Metro are sufficiently unusual that they appear to be a major reflection of the restructuring the Academy represents. A proposed schedule is created
each semester by Art, after meetings that air exactly what each
teacher would like to have. According to reports, a proposed schedule always goes through multiple versions before it is completed.
This means that in resolving conflicts and accommodating needs, the
whole thing is scrapped several times and the task launched again
from the beginning. The fall version this year represented the sixth
such take-it-from-the-top try.

Unlike most other schedules, Metro's does not divide the day
into equal segments for classes. The first class in a Friday schedule
lasts 55 minutes, the second and third, 50 minutes each. Lunch is an
hour, and the two afternoon classes each last 75 minutes. (Most
classes fall within the 50- to 75-minute period. Tuesdays, however,
have one 90-minute time block.) There are also two 10-minute breaks,
one after the second class and one just before the last class of the day.

The time classes are assigned differ according to teachers' requests: Some classes are always longer, some are always shorter, and some teachers may want one or two 50-minute sessions plus one 75-minute class. Accommodations are also made to preferences as to morning versus afternoon classes, although the more frequent pattern is to shift class time so that a class which meets at 8:30 on Monday may meet at 10:35 on Wednesday. The result is that students rarely memorize schedules, and Art posts the schedule for the day outside each of Metro's rooms early every morning.

A final illustrative manifestation of the use of the schedule to serve the needs of the program, instead of forcing instruction to fit into preset time blocks, lies in the building in of nonclass time. The staff meets regularly on Wednesdays, from 12:15 to 3:15 (and on alternate Tuesdays after school). The collaboration time is made possible by having students perform service activities in the community during this time. All students are required to provide such service weekly, and on a volunteer, unpaid basis. Assignments include such activities as helping in a legislative office, a school, a teenage treatment center, or an animal rescue group.

A third characteristic of restructured student experience at Metro accrues from the staff's determination to provide whatever is necessary in the way of student support. This determination surfaces in many ways, in the school's culture as well as in its structural features and operation. In the first place, Metro has the increasingly familiar advisory groups in which students largely explore school problems. For example, the topic in one session of Vivian's advisory group this year was "What's screwed up around here?" But this year there is also a new set of groups called Organizational Tutorials, which involve all students and meet weekly. These were started to preserve the integrity of advisory groups while also providing something of a more explicitly academic advisory setting. Before the weekly meeting of the small groups of seven to nine, each Organizational Tutorial teacher checks with the teachers of all the tutorial members' classes to find out how each of his/her tutorial students is doing in the class. There is a particular emphasis on whether work is being completed, and whether any other class-specific difficulties are occurring for each student. This arrangement was launched in the interests of proactive troubleshooting, and of trying to identify cognitive difficulties when they are emerging. It is a brief, highly task-oriented session. The Organizational Tutorial teacher goes around the circle, both asking for student response on how things are going and providing feedback from teachers. There are often suggestions about needed priorities, time management, work organization—whatever seems needed.

Three kinds of labs are operated to assure that students get needed support: Homework Labs, course-connected labs, and College Labs. The Homework Labs function as study halls and are operated for those who want them. Because some Academy students are totally without supportive conditions for doing homework outside school, such an elective fills an important function for them. The students enrolled in Homework Lab get help as needed and must arrive at each session with an assignment to work on, or one is provided for them. Students who do not elect to enroll in a Homework Lab take Independent Study instead and can pursue individual or group projects. Most select the latter and at the moment, one Independent Study group is reading Dostoevsky, another is working on conversational Spanish, and a third is doing a videotape of the school.

Another sort of lab is attached to specific courses that make heavy demands in terms of reading or writing. Such a lab might be scheduled for a course assigning an extensive research paper, or a series of short analytic papers, where several rewrites will be suggested. The intent is not remediation but the provision of proactive support to enable students to meet demanding standards. This year, American History and Television Analysis had labs during the fall semester, and the History and Issues courses had them in the spring. Just one of their unusual features is that the lab segment of each course—which meets for one separate, and longer, period each week—is, by design, taught by a teacher other than the person who teaches the course. Typically the lab teacher(s) will sit in on the course's regular classes occasionally, to remain aware of course expectations, but not in the usual role of study hall teachers.

The purposes of assigning staff this way are several: It affords students additional help because there are now two sources and two sets of resources to tap; but at the same time, it leaves the student in charge of carrying out the assignment and satisfying the class's requirements, because the lab teacher's role is to help the student, not to coteach the course; and it places Metro staff in yet another collaborative setting, giving them a view of others' teaching and perhaps prompting questions about their own. This semester lab teachers have helped the students enrolled in Television Analysis and American History to organize themselves to pursue research, to organize notes and materials for writing purposes, to get going, and to revise as indicated.

Still a third kind of lab has emerged in connection with Metro students' enrollment in college classes. The Academy's students have the option of enrolling in such classes. But based on difficulties some have encountered, and on students' insecurities and hesitations, a Metro teacher now accompanies the students and sometimes sits in on the classes in which they are enrolled. The group travels together to the campus of a local 4-year private college, or to a two-year City college, and one or two Academy teachers sit in as observers in the courses Metro students have selected. Back at the Academy, in a specially scheduled College Lab class, whatever support the students need is provided.

There are also many other sorts of support extended to Metro students, although not all of them in typical ways. There are no counselors at Metro, because every teacher is expected to fill the counseling role in the sense not only of academic advisement but also of standing as an interested and concerned adult to any student seeking help. A part-time psychologist is supposedly available to Academy students for 2 half-days each week, though he reportedly often gives many more than the hours that are expected of him. Otherwise, he maintains a private practice.

The Academy population is small enough, and there is sufficient psychic closeness in the school, that when kids are in trouble it quickly becomes evident. A teacher who happened to spot difficulty, or to wonder about whether there was some, might first address Art about it, or go first to the advisory group leader enrolling the student. Or he or she might simply comment to another teacher. It might then occur spontaneously or by design that the youngster would be engaged by a staff member attempting to discern the difficulty. Art has frequent access to the students because they pass his desk in going from the office/staff room to the student study/lounge next door. He

also stocks two aspirin bottles on his desk with M&M's. Students stop
by constantly throughout the day and help themselves to the supply
(requiring Art to refill the bottles all day long and to purchase 15
pounds of M&M's per week). This means that a student stopping for
a handful of candy may become engaged in an exchange with Art, or
with another student who is on the same mission. Art is a father
figure to the entire school, and students feel they can ask him for an
unusual range of assistance and advice. The notes mounted on the
walls around his desk attest eloquently to this:

- Hola Art. There's a leaky pipe in the Women's Bathroom.
  Check it out TODAY.
- I hate you, Art. Love, Bill
- Art, I feel crabby and/or cranky. I'm sick. Please come and get
  me in Dance A.S.A.P. — Jean
- Art, Lily is driving me crazy. Please help me. Shanti
- Dear Art,
  I have been diagnosed with "School Burnout"!!! So I'm going
  home to sleep it off.
  P.S. See you tomorrow.
  Your hardest working student, Jane
- Dear Art:
  i appriciate the fact that you have saved all the letters that i
  have given you over the years. But you should take them down
  soon, because i have grown tremendously and find them quite
  embarassing . . .
  Very happily, May

Lest these messages seem to suggest a highly indulgent environment where students do as they please, a further look is needed. An
observer who concluded that Metro Academy is a permissive school
where student whim or choice governs would have missed the essence of the school. An important contrast separates Metro Academy
from schools where students decide most things. Students are constantly consulted at Metro: They are invited to participate in
decision-making sessions, they are asked what courses they want to
take and with which teachers, and they are encouraged to express
their reactions to events and conditions. What they have to say is

listened to not only courteously but also intently; what they like and dislike gets serious consideration, as does what they find meaningful as opposed to what they find obscure or inscrutable. They are obviously taken seriously and influence events. But they are not the decision makers at Metro. The teachers are.

For instance, students' choice of courses may be overridden in the interests of getting an appropriate balance for the class, getting a schedule that makes more sense for the individual with an eye to meeting graduation requirements, or separating students whom staff feel should not share the same class. Similarly, within curriculum and content, student interests are taken very seriously, but it is the staff who make the decisions. Though students are the major determinants of what happens at Metro, their influence is not manifested through votes or statements of preference; it is mediated by staff decisions on what seems indicated in light of student preferences as well as in light of other considerations.

One final way in which the culture at Metro Academy extends enormous support to students is through the clear priorities that exist there. At most conventional high schools, it is simply assumed that adults are entitled to courtesies denied students. It is also assumed that communication among the adults who are there to run the place takes precedence over other exchanges. Thus it is not unusual in most schools for an administrator or another teacher (or a public address system) to interrupt a class or a student-teacher conversation to deliver a message to the teacher or to get the answer needed to a question. This is clearly not standard operating procedure at Metro. Classes, and student-teacher conversations have priority and a kind of sanctity, so that if a student is standing with a teacher in the hall, or seated at a teacher's desk in the crowded staff room, they are rarely interrupted by another staff member—especially if they are talking quietly. In fact, the norm is just the reverse of what one typically finds in schools. At Metro, staff and other adult conversations may be interrupted by students or teachers, but not student-staff conversations. There is too much commitment both to respect for students and to the importance of "the teachable moment" for such interruptions to occur. As one teacher put it, if a teacher and a student arrive simultaneously at Art's desk seeking his attention, it is the student and not the teacher to whom he turns first.

A rather different kind of support also prevalent at Metro Academy accrues from the dogged attempt by staff to figure out exactly why their academic expectations of students are not being met, and then to do something about it. They consistently reject answers like "They're just lazy," or "They were careless," or "They didn't think" in favor of diagnoses as to specific process deficiencies. When a full class failed to analyze material, the situation was pursued sufficiently to ascertain that they didn't know how. Hence they needed help in how to conduct the process, and the staff set to work figuring out how to provide the assistance necessary.

A consequence of such an approach is the tendency at Metro to render explicit a great deal that other schools simply take for granted. When Academy students are instructed in how to do research papers, for example, the instructions are not just as to length, and what note cards and footnotes should look like; there is an attempt to have them understand the nature of the mental processes one goes through in doing research. This marks a considerable contrast with customary educational practice: We tend more typically to tell students to "analyze," "discuss," or "appraise," and then we test them on whether they can do so; but rarely do we offer, in between, the step-by-step guidance on just how one performs these operations. It is characteristic of Metro Academy staff to try to figure out the process and instruct youngsters on how to conduct it.

Teachers' Experience

Metro Academy teachers work hard, but in several important respects their work appears different from that of teachers in traditional schools. In the first place, their workloads do not look like those in comprehensive high schools, because the array of duties and expectations is far broader than the teaching of classes. As mentioned earlier, some teachers perform regular administrative functions, like the handling of admissions or the categorizing and recording of credits on student transcripts. Others may have an assignment to accompany students to a college course, and still others may be assigned to conduct the lab portion of a colleague's course. New teachers are expected to audit one or two classes taught by a senior teacher in a related field. New teachers (and interns) also meet weekly with Art, in small groups, to discuss challenges and difficulties as raised by either party. All teachers are expected to be available to cover a colleague's class, or to assist with it (e.g., by participating in a demonstration or debate) on absolutely minimal notice (such as 3 minutes). Asking for and receiving help is common.

Although a look at schedules may show a teacher teaching during only three of a day's scheduled five periods, no teachers appear to have prep periods in the form of assigned time that commonly belongs solely to themselves. They are expected to be available at any time for whatever appears to be needed. Although some might find this an infringement on individual entitlements, it seems closely tied to the deeply rooted conviction that all are jointly responsible for making the school work—and when something is needed and one is the logical member to do it, or simply the most available member, one does it. Obviously, such an attitude could not long prevail were individuals to believe themselves exploited or victimized. But a sense of reciprocity—a conviction that one can count on comparable support from others when the need arises—prevents a sense of being exploited.

Metro's teachers clearly work hard in ways that are demanding and place a premium on invention and creativity. Working out the curriculum described in these pages is extremely demanding—particularly because change and novelty are perceived assets to sustaining student engagement. By virtue of the quality of effort required, teachers at Metro experience their work as highly professional in nature. They see themselves as performing an intellectually and emotionally challenging task and although, or perhaps because, they find almost constant reason to change and improve their efforts, they are proud of what they do and the success with which they do it. They seem to relish the intellectual challenge that their problems sometimes occasion. In multiple ways the staff project the message that educators generally would have much to gain by emulating their program and arrangements.

One reason is the sense of confidence and efficacy that is evident. The school's descriptive brochure proclaims: "The Metro Academy is recognized as a rigorous academic school serving a diverse population of students who have often been unchallenged in previous settings." As staff describe this population less formally, they say it is a group that has had trouble with authority in other school settings. What Metro does is to construe a population, which has elsewhere posed disciplinary problems, as posing a primarily pedagogical challenge instead. It seems to work. There appear to be few disciplinary problems, and virtually none of a confrontational, showdown sort. The school's sole absolute is "No fighting." I am told that it has never been violated in Metro's 9 years—and that on the sole occasion when that record was threatened, it was students who stepped in to uphold it.

There are, however, a normal number of adolescent challenges to adult authority and numerous other infractions that, in more traditional schools, might become confrontational occasions. To cite three sorts, lateness is a chronic problem for some Academy students; locker fronts sometimes exhibit displays of questionable taste; and male students often want to wear hats while walking through the hallways of The High School for Social Sciences, where hats are forbidden. Metro handles such challenges with careful inquiry into causes and circumstances, a receptivity to discussion and negotiation, and often with considerable humor. Depending on the circumstances, lateness may be viewed more sympathetically than at other schools and it is handled on an individual basis, but only after an effort to detect its reason. Sometimes the answer has been to give the student an alarm clock—or to do a morning call. Other measures have included careful scheduling to lure youngsters into arriving on time, and a support group is currently under consideration.

The challenge of locker fronts displaying sexually explicit photos, or language that would undoubtedly offend some, are more likely to turn into First Amendment discussions than personal confrontations, and staff are quite willing to applaud (even if they do not concede) when students put forward strong defenses. When students who feel they have been wrongfully censored respond with locker fronts proclaiming that message in some way, staff are willing to accept that and often to appreciate the student's stance, even though the taboos remain in force.

One of the most important features of Metro's nonconfrontational stance is a willingness to negotiate matters that are not elsewhere negotiable. Lynn talks about the hats in the halls question this way: When students begin insisting, she and Art express a willingness to negotiate it, if the students assign it a priority. Because negotiations will probably necessitate giving as well as getting, the students must decide what they are willing to surrender: their right to leave the building at noon? their right to use Walkmans in Homework Labs? When so approached, the hat issue usually recedes, although some rules have been modified through such negotiation between Metro students and staff.

The general absence of confrontational disciplinary problems doubtless contributes to the staff's sense of efficacy. They are spared a lot of struggle and unpleasantness hard to avoid in other schools. That may be a factor in the strong sense not only of accomplishment but of the group's self-sufficiency and collective competence to cope successfully with the challenges that arise.

Professional Community

Metro Academy enjoys an extraordinarily close professional community, although it does not appear to have spawned the kind of social interaction indicative of close personal relationships. There have been brief stretches when as many as two thirds of the staff go out for Friday afternoon coffee together, but apparently such practice is not sustained as custom. There may be some socializing among those who live on the Upper West Side—a group that roughly approximates the old-timers—but that does not appear extensive. Thus, Metro does not represent a place where all are close friends and personal relationships will spontaneously coordinate interaction.

Yet these are obviously people who like and respect and admire one another enormously. It does not appear that there is regularly a great deal of discussion of personal affairs among colleagues—less than in the typical teachers' lounge. But word spreads quickly among the staff of major tribulations, and there are efforts to accommodate such personal difficulties as Lily's father's illness and the lengthy terminal illness of Marcus's father. There are also many expressions of congratulation over events like Vivian's marriage and the birth of Marcus's son. Birthdays are usually celebrated with a cake at the staff meeting nearest to the event. There seems a consistent and genuine concern for staff as people and also fellow professionals.

It would be hard to find a faculty group with members more respectful of one another's knowledge and skills. One remarkable staff meeting involved a short, good-natured rivalry between Lily and Marcus about who was to present a description of a new course each was currently teaching. After the meeting I asked each privately the reason for the desire to describe what they were doing (a desire that might be expressed among most faculties only in consequence of extreme pressure). The two responded similarly: They expected substantial valuable help from the anticipated reactions so they were eager to obtain the benefits as soon as possible. As Marcus put it, each teacher genuinely seeks answers from the rest of the staff—and equally significantly, expects quality answers to be forthcoming.

There is considerable fundamental agreement among Metro Academy's teachers. Although they express it in varying degrees of detail and eloquence, they are engaged in sustaining and inducting young people into an intellectual community. Their intent is occasioning cognitive learning and development for young people, in the interests of making them independent thinkers able to function as adults both receptive to and capable of further education.

As Marcus put it, the school's several purposes are first to provide an empowering education for students that enables them to establish their place in the world with self-confidence, openness, and critical mindedness. Second, the aim is to create a community and to teach kids what it is. And a third purpose is to provide an enduring, successful instructive model of alternative teaching.

Lily expressed the Academy's purpose as "to turn students on to school and thinking." Ruth, a new teacher, put it in terms of bringing students to love learning in the interests of enabling them to be able to handle further education. Bob, a senior staff member, said simply "to create independent learners." Naomi, another new teacher expressed it as "to create a community of students." Lynn expressed it as "getting kids to buy into intellectual rigor and to see themselves as intellectuals."

Some systematic differences are discernible in the ways that older and newer teachers set priorities for the school's purposes. New teachers are sometimes bowled over by the home and neighborhood situations from which many of the students come. They often focus on "the emotional baggage weighing these kids down" (in Ruth's terms). Older teachers appear continually conscious of and responsive to such problems, but they seem to have arrived at a more clearly delineated ordering of purposes—in which responding to the problems is an instrumental purpose to be met in the interest of encouraging intellectual accomplishment and development. The differences are subtle, because all Metro Academy teachers are much concerned with the personal and affective dimensions of their students' present lives, and with their future prospects. But the professional culture at Metro is strong in insisting that all youngsters can and must become competent independent thinkers, and that contributing to this development is the Academy's ultimate purpose.

It is indicative of the strength and extent of collegial agreement among the faculty that there is comparable unanimity about taboos. Teachers respond quite similarly to questions about the worst thing a Metro Academy teacher could do as far as students are concerned. Several spoke explicitly of showing disrespect. They also replied in terms of "putting a student down," "taking away a student's self-esteem," "making kids feel incapable," and "attacking or humiliating a student." When asked what would be the worst thing they could do as far as the codirectors were concerned, they spoke of "turning kids off intellectually." And one particularly sensitive teacher, Lily—to whom many students turn—also spoke of keeping oneself "unavailable as a human being" and of a "failure to engage or connect, a 'not being there' for kids."

There is similar agreement that the Metro Academy's particular strategy for bringing about the intellectual development sought is the inquiry approach. This is the school's unique focus. When I asked each teacher what would happen were they to disavow the approach, all but one concluded that such a position would be incompatible with remaining. Bob's reply was "I'd leave; the inquiry approach is nonarguable." Marcus jokingly said "I'd be an enemy of the people." Only Lily felt that such a personal conclusion would be discussible in staff meetings, because inquiry, after all, applies to a process of searching and learning.

Lily is a highly respected member of the senior staff, and her answer suggests an important feature moderating the press for conformity to the inquiry approach. The approach is differently interpreted and differently carried out in each classroom. To some extent such differences are imposed by epistemological differences in subject matter, but even where this is the case, approaches are sought to render the material subject to inquiry. For example, the claims of algebra and geometry are not inductively substantiated, so the open-endedness and tolerance of difference that mark Art's Issues course cannot occupy the same place in Bob's math and Puzzles courses, where the questions are deductive and only one answer is correct. Nevertheless, the group work that Bob pursues in his courses places students in the position of cosearchers and coinquirers as they jointly pursue solutions. And care is taken to acknowledge more than one approach as a valid way to tackle a given problem. Many of the questions that arise in other courses fall somewhere between the open-endedness of the Issues course and the necessarily more prescriptive stance of a math course. Thus, although Art and Lynn are widely thought to offer the quintessential inquiry courses, it is recognized that the approach will not work out the same way everywhere.

Personality also clearly seems to have something to do with the particular way in which an individual teacher employs the inquiry approach. Art is nondirective with respect to the substance of students' views on the issues considered. He operates as a facilitator (which is, incidentally, the same role he assumes in faculty meetings). His most directive move in dealing with content is to raise a new question (or subquestion) that either elicits challenges to what has been said or channels response in an altered direction. Art's version of the inquiry approach is to raise a broad question, identify those who want to address it, call on them in the order in which they sought to speak, and take careful notes on everything said. He may occasionally offer a brief summary of what has been said, or raise a new question, but he does not offer or endorse any replies. His contributions are exclusively process-oriented rather than substantive. Lynn follows largely the same pattern in her Television Analysis class, beginning with a broad and provocative question thrown out to a class seated in a large circle. But the effects are different because Lynn is more tempted to exert an influence on substantive outcomes.

Other teachers pursue the approach in different ways. For instance, the descriptions just offered provide opportunities for each individual who wants to speak to do so. But it minimizes opportunities for engagement in sustained pursuit or exchange on a particular point. The purposes of the Debate course call for a different arrangement, as could frequent purposes of the Political Philosophy course and the Plays course.

Thus, the inquiry approach appears not so much a matter of particular moves and techniques as of broad intent and orientation. Teachers and codirectors both characterize it by contrasting an inquiry lesson with a developmental lesson, in that the latter begins with a particular point in mind that the successful lesson must arrive at before it concludes. An inquiry lesson, by contrast, has no such single-minded and specific endpoint, and may go in quite different directions from what might have initially been envisioned.

In further seeking the common ground that marks the inquiry approach as applied across various classes and subjects and by different teachers, it seems to represent: (a) a commitment to maximal openness and receptivity to student responses, with a willingness to pursue hypotheses even when they seem wrongheaded; (b) a commitment to exposing students to a variety of information and opinion on all matters considered, thereby expanding awareness of existing knowledge and theory; and (c) a commitment to casting the student in as intellectually an active and demanding a role as possible.

So understood, the approach appears strongly embraced and consistently reflected in all classes. It is broad enough not to pinch: Academy staff do not experience the inquiry orientation as a constraint on their own practice, but instead report a totally unprecedented degree of autonomy. The inquiry approach is also sufficiently specific that it would undoubtedly prove alien and restrictive to some teachers, but the orientation lends consistency to what students experience throughout the school. It does so by enabling Metro to stand for something, as distinct from what its faculty may stand for as individuals. And it is this that in turn enables both students and staff to select the Academy for what it represents.

But lest this suggest that the core agreement among the faculty is only to a broad or abstract set of ideals, that is not the case. Metro has honed several approaches and techniques to a high level of development, and these are used repeatedly in projects and from class to class. One is an expert panel. This is a frequent activity for opening an area or topic of study. One panel, for instance, dealt with the question of "What's an education for?" It combined two Metro teachers and two outside educators, each of whom spoke from a single, deliberately focused perspective. One advanced the idea that the central purpose of an education is to take on the culture; another, that it is to prepare the individual for a career; a third, that education's aim is to acquire the values and orientation of the family; and a fourth, that education is for learning how to think independently and to look critically at conditions and ideas.

A second frequent activity is a debate between two Metro teachers. This is a particularly effective way to make students aware of conflicting perspectives, and of knowledge bases that are not always consistent. But well-staged debates between teachers also serve several other long-range Academy purposes extremely well. They provide a platform for teachers to model how adults think about and pursue issues, and to model how intellectual disagreement and conflict can be handled. Thus, Art came in to Marcus's history course one morning to argue that Columbus was a hero for his time, and that his own context rather than ours is the appropriate grounds for judging him; and Marcus argued the position that Columbus was an exploitative business man who pillaged and murdered and is undeserving of the place history has accorded him. Lily came in to moderate the debate, and Naomi sat in to observe it. After the debaters' statements and rebuttals, Lily moderated the class discussion that followed.

Still a third technique extensively developed and often used at Metro is the "sort." A sort calls upon participants to review and assess a large number of possible responses to a broad question such as "What are the characteristics of a good parent?" or "What are the most influential documents in American history?" Participants are typically asked to arrive at the 10 best answers to the sort question, and the 10 least acceptable answers (usually out of 60 possibilities presented). They are asked to do this by literally sorting the packet of 60 small cards each individual receives into three separate piles: 10 best answers, 10 worst, and the remainder. They are often asked next to examine their own answers in relation to others', to discuss rationales, and to arrive at some agreement.

As such approaches and techniques would suggest, there is quite a bit to learn in becoming a part of the faculty of Metro Academy. Although not all of the staff seem fully aware of it, there is quite an elaborate system for inducting new teachers into the Academy's culture and readying them to develop their own style of carrying out the inquiry approach. It is accomplished largely by modeling and participation in collaborative circumstances. The 3-week project that launches every semester at Metro Academy is the new teacher's introduction to the school. The project occupies the full school day for 15 days and it immerses the beginner in intensive interaction with colleagues and students. The school's entire population is pursuing a single inquiry theme, partly in an all-school group, and partly with differentiated segments of the broader question being studied by 8 to 10 small groups of students, each led by a teacher. The new teacher begins working with colleagues, then on what is a brand-new curriculum for everybody involved. Because the content is novel for all, newcomers are just as likely to have valuable substantive contributions to offer as veteran staff. The process, however—not only of elaborating the plan for the project but of carrying out the inquiry it represents—is a 3-week demonstration epitomizing what the school stands for. While carrying it out, staff model the inquiry process for newcomers and for students. It is a good introduction to the way challenges are met at Metro, together and separately.

But the induction process for new teachers does not end in 3 weeks. When regular classes begin, newcomers are put into a series of collaborative relationships. Naomi, for instance, is a new teacher who came to Metro last spring. She had the following assignments this fall: She taught Political Philosophy and Plays, and she was also assigned (with Marcus) to the laboratory for Lynn's Television Analysis course. Additionally, she worked with Vivian on *Highlights*, the school paper, and audited Lynn's course. Thus, by the end of the semester she had had abundant opportunity to work with, and become acquainted in some detail with, the teaching of three Metro teachers. At the end of the year she will participate with the rest of the Academy staff in a 1- to 2-week intensive review and evaluation of the year, and planning session for next year.

It is probably these several sorts of association and contexts for collaboration that assure the high levels of agreement among the faculty. There are the project-generated connections, the class-related relationships, the connections built when two or three teachers find themselves working together on a specific activity or challenge (a frequent occurrence), plus the full-staff involvement of the weekly regular meetings and the biweekly curriculum meetings. When these activities are added to the proximity of office space described earlier, it becomes clear that new teachers do not long remain on the fringes of life at Metro. It is these several factors that also sustain some other prominent and very fundamental tenets of the Academy's culture, the largely unspoken, taken-for-granted realities.

The Professional Culture's Core

Assumptions about collaboration and change probably underlie most of the more explicit tenets and themes observable at Metro. As Jan speculated, the capacity to collaborate probably operates as a screening criterion for teachers applying to Metro. The willingness and ability to do so are essential to the school's operating procedures, and the assumption that almost everything is done collaboratively runs deep. As Hank expressed the sense that accompanies such practice, "The key to this place is a shared sense of responsibility." It is also a strongly felt shared sense of ownership. As Lily put it, "It's *our* school."

An additional widely shared and pervasive part of the taken-for-granted reality of Metro Academy—an assumption that goes far toward determining daily activity—is the conviction that a successful school is always in the process of changing. As Marcus put it:

> Here, courses are constantly revised, the amount and quality of learning is constantly examined, we're always looking for effective ways to offer support to kids. The grading system, the approach to colleges, voluntary community service have all changed. In traditional schools, changes are implemented and if they don't work the kids are blamed. Here, it's back to the drawing boards.

As both meetings and conversations attest, there is a shared assumption that very little about the school is beyond question, that virtually everything can be done better, and that what they are there for is to try to do just that. It falls well short of flux, because there are durable fundamentals. But change is constant.

These commonalities as to beliefs, values, and assumptions yield several themes that seem to pervade most of the arrangements and practices at Metro. Five elements of this cultural core assume particular prominence: the nature of school structure; the centrality of the mission; efficacy and hence obligation; professional autonomy, and responsibility and conformity expectations; and teacher sense of affiliation.

Structure

Structure serves consistently as a highly manipulable instrument or means at Metro. The school and the way it operates are an effective counter to those tempted to see organization and structure as tools used only by bureaucrats and traditionalists to standardize and create rigidities. At Metro, such structured regularities as schedule, task assignment, and roles must constantly bow to achieving purposes.

Structure, as we have seen, is carefully used to sustain professional culture and community. This occurs naturally, in consequence of physical structure—the physical proximity of crowded office space, and the need to share classrooms; but it is encouraged even more specifically through the intricately interwoven patterns of interaction and assistance built into the Academy's work patterns. The teacher collegiality so sought after today can range from "parallel play" situations—where side by side each does his or her thing independently—to high degrees of mutual interdependence. Even the parallel play arrangement may be an improvement over the solitary traditional circumstances of the teacher, but it is a long way from genuinely collaborative interaction.

Metro's structure stimulates collaboration in several ways. It puts teachers into multiple relationships of mutual dependence as they together generate and design two 3-week, cross-disciplinary projects annually; as one teaches the lab section of another's course; as one serves as a presenter in another's course, providing a requested perspective or set of data; as they together pursue new solutions to the challenges introduced at staff meetings; as advisory teachers obtain student feedback about how things are working and bring it before the full staff; as Organizational Tutorial teachers follow up on explanations from students about why they are working hard in one class but not in another. Both program and organizational arrangements are constructed to maximize contact among teachers, both individually and in groups. They do so, assuring frequency of contact, contact with a number of teachers, and intensity of contact through task assignments that create interdependency. It appears a highly effective way to sustain the culture within the group and to induct newcomers into the school's professional culture.

Mission Power

Metro is a rare example of a school that does what it says it sets out to do—where the announced mission serves constantly as the criterion and desideratum for everything: for selecting content, materials, activities, processes, structures, assignments. The influence and control exerted by the school mission are evident everywhere, from the bulletin boards to the all-school projects, to trips taken and the particular way the surrounding community is used as the object of inquiry, to the way each class is conducted, to the way teachers address and query students and the way they address and query one another. The determination to make the school an inquiring community, where intellect is valued, pursued, and exercised, is visible in all that goes on.

One reason for such consistency and power may lie, as the directors believe, in the fact that Metro's theme or focus is pedagogically centered rather than substantively centered or focused on school governance or elsewhere. Such a pedagogical focus obviously responds to a central concern of teachers. It connects closely with what they all do and decisions they must all make constantly. Such a focus is also of sufficient logical centrality to a school's operation to bear relevance to most of the decisions the school must make. This contrasts with many of the themes articulating school reform and restructuring efforts (e.g., school-based management and/or shared decision making) and with the themes often selected as the focus for a magnet school (a particular discipline or a cross-disciplinary topic) that lack such advantages.

Efficacy, Therefore Obligation

Metro Academy teachers have a strong sense of their power over the life chances of their students. They are sensitive to the difficulties these youngsters face, with respect to their current lives and their chances for the future. And they are totally convinced of the importance of learning to use their minds as effectively as possible, to the long-range opportunities these young people will enjoy. Metro staff have a high opinion of just how much previously unchallenged youngsters can do, and they have a high opinion of just how much they can accomplish as teachers. This generates what Lynn called "a sense that all is fixable." And teachers' sense of their own power to realize their goals is buttressed by their faith that the school's co-directors can get them what they need to function well. To date, this assumption has proved justified, because over the years Art and Lynn have managed to obtain private support for a number of projects and activities that public funding could not cover.

If the perspective appears a bit too rose-colored, given the backgrounds and prior histories of many of these students, it does not yield that sort of optimism assuming things work out and will take care of themselves. Indeed, almost the opposite seems true: If it is so enormously important for these kids to learn to use their minds well—and if they all can do so—and if outside support and means can be found if needed—then it becomes a moral imperative for the school, and each teacher within it, to make this come about. Thus there is a constant drivenness and urgency at Metro, generated by a shared awareness of youngsters' needs and teachers' power to meet them. This is the unarticulated driving force of much of the Academy's persistent efforts to improve what they do yet further.

Professional Autonomy, Responsibility, and Conformity

Teachers at Metro Academy feel they enjoy much more autonomy than in previous schools where they have been assigned—save for one teacher who came to Metro from another alternative high school. To a considerable extent, Metro's teachers are free to select or design the courses they will teach and the content comprising those courses. The desire to make offerings enticing to students places a premium on variety, so one need not teach the same thing semester after semester. Instead, teachers are encouraged to design new courses. They are also encouraged to offer courses based on hobbies or personal interests, and in accord with the "generalism" espoused by the Coalition of Essential Schools, they are encouraged to teach outside their own specialization. Thus, Lily, the psychology teacher, has offered a horticulture class; Bob, whose subject is math, has taught a course in ancient history; and Jan, the science teacher, teaches a course in novels.

But as Art points out, teacher freedom and autonomy are not total, and their justification is not academic freedom. An Academy teacher's freedom is limited by two kinds of constraints: One is a matter of responsibilities to the school operation, the other is a matter of conforming to the school's mission. The first can limit the time and other resources to pursue one's own classroom needs, and the other defines the range of possibilities deemed acceptable in the school.

Each Academy teacher is responsible for the success of the total enterprise. This means that individual responsibilities are not sharply delineated, and if there is a need, one is expected to simply step in and fill it. A student's need to talk, or a colleague's need for assistance, is normally expected to take precedence over the sanctity of any unassigned time. In recognition of this, although Metro teachers have unscheduled class periods, none is designated as personal preparation time.

The school mission also restricts the range of a teacher's choices. The inquiry method delineates acceptable instructional strategy, and if a teacher wanted to present developmental lessons instead, such a pedagogy would be found incompatible with the Metro Academy orientation. Art has no hesitation in stating that this is the toll exacted by a strong mission orientation and a consensual commitment to it. As far as the school is concerned, its integrity cannot be maintained without this operational conformity by all involved. So far as the individual teacher is concerned, the pedagogical restrictions could prove considerable. The trade-off is that those who accept the parameters thus imposed will find unprecedented amounts of professional freedom within the school. But a faculty member who did not accept the mission and its parameters could not find the Metro Academy a comfortable place. And given the public nature of teaching there, it would be impossible for a dissident to conceal or downplay divergent practice, or to retreat to isolationism as the comprehensive high school allows. This is the reason joint selection of faculty—as exercised by a prospective candidate and also by the school—is seen as critically important at Metro.

Teacher Identification

A final theme that underlies professional life at Metro is the priority teachers assign their affiliation with it. For many teachers elsewhere, the primary identification is as "a New York teacher," or as a member of an occupational/professional group epitomized by the union, or as primarily a teacher of biology or of reading or of special needs students, or as a professional of a particular persuasion (e.g., a whole language or an inquiry learning advocate). Most Metro Academy teachers report primary identification not with these but with the Academy. Although they maintain other loyalties and experience other points of identification, their strongest affinity is evidently with the school.

This assumes particular importance in a city where the union is strong, and where most teachers may come to see it as having a primary claim on their loyalties and obligations. This appears not to be the case at Metro Academy. There is a union representative, whose teaching field (history) has made him highly knowledgeable about union matters. Furthermore, his own political orientation would render him responsive to and sympathetically disposed toward union contributions. But the teachers union's agenda simply does not loom large in this school. The union rep explains this by noting most decisions are jointly made by staff and administration, and no grievances are filed by the school's teachers—both somewhat atypical features for a New York City high school. Indeed, because staff participate in interviewing prospective new teachers, they rather quickly arrive at a sense of the incompatibility of the union's insistence on seniority transfer rights with the sustenance of Metro Academy's mission and mode of operation. Their inclinations under such circumstances seem clear. (Formally, the Academy is bound by the New York City-United Federation of Teachers contract and its transfer provision. Transfer rights have never been invoked by an applicant, however, because prospective candidates who would prove incompatible with the school's orientation are carefully supplied with enough insight when they visit to perceive that.)

Conclusion

Is the Metro Academy, then, an educational nirvana in which all goes well? Staff certainly would and do deny that this is the case. And certainly Metro's priorities necessitate that some concerns others hold important get less attention. Some alternative school analysts, for example, would say that the building of a stronger sense of community among students would be desirable—because most of that sense now rests on student-teacher interactions rather than on deliberately cultivated student-student patterns. Advisories are elsewhere sometimes used as support groups, supplementing adult efforts on dealing with out-of-school and in-school problems. Others might seek fuller development and instructional use of the service learning component—or wish that even more extensive efforts might be extracted from students. And many researchers would find the inaccessibility of data difficult. (It is hard to get a definitive picture at Metro of some features that might elsewhere be simple and clear-cut—for example, the number of students enrolled, because some students sometimes disappear for a while or others receive help in GED preparation instead of attending classes.) But whatever reservations one might have, it seems difficult to imagine fuller development of professional community.

Such a conclusion is not unprecedented. One of the most extensive investigations of professional communities yet undertaken in high schools found quite a comparable situation in the alternative schools it studied. Stanford's Center for the Context of Secondary School Teaching did extensive studies in 16 schools across the nation, and they compared their own findings with those of a national sample of high schools. The investigators concluded that the dimensions of professional community were etched more clearly in alternative schools than in any of the other schools they studied. In a report they gave to one such school, Horizons High School, they said they had found this alternative school in Wyoming, Michigan, to be "scoring higher on most dimensions of a professional community than any of the other schools in the CRC study. In fact, Horizons High School scored higher than any of the other 16 [sic] high schools on 7 of the 8 indicators of the professional community. On all 8 dimensions of the professional community Horizons High School is at least one standard deviation (and at times two and three standard deviations) above the national mean" (CRC, 1991, p. 1).

Thus, other investigations would also lend credence to the conclusion of this one: that the professional community at Metro Academy is a remarkable achievement.

4

Thomas Paine High School

Professional Community

in an Unlikely Setting

JEAN A. KING
DANIEL A. WEISS

This is a story about change in an urban high school long viewed as the "worst in the city." But teachers who have taught in the school for years report recent changes. One noted that "[Thomas Paine] has changed. This is a much more friendly, supportive school. . . ." Another put it this way:

> When I first came to Paine High, it was not what it is today. This is a much better place. The school population has changed, but I see students who are very friendly. I see students who are happy. I see students who are more willing to do better work. I see more involvement in the classroom than I did before.

A third teacher summarized:

I've been able to just sit and think what was the school like when I came, and it is very different. A lot of it is not just what you'd see as you walk down the hall. A lot of it is a feeling of real aliveness, that there are possibilities for change, and that things are growing. . . . Now [teaching at Paine] is great. We've got all these ideas, and the only thing that keeps us from getting them all done is that we don't have enough time or energy.

What follows is one chapter in the ongoing story of how Thomas Paine High School continues to improve as committed teachers—the same group who was there when it was "the worst"— strive to create successful educational experiences for their students. And unlike that of so many schools of its type, this story is struggling toward a happy ending, in large part due to the emergent professional community created among its faculty, administration, and staff.

Some features of Thomas Paine are to be expected. As you first approach, the building looks like a bastion of traditional education. Three stories high, it occupies an entire block of a large city in the Midwest. Two additions, including a fairly recent gym and shop complex, expanded Paine's original brick building to its present structure. Its extensive athletic fields occupy another block nearby in a blue-collar neighborhood less than a mile from the city's suburban border. There has been a longstanding tradition of support for public schooling in the community and, in the past, for Thomas Paine as a school. In the 1940s, its athletic teams captured state trophies in several sports, establishing its reputation as an athletic powerhouse with a stable academic environment—in short, a school students wanted to attend. Bastion or not, however, Thomas Paine in the past 30 years has faced problems common to many urban schools, problems that have replaced its positive reputation with a negative one.

Unlike many schools, however, Paine has both the resources and the will to tackle its problems, problems that might stymie a lesser staff. What follows is not another discouraging description of failure in an urban environment. It is instead a story of how, despite continuing negative pressures, restructuring at the school has fostered the ongoing evolution of professional community. The story of how the teachers and administrators of Thomas Paine High School have worked together provides strong evidence that, although the barriers are many, urban schools can effect meaningful change that can directly affect the learning and lives of their students.

The World of Thomas Paine

Formerly the pride of the neighborhood, Paine's dramatic slide began in the 1960s, following desegregation of the city's schools. Since then, community support for the school has waned. Minority enrollments have risen dramatically, accounting now for more than half the student population. A number of apartment buildings nearby serve as short-term housing for many, particularly minority, single-parent families. Students from these families often attend Thomas Paine for short periods, then move to other schools, frequently attending several high schools during a single academic year. Furthermore, the city has open enrollment so that neighborhood students living near Paine routinely opt for schools with better reputations. The presence of a district-wide program for severely emotionally and behaviorally disordered (EBD) students at Paine was, until recently, its only magnet in a district committed to the use of academic magnets to draw middle-class students. This did little to enhance its status.

Like other high schools whose students ride busses or take after-school jobs, Paine has struggled with extracurricular activities in recent years. Cheerleading, dance line, and athletics survive, although the outcome of Paine's athletic programs place many of its teams at the bottom of their leagues. There is an elective choir and band that can practice only during the school day. In recent years there has been no drama club or annual school play, and the student council was disbanded when the student body purposely elected a group of less than serious representatives.[1] On the positive side, Thomas Paine is known for its top-notch speech team; in fact, a Paine student won the state speech championship for 1994.

For the past decade, Thomas Paine has ranked at the bottom of the district in both academics and athletics. With disturbing consistency, Paine has scored at the top of negative measures, such as average daily attendance and student turnover, and on the bottom of positive measures, such as achievement test scores. External pressure from gang-related activities is a constant force in the school, and aides continually patrol Paine's halls, checking passes and enforcing rules. A uniformed police officer is routinely visible in the halls as well. Though violence has not begun to approach the level found in other urban schools—in recent years the most serious offense inside the school was one gun found in a school locker—the threat of violence is still a determining factor in school climate.

One example came in fall 1993, when a gang member pulled a fire alarm. When the building was emptied, members of the gang outside grabbed a Paine student who was a member of a rival gang and attempted to assault him. Thus began a series of student-initiated fire drills throughout the fall that quickly made teachers highly aware of their vulnerability in their rooms, and reduced faculty morale. Such threats of violence, gang activity, high dropout rates, teen pregnancy, and low attendance (one quarter of the student body is absent on any given day) challenge school work on a daily basis. Administrators in the building often become embroiled in discipline-related affairs, making it difficult for them to spend time on instructional or professional development issues. Until quite recently, teachers assigned to Paine usually bid out to other schools as quickly as possible.

Upon entering the building, the most visible and striking feature is that of peeling paint. Throughout much of Thomas Paine, large strips of paint dangle off the walls, dramatically altering the effect of brightly painted designs. Students from a local college who visit Paine unanimously point to this feature as documentation of a troubled school. But this condition inaccurately gives the impression that Thomas Paine lacks resources when, in fact, its facilities are surprisingly adequate, especially in comparison to urban schools in other cities.[2] The district's new superintendent is eager to maintain the momentum created by the passage of a levy referendum that explicitly reduced class sizes for elementary students, and he is committed to maintaining the resource base for all of the city's schools.

Teachers at Paine expect to have sufficient books and instructional materials for their students, and at the end of the 1993–1994 school year they were busy ordering new materials. Paine's copier is available to teachers as they need it. The school has a well-supplied and extremely active media center and computer lab. In the media center and an adjoining classroom, there are more than 40 computers; many teachers also have individual computers in their rooms. Most Paine classrooms are large and bright. Bulletin boards and trophy cases display student awards, pictures, and newspaper articles related to student achievement and activities. Student artwork is displayed in many classrooms and hallways, and brightly painted papier-maché animals cover the display areas of the media center. The school has a fully functional gymnasium, several athletic fields for its physical education program and team sports (both male and female), and access to a neighboring ice rink. An enthusiastic team of building engineers keeps the building in spotless condition and good repair, peeling paint or not.

Since 1990 the school has had three principals. Principal Rita Mease, a tall and dynamic African-American, began a long-term change process to rebuild Paine's programs, focusing on student success and empowering her faculty to take risks and alter their practice. Under her leadership, teaching teams were created, including a team that sought to carry out the principles of the Coalition of Essential Schools and an open team. Teachers developed an International Baccalaureate program that has successfully attracted academically motivated students to the school. Two collaborations with external agencies—a local bank and a teacher education college—became important sources of ideas and support.

Unfortunately, Ms. Mease developed a serious illness during the 1991–1992 school year, missing many days of work and, by her absence, creating an unavoidable leadership vacuum. Once it became clear that she would be unable to return to Paine full-time, the district assigned an interim principal—an experienced central office administrator—until determining a permanent replacement. When Assistant Principal (AP) James Hissop was named as the permanent principal, many were visibly relieved. Hissop, though fairly new to the building, had a reputation in the district as a thoughtful and gifted administrator, an American Indian who brought an unusual style to his work. In contrast to the directive style of traditional building principals, Hissop works indirectly to carry out his ideas for change through encouraging others to take ownership and assume leadership responsibilities. Paine is now led by a four-person administrative team: Hissop, two African-American male APs, and a third AP who jokingly refers to herself as the token white female.

Although the physical plant could house 2,000 students—and once did—Paine today is a small high school. In recent years there were regular rumors that the district would close the school and send Paine students to other, more popular and populated buildings. In 1993–1994, the student population increased slightly to 730 students, almost half African-American (47.9%), a smaller percentage of whites (41.7%), and the remainder a mixture of other minorities (6.5% Asian, 2.5% American Indian, and 1.5% Hispanic). Paine has a teaching and support staff of approximately 40, almost entirely white, 19 of whom were new to the building in 1993–1994. That figure is somewhat misleading because 9 of the 19 new positions were cofunded by regular and special education funds during the past year, but filled in several cases by returning faculty; other replacements were due to early retirements. It does mean, however, that Paine has had an infusion of new blood; people, in some cases hired explicitly, who bring a variety of skills and interests to the building.

The official school day begins at Paine at 7:15 a.m., so that most teachers get up between 5:00 and 5:30 in the morning to make sure they are at school with sufficient time to prepare for the day's activities. For much of the year they arrive in the dark. First "lunch" begins at 10:39 a.m. In 1993–1994 Paine's teachers taught five of the seven periods (six during one trimester), using the other class hours for meetings or preparation time. Duties (e.g., hall monitoring, cafeteria supervision) are largely handled administratively. Due to the high level of student absenteeism, actual class sizes tend to be small, but inconsistent attendance makes day-to-day teaching a challenge. In addition, Paine High experiences an extremely high rate of student turnover so that class rosters are in constant flux as student names are added, deleted, and sometimes added again throughout the year.

By 2:00 p.m., when the school day officially ends, Paine's teachers are often exhausted, but they routinely attend after-school meetings on a variety of topics. As one teacher quipped, "Boy, I'm forever meeting with people!" There are occasional meetings of the whole school staff, committee meetings (e.g., staff development, accreditation, Leadership Council), team meetings, and departmental meetings, besides meetings with individual students, teachers, and parents. One teacher noted the importance of smaller meetings:

> In the small meetings, everybody gets a chance to talk. They get a chance to voice their opinions. The [smaller] meetings that I have been in . . . I think there's a higher level of trust. So that you are more willing to express opinions whereas you probably wouldn't say them in one of the staff meetings.

As the opening paragraph of this chapter suggested, the teachers at Paine are well aware that the school is changing. A teacher who has taught in the school for more than a decade notes the effect this has had:

> If you decide that what you want to do is teach out of your file cabinet day by day, then nothing is going to change what you decide to do. [But] that percentage is getting smaller and smaller. . . . Too many teachers are doing innovative things, and the students have complained about the ones who are teaching out of their file folders.

Paine is no longer a "place [for teachers] to hide out," and good instruction is at the heart of teachers' daily activities. Staid and negative teachers are opting to retire or to leave the school:

> There are some naysayers like everywhere, but there are fewer than there used to be because it is not a comfortable place to be if you're a stick-in-the-mud because people are always saying to you, "Well, if it doesn't work, let's fix it." That gets to be a real drag to a person who wants to do everything the same as they have always done it.

"People who have not wanted to get actively involved with reform— many people—have transferred out." One teacher perhaps said it best of all. In discussing ways in which Paine supported long-term improvement, she asked, "What could be better than to do some dreaming and then bring it back [to school] and find out that people say, 'Yeah, let's go for it'?"

Structure:
The Means to an End

The evolving structure of Paine High School directly promotes interaction and discussion among staff, who meet in a variety of groupings throughout the school year. Several traditional structures facilitate this. Periodic all-faculty meetings are held, but only when there is a compelling reason to do so, and then only for 1 hour no more than twice a month, typically on Tuesday afternoon. In the past year, for example, topics included presentations by faculty from the district's multicultural magnet school, a description of programs supported by Paine's business partner, and an emergency meeting to plan an assembly to discuss student-initiated fire drills. One teacher noted, "Most of the meetings are relevant, and they do answer questions." The departmental structure of a traditional high school continues to exist, although some teachers find it weaker because of the team emphasis. Nevertheless, teachers from the same discipline generally meet two to four times a month, which varies according to the department. Teachers also serve on and lead a variety of committees related to building functions (e.g., Paine's site-based Leadership Council, the staff development committee, Outcomes Accreditation target goal committees, and committees related to the collaboration with Paine's business partner). Equally important, two fairly new structures—instructional teams and a multifaceted professional development program—have created opportunities for Paine faculty and staff to interact regularly concerning individual students, teaching and learning, and professional development.

Teaching Teams

The most active and vital structure now focusing the energies of most of Paine's teachers is that of the student/teacher team. In contrast to some restructured schools that team teachers and then randomly assign students to teams, Paine's teams are student-centered and based on different learning styles and content. In other words, at Thomas Paine teams of teachers teach teams of students, many of whom have chosen their placement. Completing the restructuring that Rita Mease supported, the school is now organized into six instructional teams, four of which (International Baccalaureate, Essentials, Open, and Comprehensive) have at least one teacher each from the English, mathematics, science, and social studies departments:[3]

The International Baccalaureate (IB) and Pre-IB Team (260 students; 36%). Added to Paine as a magnet to attract academically oriented students, the IB is an international, college-preparatory program for 11th and 12th graders that focuses on international education and standards. High school students from literally around the world take standard IB exams to attain special diplomas or certificates that can lead to advanced standing at colleges and universities. Entering the IB program after 2 years of preparation, Paine's IB students must maintain high levels of achievement or risk being dropped from the program.

The Essentials Team (58 students; 8%). After several Paine faculty were exposed to Theodore Sizer's work during a class at a local university, they proposed and developed the Coalition of Essential Schools program with assistance from the woman who taught the course, adjunct faculty at the university, and a longtime employee of the teachers union. The Essentials Program now serves 9th and 10th graders and focuses on an interdisciplinary, activity-based curriculum and demonstration of learning.

The Open Team (95 students; 13%). Developed around the concept of the open school, the Open program's goal is to have the students develop initiative, self-management, and intellectual curiosity. Students work in interdisciplinary team-taught blocks.

The Comprehensive Team (250 students; 34%). Students who do not choose to go into one of these three programs are placed into what has euphemistically been labeled the Comprehensive Program, which in the past has merely meant a schedule of classes taught by individual teachers, rather than by a team. Recognizing the power of team planning and discussion, faculty are now working to create a distinct and more cohesive program. Given its origins, the Comprehensive Program is more traditional in nature, where the teachers provide a controlled set of options for students within a routine schedule.

The Electives Team (no students directly assigned). With most of the core subject instructional faculty placed on teams, it made structural sense to group remaining teachers into their own team, even though they function independently. The electives include family studies, computers, music, art, foreign language, industrial arts, drivers' education, and vocational education teachers.

Special Education and the Special Program for Reaching Every Adolescent Daily (52 non-SPREAD special education students and 24 SPREAD students, for a total of 76 Paine students with "Individualized Educational Programs" in special education; 10%). Paine has a well-staffed program to serve special needs students, many of whom are mainstreamed for part of the day. The group implemented a number of major changes, planned in spring 1993, to move collaboratively toward a continuum of services model. Although the SPREAD program enrolled only 24 students last year, it nevertheless exerts a powerful influence in the building. In extremely small classes, it focuses on "improving students' social, behavioral, and academic skills by providing vocational awareness training and on-site work experience." Many Paine teachers view the team structure positively. One teacher, for example, commented,

> Most of it has to do with the relationships that the individual teachers have with the kids and their families. You want to have individual relationships with the kids. I think also [it is helpful] having teams within the building, teams that meet on a regular basis to discuss the needs of the kids. That helps a lot.

Another noted:

> When you have the group of needy students that we have . . . you've got to have teachers talking with each other and sharing the load of home contact. Just knowing students well

has been very, very important. They're so fragile and they slip away so fast, even when you know them well.

There were seven periods in the 1993–1994 school day, and every teacher had at least two to use for prep or meeting time.[4] Teamed teachers share groups of students and, in all but one case in 1993–1994, common planning time and a behavior "dean" (a teacher given that special assignment), enabling an ongoing exchange of information and support. Most teams meet at least twice a week as a team and sometimes more often. At the end of the school year, for example, Mr. Hissop charged each team with creating its desired schedule and staffing for the next school year and determining what instructional resources to order, resulting in a flurry of informal discussions to get the job done. For the first time, in 1993–1994, teaching positions cofunded by regular and special education placed special education expertise on each team. Requiring an unusual waiver from the district and state, these cofunded positions were a vital component in making special services immediately available on a daily, as-needed basis to the teams' students. In the upcoming school year, special education resource teachers (SERTs) will work directly with specific teams, providing additional support for the teams. Teachers and administrators are working to create an increasingly effective structure that will allow for the timely assessment and cross-teacher discussion of student needs so that Paine's students can focus on their learning in an environment that supports them as individuals.

Professional Development Activities

Three distinct efforts have resulted in a wide range of professional development opportunities for Paine's teachers: (a) the creation of a professional development school (PDS) at Paine; (b) the development of a district professional development planning process; and (c) teaching improvement programs supported by the state department of education. Each has a place in the school's organizational structure and provides teachers opportunities to reflect collaboratively on their practice.

The evolution of Paine's PDS has been an important source of professional development activities and of increased human resources within the building. From 1990 to 1993, faculty from Paine and a local college of education received support as part of a national project to establish a PDS in the building. Working first as a distinct subgroup—both in the school and in the college—the group over time created structures to establish the Paine "continuum of teacher development." Now fully developed, the continuum ranges from preservice college student involvement (observation, practica, student teaching) to induction activities for initially licensed teachers (residency, support during probationary years) to career professional work (e.g., mentorship, teacher education, curriculum development, program coordination, and related forms of teacher leadership). In October 1993, Paine's Leadership Council voted unanimously to make all teachers in the building active participants in the PDS, pointing to the potential for a cross-cutting, integrative function, in direct contrast to the original work of a small group of enthusiasts.

Two major structural mechanisms support the activities of the PDS continuum. Paine's residents (formerly called interns), who are newly licensed teachers with no previous teaching experience, teach two classes of their own each day, then spend the remainder of their workday observing and assisting other teachers, engaging in professional development of their own (e.g., by visiting other sites or reading articles), or releasing teachers who themselves have professional development work to do. There is consensus that everyone wins in this arrangement. Although the residents receive less than a full-time teacher's salary, they report satisfaction at easing into a teaching career in a highly supportive environment; Paine teachers who mentor them express great relief at having competent individuals with whom to leave their classes while they engage in professional development activities. The idea of having meaningful professional development time during the workday, without having to abandon students, excites teachers, and by the end of the year, competition for the residents' services became fierce. In August 1994, the PDS would hire four new residents for the 1994–1995 school year: one funded by the PDS sponsoring college; one by an exemplary staff development grant from the district; and two paid for from teacher/coordinators' release time funding. This will be the first time that four residents have been in place on the first day of school, and expectations are high as to the effect this will have in the building.

The PDS also uses a second and more traditional structure to provide a time and place for professional discussion: the meeting. But PDS meetings are nontraditional in that they are often places where teachers can openly discuss professional issues and seek one another's support and solutions. Each Wednesday, many teachers and college students meet during their lunch hour at the PDS brown bag lunch. People bring their own lunches, and the PDS provides chips, cookies, and beverages. There are occasionally set topics (e.g., tips for good parent conferences, designing an exit survey for seniors), but more typically people raise their own issues of concern. One week, for example, a student teacher wanted to discuss a specific classroom management problem that was causing him to lose sleep. Several experienced faculty (most of whom knew the student) commiserated and gave explicit suggestions for him to try. By the next week, although the situation was not entirely resolved, much of the tension had been alleviated. At other times, the lunches have been a venue for college faculty to meet a number of teachers conveniently (e.g., the chair of a college department who wanted to touch base on high school reading programs), to try out an idea (e.g., developing questions for a seniors' exit survey), or simply to discuss professional matters in an informal setting.

In addition to the brown bag sessions, the PDS sponsors other meetings to encourage continuing discussion. This past year, the entire faculty from Thomas Paine was bused to the college campus for a meeting with college faculty in October; a reciprocal meeting was held 2 months later at Paine. The president of the university visited the school in February, spending an hour discussing the college's role through the PDS in improving education both at the college and at Paine. In April, a more formal conference celebrated the successes of the PDS, by inviting representatives from teacher education institutions in the area to a discussion that featured Paine faculty together with two colleagues from out-of-state universities. Plans for 1994–1995 include a three-credit course that will run throughout the school year, cotaught by college and Paine faculty, to study the latest research on school change.

A second source of professional development activities comes from the district. At the same time that teachers and college faculty developed the PDS, the district's central office established a flexible process for teachers to create individual professional development plans (PDPs) as part of both the teacher evaluation cycle and the district's focus on goals. One teacher at Paine became excited about the process in 1992–1993, putting together a PDP and a computer program to simplify the process, which became an exemplar for the district. Quickly recognized as a potential trainer at the district level, this individual was given the task of consulting individually with Paine residents and faculty to develop their PDPs. When she was forced to leave the school in January 1994 for medical reasons, another teacher—new to the building, but extremely enthusiastic about the process—took over and was quickly accepted as a trusted colleague with whom to discuss professional matters. He met individually with more than a dozen teachers, including the teaching residents, and showed them how to connect district and building goals with their own development needs related to teaching and student learning. The discussions were directly related to improving classroom instruction. For example, one teacher who was new to teaching came to understood through the PDP process how he could work with students on one of Paine's targeted areas for improvement (critical thinking) as part of his daily lessons and track his own and their progress. His focus on explicit ways to foster critical thinking will continue into the next year.

The third source of support for professional development activities comes from the state. A statewide teacher mentorship program has for several years provided minimal funding ($500 per mentor) to several of Paine's career professionals to serve as mentors to newer faculty. In some cases the mentoring has been extremely positive, for example, helping an inexperienced science teacher maintain control in her classroom. In other cases, mentors have become frustrated when their mentees were unable to work successfully with Paine students; the question of exactly how much mentors (as opposed to administrators) should or even can help weak teachers has generated tension for some.[5] A state teacher residency program—created in structure, but not yet fully funded by the legislature—is a second source of support, one that has given Paine's continuum of professional development visibility because Paine is to date the only fully functional professional development school statewide.

Teacher control of certain staff development funds is a third example of professional development activities supported by the state. Recent state legislation mandates that a committee of teachers within each building allocate certain state staff development funds, and district guidelines require that the committee document outcome indicators for the activities supported. Paine's staff development committee, along with the administrative team, sets an agenda and theme for group staff development activities during the year, and teachers can then apply for funding for individual projects (e.g., attendance at professional meetings, specialized curriculum development).[6] Individual activities must match the building theme or "fit toward the school improvement plan"; teachers "have to determine how that conference they wish to attend fits into the theme for the year." In a somewhat awkward example of teacher empowerment, during the past year Paine's administrative team applied to the committee for money to support special management training, and the teachers insisted on including some form of assessment of its outcomes. One teacher noted, "There's some strategic leadership within staff development. There're representatives from the different programs and their administrators, and they pick out a vision or a theme [for the year]." Another said, "Staff development . . . is much more useful stuff this year. . . . It seems much more tied together."

In summary, a reason given by Paine's teachers in May 1994 for enjoying teaching in the school is that people interact regularly about professional matters. Teachers have many opportunities to discuss the students they teach. Experienced teachers work directly to support those newer to the profession. And many forums exist for the development and exchange of ideas about teaching. Besides traditional faculty, departmental, and school-wide committee meetings, continuous involvement with teaching teams and professional development in a variety of forms enables teachers at Paine to remain active learners about their students and their craft.

Coming Together
Around Issues of Student Learning

Structures that promote professional dialogue may be necessary for change to occur, but unless the discussions directly address the troublesome issue of student learning over time, they may miss their ultimate target. For a school like Thomas Paine—infamous for its low standardized test scores—the need to focus on student achievement is vital. Like the team structure, this focus is a legacy of Principal Mease, who, when approached with a possible change, would reportedly ask two questions: What will this do for students; and how exactly do you propose to put it in place? Several examples document the ways in which the faculty and staff continue to actively address this issue of student learning at Paine.

One example is found in two all-school programs that explicitly focus on student achievement. Thomas Paine is one of only two schools in the state implementing the Multiple Options, Multiple Opportunities program. For 5 years (albeit quietly and without a great deal of teacher involvement), the program has encouraged Paine's students to take specific courses that will enable broader academic or vocational opportunities after graduation. In part because of the program, all 9th graders at Paine take algebra; there is no general math class offered. The Renaissance Program, which offers incentives for students to increase attendance and achievement, is a second all-school achievement program, one started together with several local businesses.[7] Students who make the A or B honor roll, increase their grade point average by .5, and/or have excellent attendance receive cards that entitle them to free or discounted admission to school athletic events, coupons given by local merchants, and special awards such as T-shirts, movie passes, bumper stickers, and so on. When the program started, many students thought of it as a joke. However, as the rewards became more apparent, the program caught on with many students: The total number of students honored in 1990–1991 was only 185; in 1993–1994 it was 404, more than half the student body. Impossible to imagine a few years ago, all-school Renaissance assemblies—"auditoriums" in Paine's vocabulary—have become proud celebrations of student success.

A second example is specific to one department known to have some of the strongest teachers at Paine. Shortly after Paine's math department had collectively come to the conclusion that the current math curriculum was "not working," math teacher Donna Borich attended a seminar on the Interactive Math Program (IMP), an innovative approach to teaching mathematics that focuses on making math understood by and applicable to all students, regardless of their skill level. Ms. Borich (representing Thomas Paine) and two other teachers from the district then wrote and received a grant to implement the IMP in their respective schools. When she approached the math department with the possibility, they agreed that they should try the IMP, as did the principal. Because it is a fairly extensive curriculum, teachers must receive training to teach it; in the first year (1993–1994), only a few teachers from Paine were trained. But when they tried IMP in several classes, they found it to be extremely successful. Their regular discussion of specific IMP lessons, and hints of what worked and what didn't, occupied many brown bag sessions.

During several meetings midyear, the math department reexamined the IMP, eventually deciding that it should become the school-wide math curriculum for all 9th and 10th graders. "That was a math department decision. . . . We felt we were able to make that decision ourselves." As Donna Borich put it:

> Our real common vision in the math department . . . [is] to increase kids options, and we want them not to be locked into a certain thing at a certain point and not be able to do other things. . . . We said, "Why not IMP for everybody? Why do we have to categorize kids in 9th grade?" For the rest of the time they're going to be categorized and not be able to do anything else, which is what happened previously. . . . For instance, we used to have kids who were in pre-IB [math classes]. . . . All of the kids didn't get in. It was definitely tracking, but it was tracking students did to themselves. Nobody followed them around and said [take this pre-IB class]. . . . Kids could break in or break out occasionally, but not very often. And we said, "Maybe we could have lots of kids do IB if they were prepared for it."

Over the summer, the rest of the math department would receive IMP training, and in 1994–1995 all of the teaching teams will implement IMP in heterogeneously grouped 9th-grade math classes.[8] The goal is not only effective mathematics instruction; it is explicitly to increase the potential number of minority students who will be eligible to enroll in the IB program ("It's for a racial mix as well that we want to get"). Creative offerings in other departments (e.g., a humanities course team-taught by the art teacher and a colleague from social studies) also seek to engage students' minds in nontraditional ways.

A third example of how Thomas Paine faculty are directly examining student achievement is through the implementation of the North Central Association's Outcomes Accreditation process. A former superintendent made the decision that all district high schools would switch to this innovative accrediting process, through which schools first decide upon documentable areas of weakness and create target goal areas, then collect baseline data, identify specific subgroups of students to track, and plan and implement interventions. The final step, 5 years after initiating the process, is to collect followup student data to document the success or failure of what was done. At Paine, then-principal Rita Mease gave the OA charge to Ellen Carlsen, a highly organized, longtime Paine elective teacher who had pulled together the mandated district building profile, an extensive compilation of school-level data. Linking the existing building profile to the OA process, Ms. Carlsen has now managed the OA process through its third year. She was helped this year by a special educator who was released, in a district pilot test, one class period a day to access and download data from the district's mainframe computer.

As mentioned earlier—and as the OA process requires—some of the five target goals are academic (math, language, critical thinking) and some are affective (self-esteem, respect). Although the process has not been entirely smooth (OA committee meetings are often poorly attended, certain target goal committees have had to begin from scratch when key personnel left Paine, some committees have been poorly organized or unable to focus), it had by the spring of 1994 generated provocative data about student achievement in the target goal areas. The subgroup identified for special study is students who attend Paine regularly for 4 years, that is, those students who actually experience what the school has to offer. Teachers will put planned interventions (e.g., the IMP for all 9th and 10th graders, and "Power English" for those identified as unable to read) in place school-wide, beginning in the fall, and then monitor what happens. Faculty will collect 5th-year achievement data in 1995–1996, completing the first OA cycle.

A fourth example can be found in the function of the IB team. Operating within the external standards of an international program, it must maintain exceptionally high standards if Paine students are to become successful diploma candidates. As a result, IB teachers pay close attention to individual students' work, often checking with other teachers if there seem to be problems, or spending time tutoring students during prep hours or after school.[9] For example, when the three students who sought a formal IB diploma formatted their extended essays on the day of the deadline for external review in England, two IB teachers and the IB assistant principal helped solve a last-minute printing glitch so the papers could get in the mail by the deadline. Their emotional and technical support was essential to completing the task.

A collective focus on student learning is also apparent in James Hissop's direct support for teachers' and administrators' use of data. He is constantly asking, "What is working, and how do we know?" and expects that staff over time will do likewise. A good example of this comes from a spring 1994 action research study of Paine's special education delivery system. Knowing the importance of improving special education functions in the building, Hissop asked a team of special education teachers to design a dramatic change plan for 1993–1994. The plan ultimately included increased mainstreaming of the school's most challenging emotionally disturbed students, a behavior intervention room, cofunded positions that would allow special education certified staff to work on instructional teams, and use of the school's conflict resolution program. These innovations—actively working to integrate special education students into the mainstream of Paine's academic life—held the dramatic potential to affect the students themselves and their teachers, both special education and regular. With a small grant from the state department of education and the help of two college colleagues (one professor, one research assistant), Hissop directed a collaborative study of these changes. As he framed it in an introductory meeting, "Anything we do, we try to measure. . . . If we are doing some things right, we all need to know that. . . . As a professional, we expect you to be an evaluator."

Volunteers, including the AP over special education, teachers, and human services staff, determined the study's questions: How can we know if what we're doing is working? How do issues of race and culture affect special education services? and How can we encourage collaboration across programs? They reacted to data, split into working groups, and eventually developed an extensive plan for additional changes and further action research in 1994–1995. One piece of data led teachers to wonder if perhaps the changes made were actually affecting student attendance and, presumably, student learning: If students in the 9th-grade Comprehensive program attended school at all, they attended extremely regularly, suggesting perhaps that something in the program kept them coming. Tracking these students in their 10th-grade year will let teachers see if this is the case. Supported by the college's PDS co-coordinator, several additional action research studies will generate data on student attitude and achievement during the 1994–1995 school year.

In summary, there are many ways that the staff at Thomas Paine—both in groups (e.g., the math department, the IB team, or action research volunteers) and as a whole (i.e., through school-wide programs)—focus on student learning to celebrate student success and to improve instructional practice. Nevertheless, one of the most frustrating things about teaching at a school like Paine is the relentless power of nationally normed test scores to reinforce publicly students' achievement problems. In March 1994, when the district released the 10th-grade achievement test results, the Paine staff noted with pride that, for the first time since anyone could remember, Thomas Paine students' scores were not the lowest on the chart: For both the mean and median composite scores, Paine's rank order was not the bottom position. Although one could explain this result in a number of ways (e.g., the percentage of students tested at Paine was smaller than at any other school, and it was not clear exactly who took the test), the psychological effect of a visible success was not altered, and it brought smiles to many faces. Perhaps at last the multiple and collaborative efforts of staff have begun to pay off in one of the most important measures a school can report.

The Continuing Development of Professional Community

The past 4 years have brought many changes to Thomas Paine. Once it was a school where teachers could close their classroom doors and isolate themselves from colleagues, but one teacher noted that "you can't hide out at Paine any more." Nor, reportedly, would faculty want to. Teachers no longer bid out of Thomas Paine; district rumors now circulate among those who know that Paine is a desirable school, a good place to work, and Paine's administrators now must control who bids in and who is hired on staff. At Paine, teacher empowerment is more than hackneyed jargon; it has literally come to life in the multiple structures that promote teachers' collaborative involvement with other teachers around a variety of school issues, including the improvement of professional practice in a personal and collective sense. Teachers care about students and want them to succeed academically. For example, a social worker reported this year that 80% of female Paine students who had children (16 out of 20) graduated on time with their class, testimony to the support given to the young women.

Teachers also care about one another and work hard (on their teams, through the mentor program) to help colleagues who need it. Paine's teachers are professionals, charged with charting their own course. As one teacher put it, "I think people have to . . . decide what's best for themselves. They have to really think about it." The work of individual teacher leaders documents their power to effect change:[10]

- Hanna Ten Elshof first came to Paine on an assignment in an introductory education class. She then did most of her clinical experiences at the school, including a teaching residency, proving along the way her ability to work effectively with Paine's students. Now in her second full year as a math teacher on the open team, she directed the PDS's practica assignments last spring, ensuring that teachers and college faculty were clear on each other's expectations and needs.
- Donna Borich, mentioned earlier as a math teacher involved in implementing the IMP, is a 12-year veteran of Paine. A lively and outspoken member of the faculty, she heads the Renaissance program, organizing three plus major "auditoriums" during the year to honor Paine's student achievers. She is known as an exceptional teacher, and her work with college students during the past year included a session during which

she publicly discussed and critiqued a videotape of one of her classes.

- Susan Hopsicker has taught at Paine for more than a decade, a mainstay of the SPREAD program. Her commitment to SPREAD students is unflagging; when one of her student's babies was hospitalized, she visited regularly. As a mentor, she spent hours supporting a first-year teacher who had considerable difficulty with classroom management. In addition, because she is interested in computers and data management, over the course of 1993–1994 she became the only teacher in the district with direct access to data from the district mainframe. Her assignment was to work with the central data department to determine how to download data, format it for use in the building, and get it to Paine staff. Although the project was fraught with technical glitches, her enthusiasm never waned.
- Steve Fuhrman is a second-year science teacher at Paine, who worked each year with a sizable number of science practicum students during the winter quarter. As coordinator of the open program he is responsible for its smooth functioning. This year he also wrote a grant to a local foundation for external funding of special chemistry equipment.
- Susan Travers, who has taught social studies at Paine for a number of years, exemplifies lifelong learning and professional development. She was instrumental in the success of the PDS and continues as the Paine coordinator for teacher education activities in the building, scheduling visits and practica, monitoring student teachers, and running the residency program. She is active in professional organizations and recently completed a highly competitive leadership training fellowship.

Does having such teacher leaders in the building mean that Paine has solved all its problems? Indeed not. The nature of an urban school environment suggests the impossibility of that goal, and faculty and administrators alike point to problems the school must face in the coming year. Even though professional community is clearly in evidence at Thomas Paine, several issues continue to impede the development of a school-wide professional community.

Concerns With the Team Structure

Although virtually all teachers value the team concept for Paine, there are nevertheless three concerns about its implementation. Some electives teachers report frustration at their inability to influence decisions within the new team structures. Because they are not assigned to work directly as part of a core academic team, they—through no one's fault—become "second-class citizens," out of the loop on important discussions. Human services staff also wonder whether the team structure might encourage teachers to take on more than they are trained to handle. In addition, some teachers worry that the return to a six-period day for 1994–1995 may exacerbate this situation as there is less flexible time for discussion and consultation.

A second concern is that although there can be no doubt that professional discussion within teams has enriched professional practice in the building, any cross-team/whole building focus must compete with team discussions that are more immediate. In the busy, often frenetic world of Paine, these larger discussions may take a distant second place in the competition for teachers priorities. As one teacher put it, "I think the teams . . . have a tendency to take and break the faculty apart. Break apart maybe isn't the right word, but they have their own little group and they have their own agenda. . . . It's very difficult to try to get everybody to work together towards the same agenda."

Some programs overcome this. For example, activities sponsored in conjunction with the local bank that is Paine's business partner receive wide support, and teachers enthusiastically assist their peers who spend hours on this work, including school-wide quarterly "auditoriums." Other building-wide programs seem to have more difficulty in establishing teacher participation. The OA process, for example, has established school-wide teams, some of which (e.g., math) have moved in a straight line and have already planned interventions to improve student achievement; others (e.g., critical thinking) have struggled just to get people to attend meetings. For teachers busy with team activities, OA discussions may seem less related to daily practice and necessarily less compelling, causing some to question how real the OA process is. Two other areas—teachers' involvement in teacher education activities and their commitment to addressing issues of multiculturalism, diversity, and varying learning styles—also compete for whole-staff attention. The staff development committee has made diversity the unifying theme for all professional development at Thomas Paine in 1994–1995, tackling head-on a topic with dramatic potential to both engage and enrage faculty in light of the school context.

A final concern about the team structure is that although it makes sense programmatically, it may have inadvertently segregated and/or tracked the school. Most students participating in the IB and pre-IB programs are white (57.3%, 62.6%);[11] the majority of students in the Essentials, Open, and Comprehensive programs are African-American (69%, 56.8%, and 61.2%, respectively). Furthermore, some students in the Comprehensive and Open programs report feeling that IB students receive more of the school's resources (e.g., the better teachers).[12] One math teacher active in establishing the IMP as Paine's only math program stated strongly the negative potential of teams:

> We've really had to get people to realize—we don't want to shoot down teams. That's not the point. But we think that teaming them at that point [i.e., 9th grade] is tracking them at that point, even though, yes, it's real cuddly, cozy to be in this class and to know everybody and have them be the same all the way through. It also limits them to those people. And if you're putting them with the lower level kids—*all* lower level kids—you're going to be lower level than if you were put in with a wide variety.

Coordination and Focus

A second general problem with building school-wide professional community stems from the number of initiatives currently under way in the building. As mentioned earlier, the administration has been highly supportive of teacher initiatives. One teacher described the "empowerment we get from our administration . . . you know that your ideas are valued." Virtually any good idea that anyone has can be tried out. In fact, one of the jokes at Paine is that "we never met a program we didn't adopt." During the summer of 1994, for example, Paine's teachers developed still more ideas: three support staff attended a university institute to plan cross-grade home rooms and student wellness programming; others attended a 4-day Multiple Options, Multiple Opportunities training in the Southwest, returning enthusiastic and eager to expand its function in the school; 10 teachers attended a multicultural training session to write curriculum for next year; the vocational education staff refined a major 5-year plan; and so on. It is hard to even keep up with the number of innovations in the building, let alone their content.

At this point, however, Paine's openness and acceptance of innovation may have become a fault. By having so many different programs on its collective agenda, the Paine community is pulled in multiple and sometimes competing directions. As one teacher put it, "There's many visions. Not double vision, but double, double, double visions. . . . Not that there can't be more than one vision, but there's not one clear vision." To date, the administration has not sought to forge (or perhaps force) such a vision for Thomas Paine as a whole. Indeed, the assignment of the three Assistant Principals to specific programmatic and team responsibilities reinforces the divided approach, and works in some sense against school-wide community. Some teachers do not see this as problematic:

> I think there're different groups within the building that have
> a vision, and I think the visions have been very compatible;
> and as long as they don't get in each other's way, I think it's
> all right to have those people working on [different] goals.

Others believe there is, in fact, a broad, unifying vision:

> There is a large group of people who have similar, common
> goals. . . . We definitely share a common vision. . . . Probably
> a lot of people are not going to be able to mouth the words,
> but I think the large percentage of people truly do believe
> [that all Paine students can learn].

Or, as another put it:

> There is an increasingly shared vision that all students can
> learn and that we need to have high expectations for them.
> And that traditional ways of teaching are not necessarily the
> best. There're lots of new things that need to be explored. I
> don't think we have thoroughly agreed on what those
> things are.

It is not clear at this point the role that an explicit shared vision would
play at Paine as it continues its evolution. What is clear is the need
to raise the issue for discussion.

Another problem associated with Paine's openness and flexibility is related to the teachers who are less than competent or who are
dissociated from the change program. How open and flexible must
the school be with colleagues who are slowing the change process
because they are either unable or unwilling to change? There is a need
to balance the needs of adults with the needs of students, and staff at
Paine attempt to achieve this. Less than effective practice is still
clearly present at Paine, and the administrative team identified and
worked with a number of teachers during the course of the year. In
some cases mentoring or administrative intervention was successful;
in others, it was not. Two teachers eventually went on long-term
medical leave, and five other teachers will not return in the fall (three
first-year teachers' contracts were not renewed; and two tenured
teachers were strongly encouraged to leave). Although teachers acknowledge the importance and value of such actions, it unavoidably
creates an awkward tension in a school that is committed to openly
helping people improve their practice.

Communication

A third major challenge to the development of professional community at Thomas Paine, one related to the second, is the lack of an
effective communication system. There are faculty mailboxes, but by
the end of the day they are often full of paper. Messages and announcements may go unnoticed. There is a loudspeaker that is used

for student announcements, to announce staff meetings, and for individual requests (e.g., to get individual teachers' attendance sheets or to page individual teachers or students). However, apart from actually finding a person in the flesh, there is no systematic way to get information to the building for use by various individuals, teams, or the whole school. Even for teachers who have telephones with outside lines in their rooms—and not all do—there is no voice mail. At the end of the year one teacher complained: "We don't even have each others' phone numbers. So if people want to communicate with someone about something in the evenings because we get busy during the day, I had to call one person to another to try to get . . . numbers. There was never a directory of phone numbers."

Few teachers have access to electronic mail, and even those who do may not have the time to use it. It is sometimes difficult, therefore, for parents and others outside the building to get messages through to Paine staff. Despite efforts to the contrary, there are simply no guarantees that a message will be received and responded to in a timely manner.

The emergent professional community at Thomas Paine High School speaks eloquently of the power of urban teachers and administrators to come together in support of effective programs for students. The continuing challenges to the development of this community—problems associated with the team structure, the need to balance openness and flexibility with coordination and perhaps even centralized control, and communication issues—are not insurmountable. Because there is professional community, the mechanisms (e.g., the Leadership Council, the administrative team, the team leaders, the OA steering committee) exist to address them. Continuing study will record what happens as Thomas Paine moves forward.

Notes

1. The student council has been reinstated for the 1994–1995 school year.

2. The reason that the paint is peeling off the walls, teachers quickly tell visitors, is that a fish oil-based paint was put on the walls during World War II, which causes all new coats of paint to peel off

and would be, unfortunately, very expensive to remove. It is cheaper to repaint the interior of the building ever 3 or 4 years than to pay to remove the traces of the bad paint.

3. In addition, the district has a postsecondary program for students. Eleventh and 12th graders may take courses at local universities and colleges if they are not offered at their high school. In 1993–1994, 12 students from Paine used this option.

4. During one of the three trimesters, teachers offered an elective course, eliminating one of their planning periods for that trimester. In 1994–1995, Thomas Paine will revert to a six-period day, a change with the potential to limit teachers' time for meeting.

5. The contracts of two first-year teachers who had spent hours with their mentors were not renewed for 1994–1995, raising difficult questions for the PDS that purports to help all teachers.

6. For the past 2 years Paine teachers and administrators have petitioned the school board for, and received, 3 staff development days beyond the set allotment. These additional days provide more opportunities for teacher-planned activities.

7. Teachers are also recognized by their efforts and are given gifts such as T-shirts, portfolios, clocks, and the like. Like the students, they are very receptive to the program. As one put it, "It seems kind of corny that we get together and get prizes and stuff—I got a beach towel—but it is really nice to know that we are being recognized for our work. We are appreciated." Another teacher said, "It's nice to get together on something positive for a change."

8. Next year there will be 10th grade IMP classes for those students who had IMP in the 9th grade. In 1995–1996 all 9th and 10th grade students will study IMP math.

9. Other teams' teachers also confer with colleagues and provide individualized instruction during free time, but without *external* standards for student learning.

10. In interviews two people noted the matriarchal nature of Paine's teacher leadership. "It's more like an elementary school where people say, 'Let's try it.'" It is the case that, with one exception, the most visible teacher leaders in the building are all women.

11. Though it is true that the majority of IB students are white, it is also important to note that a sizable number of minority students (42.3%) remain in the program as juniors and seniors, a feature that makes Paine's IB program different from many. In fact, two of the three diploma candidates in 1994 were African-American.

12. Some teachers report having a similar feeling toward SPREAD, which has a 6 to 1 student/teacher ratio. The high percentage of African-American males in special education is of some concern to the Paine community, although the special education action research study this year found that these students are identified long before they arrive at the school. Paine inherits special education students; it does not create them.

5

Catalyzing Professional Community
in a School Reform Left Behind

SHARON ROLLOW
ANTHONY S. BRYK

In 1989 the Center for School Improvement (CSI) at the University of Chicago initiated a partnership with Alexander, a kindergarten through eighth-grade elementary school that serves 650 poor, African-American students on Chicago's west side. Initially, we offered to help the school community implement Chicago's new reform legislation. Subsequently, we targeted our efforts to working with the faculty and organized our activities around a literacy initiative.

When our work started, we expected to help the school make a transition from a bureaucratically controlled organization to a professional community. What we learned, however, was that a family metaphor more appropriately characterized the initial condition of this school, and that this was a troubled family. The fact that urban schools may be like families, both healthy and dysfunctional ones, puts an extra burden on intermediate support organizations. Despite the enthusiasm of teachers for enhanced professionalism, such schools may need more than technical knowledge and sustained support to catalyze professional community.

This case cannot be extricated from its district context. Chicago is part of the country's most significant experiment in radical decentralization in a major metropolitan area. As part of state law, each school's policies are officially governed by an elected Local School Council (LSC), composed of six parents, two community members, two teachers, and the principal. The law, which is highly complex, also decentralized significant new budget control to schools. For example, the bulk of federal monies allocated for disadvantaged and other categorical programs now is allocated directly to the schools. The principal serves on a performance contract at the discretion of the LSC, although teachers retain traditional tenure rights. In theory, this system is intended to revitalize community involvement in schools, to enhance responsiveness to the specific student population in the schools, and to ensure that discretionary budgets are allocated to local priorities rather than distributed by a general district formula (Bryk, Easton, Kerbow, Rollow, & Sebring, 1993). In short, the goal is educational revolution through local empowerment. In Alexander, however, we see some limits to theory that are imposed as a consequence of organizational and community conditions.

Alexander's Context:
Lack of Social and Community Resources

Alexander was built 30 years ago to serve an expanding African-American neighborhood on Chicago's west side. Although poor and racially isolated, there were storefront churches and local businesses, recreation centers, and a smattering of city-sponsored health clinics and social service agencies.

Today, in contrast, this is a "truly disadvantaged" neighborhood, with dilapidated housing, a preponderance of female-headed households, an absence of middle-class and male role models, a loss of population and community institutions, and a diminution of political activity (Wilson, 1987). Most important, this community lacks the extended social networks of family and neighborhood that supported its population a few decades ago. Without this social resource the consequences of poverty, drugs, and violence appear much more devastating here, especially to the "young moms" who struggle to survive and keep their children safe. The present also contrasts with a not very distant past when mothers—in this neighborhood and others just like it—were generally older, somewhat more advantaged, and less hesitant to talk to teachers and be involved in the school. Fathers and grandparents were also more likely to be active. Today the educators in the school know that there aren't many men to call upon: "There's boys and old men but the old folk are afraid to come out of their houses. Everything in between is in jail or dead."

A small group of mothers still participates regularly in the school as classroom volunteers and LSC members. The staff appreciate their efforts, but the mothers complain of being too few and consequently burned out. This leaves the young moms as the main group with potential to become a viable presence in the school. The LSC chair tries to get some of them involved, but it isn't easy. Safety is an issue. The school does not want to be responsible for people being out in the neighborhood after dark, so meetings are scheduled during school hours or at dismissal. Consequently, working parents can never attend meetings. A problem for a second group of parents is embarrassment about their own academic skills, and their consequent reluctance to converse with educators. Finally, there is a latent hostility that keeps other parents away. Some parents have negative memories of their own experiences at Alexander, or a school just like it, and they believe that teachers regard them with disdain. The LSC chair answers her own question about "what kind of role models are these moms for their kids when they feel so hateful and hated? It can't be good."

Maternal Leadership

Being the principal of a truly disadvantaged school community is difficult. Mrs. Betty Green has to do double duty, with parents and teachers, to overcome their isolation, hostility, fear, lack of confidence and skills. Betty has taken on this challenge by becoming, not only the school's principal for the past 10 years, but, perhaps more important from her own and others' point of view, the school's "mom."

While Betty is afraid to relinquish control, she also feels trapped even as she rationalizes and defends her actions. She recognizes that some parents' and teachers' dependence and debility might be because she does too much for them (Feldman, 1982).

There is also a personal toll. Betty has been chronically ill for years with arthritis. In the third year of the school's partnership with CSI, there were rumors that the stresses of the job—taking control of the building she inherited, dealing with the mandates of the new reform legislation and also trying to adequately care for her own biological children and extended family—overwhelmed her. She was absent a lot—a day here and a day there—and sometimes even when she was in the building she was not be found. Some teachers and office staff referred to her "fragile condition," but they covered for her and took responsibility for getting her work done.

Limited Parent and Community Involvement

The LSC at Alexander contains a core of hardworking and well-intentioned women who are between the ages of 25 and 30. The chair has told us often that she is proud that there is no fighting on her council, or in the school, as there is in some neighboring schools. Unfortunately, there is also little sustained conversation or activity.

When Chicago's reform was enacted in 1989, it looked like the Act might make a difference. Many in the school and community were curious about the new law and wanted to be involved in its implementation. One of the LSC's first challenges in 1990 was to evaluate Betty's performance as principal, and offer her a 4-year performance contract or recruit her replacement. Although training was available to support this process, the many impediments to sustained participation in this community discouraged more than minimal participation and discussion by the LSC and/or other teachers and parents. By unanimous vote the council skipped her evaluation. They awarded Betty a new contract.

Excitement about community control dissipated by the second year of reform. The LSC called obligatory monthly meetings, but there was rarely a quorum, never an audience, and except for the principal's report, not much was discussed. There was another flurry of activity during the second year, when a system-wide financial crunch threatened the school with closure. Alexander stayed open, but the experience did not unite the school community. The LSC chair, Mrs. Jones, felt tired and discouraged when only 50 parents showed up for a "Save Alexander" rally she had organized. Betty expressed her frustration, too, calling parents "the most apathetic bunch" she had ever seen. Once the crisis passed, the principal and Mrs. Jones called meetings to discuss how the school might distinguish itself to avoid future closing lists. The meetings went unattended.

Blaming the Victim: Frustrations
of an Isolated and Demoralized Faculty

The LSC's reluctance to act is mirrored in the experiences of the larger faculty and Alexander's Professional Personnel Advisory Committee (also mandated by the Chicago school reform act) as it grapples with local school governance. Sixteen candidates competed for the first PPAC election because many were curious. Teachers quickly became puzzled, however, about the committee's identity and purpose. Many confused it with the Professional Problems Committee of the Chicago Teachers Union. Others knew that the PPAC was to be advisory on issues of curriculum and instruction as set out in the reform law, but they were unclear about its independence from the principal. Some members argued that they could not discuss pedagogy without the principal; others insisted that they could never develop an independent voice if she joined them.

The PPAC never recovered from this initial controversy. The principal dropped out when she was apprised of the problem surrounding her participation, and so did most of those who wanted her involved. The chair abdicated next, and another teacher replaced her at the principal's request. When no candidates came forward to replace those who had resigned, the chair asked a few of her friends on the faculty to volunteer as a personal favor. The new PPAC met once in the fall of 1992. It has not been convened since.

In addition there are other impediments. The faculty voted to go on closed campus several years ago, a move that shortened the teachers' school day, to one that ran from 8:30 a.m. to 2:30 p.m., by eliminating some preparation periods and allowing teachers only 20 minutes to eat lunch with their students. The rationale behind closed campus in urban districts is to keep children in the building under adult supervision and safe from gangs, drugs, and crime; but in elementary schools it means that children and teachers go without a break from each other all day, and there is no time for teachers to plan or meet with colleagues. The shortened day also means that routine professional development and governance activities always require staying after the school day.

In spite of conditions that militate against teachers' extended engagement (Johnson, 1990), there are teachers at Alexander who are caring, hardworking, and deeply concerned about the students. This is the core of hardworking and burned out people whom the principal drafts to serve on committees to plan for the special activities (spelling bees, Academic Olympics, and various social events) that crowd the school calendar. These teachers would like to serve students better and over the years have enrolled in countless courses and bought dozens of programs, but nothing seems to raise student achievement. Some persist in their individual efforts, but others have given up, and this portion of the veteran faculty is "riding out their time" until retirement. Convinced that the family and community circumstances of Alexander's students make their academic success highly unlikely (Easton, Bryk, Driscoll, Kotsakis, Sebring, & van der Ploeg, 1991), they insist that over the years they "have tried everything." Betty complains that their lack of motivation is the most serious obstacle to school improvement. According to Betty:

> They are convinced that they are fantastic teachers. They have had successes through the years, but things have changed. Getting them to understand that and to change is the most difficult kind of thing. Take our primary teachers. . . . I have some teachers here who have not gone back to school since they got, and this is the honest to goodness truth, their diploma in 1959. Now reading alone has changed, the whole philosophy has changed in the last 5 or 10 years and they're still doing things like then. This is a poor neighbor-

hood, the social family structures have changed a great deal, and for many of our teachers, they are teaching to the students that we had in 1963 and we don't have that kind of student any more.

It is instructive to note that most of the teachers at Alexander attended Chicago schools. Most were then certified in Chicago, and have subsequently spent their entire careers at Alexander, or a school just like it. Thus, they are hard-pressed to imagine alternatives. This poses a significant obstacle to Chicago's reform, because the heart of this legislation is the opportunity, in each local school community, to create alternatives (Bryk & Rollow, 1992, Hess, 1991; Moore, 1992). For example, when we asked the assistant principal to describe for us a "good school" he said, "off the top of my head, that's hard for me to say. . . . I haven't graduated to that way of thinking yet."

Early Interventions at Alexander: 1989–1991

The university's Center for School Improvement piggybacked on the new reform when it initiated a partnership with Alexander in 1989, offering to help the school community with organizing the LSC and PPAC, conducting a principal evaluation and needs assessment, and developing a 3-year school improvement plan (SIP). Over time we hoped to expand our involvement such that we might be a source of motivation and support to Alexander to engage a comprehensive restructuring.

The Limited Role of Service Provider

As noted earlier, however, in spite of the availability of training, most early activities associated with the legislation were minimally executed. Three years into the city's reform effort, Alexander was "a school reform left behind" (Moultrie, 1992). CSI concluded that we needed to become more involved, moving from an on-call service provider to a more active change agent. We were learning that in

Alexander and other schools like it we needed to provide more hands-on support if we were to have an impact. Such schools were offered a choice between two highly structured academic initiatives in mathematics and literacy. Alexander chose literacy.

Restructuring Relationships and Roles

A key component of CSI's initiative was to simultaneously support all of the professional staff—principal, teachers, and a school-based literacy coordinator who was recruited from the teaching staff. In contrast to other interventions that concentrate primarily on teachers, helping the principal to fully support the faculty's efforts to change was a core element of the strategy. Alexander, like other urban schools, suffers from a legacy of top-down control, where good principals, and subsequently good teachers, follow orders from above. We knew that the move from a chain-of-command mentality to a collaborative, professional community would be taxing. To support Betty's change efforts, Sara Spurlark, a former principal in the CPS, was given the role of her mentor. Another of CSI's staff members, Hal Gershenson, was available to help the literacy coordinator, who was chosen from Alexander's faculty and would work directly with the teachers. In schools as disadvantaged as Alexander, nothing short of this intensive intervention could catalyze professional community.

What no one knew as we made these plans was that Betty's illness would flare up at this time. Because Betty was such a central figure, her every move had repercussions for the faculty. Her many absences in the fall and winter months meant she could not participate in the workshops alongside her teachers, nor could she directly encourage their involvement. In Betty's absence it was the school's new literacy coordinator who largely took responsibility for working with us to carry out the initiative.

Developing Teachers' Pedagogical Knowledge

Our work began with the nine classroom teachers in the kindergarten and primary grades. Alexander had recently purchased a basal series that, although advertised as interactive and literacy-based, in fact emphasized phonics. Although Alexander's teachers had expressed a desire to move to a whole language approach, they had been unable to move beyond the basals. The primary teachers had also chosen to group their students homogeneously, with the most at-risk students segregated from their peers. Discretionary money was used to reduce class size in first and second grade to better meet the needs of these students. However, teachers had done little to change the instruction that children would receive in the smaller classes.

Work with the primary faculty was organized around 10 Saturday morning workshops developed and presented by staff from Reading Recovery and the Martha L. King Language and Literacy Center at Ohio State University (OSU). The workshops built on both the pedagogy of literacy instruction and individual student assessment developed at OSU, and their extensive experience with teachers' professional development. At an interpersonal level it connected Alexander's faculty with people: university consultants from OSU, CSI's staff, and teachers from another school who were also engaged with the Center in the literacy initiative. At a professional level it connected them with external sources of expertise and national standards of best practice. This design was of critical importance as it was intended to catalyze and sustain an informed conversation within the school and among the faculty that focused on practice.

Specifically, the workshops engaged teachers in continuing conversation about children's learning. It provided role modeling, hands-on assignments, and other supports for teachers' change. The sessions focused on classroom teaching techniques and diagnostic assessment of individual students. Building theory inductively and familiarizing teachers with new instructional strategies were at the core of the strategy.

One anticipated problem, however, was developing teachers' practical strategies and theoretical learning in tandem. Teachers naturally gravitated toward new techniques. Without a theoretical grounding, however, these remained isolated practices. During the first part of the school year most of the faculty did not know how to incorporate the new techniques into their regular program of instruction. Moreover, teachers were not convinced that they had the principal's permission to use the new strategies. Although Betty offered teachers a stipend, she did not attend the workshops with them, as noted earlier. Nor had she made clear her expectations about changing their classroom instruction or using materials additional to the basals. Furthermore, Betty had not released teachers from their obligation to cover the traditional curriculum, and in the past she had said that insufficient coverage was one reason for low test scores. Without a clear directive and daily encouragement from Betty, most of the primary teachers were reluctant to take risks.

Collectivizing Responsibility for Instructional Leadership

The heart of CSI's intervention was establishing a role for a literacy coordinator, someone who would work with teachers to ensure that the ideas, techniques, and materials introduced in the workshop series would become integral to their classroom practice. We anticipated that the coordinator would conduct demonstration classes, classroom observations, and follow-up conferences. Moreover, we envisioned the literacy coordinator as someone who would facilitate the faculty's sustained professional dialogue, both at faculty meetings and in other settings. What is most important, creating the role was an attempt to ensure that responsibility for instructional leadership became a more general attribute of the professional staff, rather than residing solely with Alexander's already overburdened principal.

Finding the right person for the job was critical. Sara talked with Betty at length about specific criteria and viable candidates. The literacy coordinator needed to be an excellent teacher of children. Additionally, she had to have the tact, sensitivity, and interpersonal skills to be an adult educator. Finally, she needed to have the principal's respect and confidence. The selection proved difficult because Betty was reluctant to move a good teacher out of the classroom. She wanted to select someone from her auxiliary or administrative staff. This was not acceptable to us, because we knew that she was protecting a few individuals out of longstanding friendship to her and loyalty to the school, rather than their professional abilities. A compromise was reached when Betty offered the job to her reading resource teacher. This teacher turned it down, however, because she said that supervision was the principal's job. She did not want a potential conflict with the principal.

Eventually, Ruth Povlovsky, a special education teacher for intermediate and upper-grade children who had been at the school for 10 years, was selected. Ruth was one of the teachers that Betty relied on whenever she needed administrative help. She liked the fact that Ruth was a perfectionist, because it meant that when Ruth volunteered to do something, it was done right. Betty also said that in spite of having only a bachelor's degree, Ruth was very bright and would do well.

Betty and Ruth anticipated a problem, however. Ruth did not have special training in reading, as did some teachers on the faculty, and they thought that this might create resentment and make Ruth's job more difficult. Sara reasoned, however, that initially the faculty would have a hard time accepting anyone in this new role, because teachers at Alexander, like other urban elementary schools, are not accustomed to being supervised by anyone other than the principal. Furthermore, Sara said to expect a certain level of suspicion at first because promotions are so often used in schools politically—to pay back, or perhaps even coopt, an individual (Ball, 1987). Sara suggested that Ruth would have to be strategic in her first efforts at helping the faculty, be patient with their insecurities, and trust that over time they would come to value her work.

A second problem was protecting Ruth's time. Urban schools like Alexander are chronically understaffed, especially in clerical and administrative positions. The time of "freed" teachers is swallowed up by principals who need help, and teachers too make demands because they know that these individuals have no direct responsibility to students. Although it was our understanding with the principal and Ruth, at the beginning of the year, that Ruth was to work full-time on the literacy initiative, we knew that this would be a struggle. Betty's illness exacerbated this strain. Just as the initiative got under way, Ruth took much informal responsibility for running the school.

Finally, as Ruth's role and expertise changed vis-à-vis the principal, their longstanding personal relationship would be tested. Although in some urban schools this might be a change from bureaucratic control to a professional community, at Alexander the projected changes were more akin to shifting from a mother/daughter relationship to a collaboration of peers, where leadership, knowledge, and responsibility for outcomes would be shared. We assumed that the

because she did not think that the teachers would have anything to say if they were not complaining about the kids. Finally, she wanted to know how to get the teachers to come to school early when they did not have to.

Hal thought that some of the more suspicious or jealous teachers would come just to check on Ruth, and a few others would come because the meeting was a novelty. He suggested that Ruth also rely on personal favors and bribes to get the rest to attend. In addition to coffee and cake, Ruth might advertise a door prize when she announced the meeting, and ask all of her friends on the primary faculty to make a point of showing up. Then, once she got people there, Ruth needed to start with some ground rules. She needed to remind teachers that they were convened to discuss only two things: questions or comments about the workshops, and their homework. Also, Hal advocated a no-gripe policy, a rule that no one could talk unless their comments were positive. Ruth appreciated these suggestions and also the structure they would give to the meeting. She felt more comfortable and thought that her teachers would relax, too, if they knew what was expected (and what was off-limits) in this new setting.

The first meeting was a huge success. Almost all of the primary teachers came, out of curiosity, and once there Ruth plied them with food and children's books. She kept everyone to her script and as a result the discussion was substantive and positive. When the 9:00 bell rang teachers were still talking, so Ruth asked if they would like to meet again. There was some hesitance and even embarrassment about volunteering to come to school early because it was so far from their norm. Several cautiously said, however, that they would "come if they could" or "maybe they'd come" or "they'd try if traffic wasn't too bad" and "if it didn't rain." They did come back, and weekly mini-meetings, facilitated by Ruth and focused on the workshops, became routine. Over time there was less need for the agenda to be so controlled and circumscribed, and the substance of the meetings expanded beyond the workshops to include teachers' general concerns about their work. Significantly, teachers began to bring up problems they were having in their classrooms—focusing on their teaching, as distinct from the past when they had complained about problem students. They began to turn to Ruth and their colleagues for advice.

Organizing and sustaining the mini-meetings was a significant accomplishment. This was a school where teachers had little experience with sustained, substantive conversation or collegial exchange. Nor were they accustomed to meeting on a voluntary basis and without their principal. This struck us as a further step toward a professional, teacher-led community at Alexander School.

Integrating Theory and Practice:
A Focus on Teaching and Learning

Ruth and Hal debriefed after each mini-meeting. With Hal's help Ruth was able to expand her work, and she began to visit more classrooms and to follow up on observations with private conferences. These advances were possible because the mini-meeting generated trust in Ruth, and teachers became accustomed to a public discussion of their teaching. In addition, Ruth was developing as a teacher leader in literacy because of her attendance at the workshops and her continuing exchanges with the OSU consultants and Hal. Her emerging expertise enabled her to identify areas where teachers needed help and offer technical assistance. Ruth's growth as a leader was shown by her initial efforts to provide advice to Hal about how CSI's initiative could be made more effective at Alexander. For example, Ruth argued that individual teachers were at different places with regard to their use of the new teaching techniques. Some had experimented with them more, and some less. Most did not understand, at this point, how they could or why they should relate an assessment of an individual child's reading skill to their classroom practice. Ruth suggested that further work with assessments be delayed in favor of continued work on teaching strategies.

She also took it upon herself to initiate conversations with Betty about the encouragement that teachers needed from her. While the initiative was advancing without Betty's attention, Ruth told the principal that much more progress would be made if teachers knew that Betty was supportive of their work. She also told Betty that some teachers were still reluctant to use the new techniques, and that they would not feel free to do so until she gave them a green light.

In response to Ruth's suggestion, the next phase of intervention focused on integrating reading and writing into the whole school day, not just language arts. The trainer, an experienced elementary teacher, showed them her schedule and how she achieved this integration. She then demonstrated for the Alexander teachers how she used individual assessment in classroom teaching. She suggested that only by knowing the strengths of each individual child can teachers make informed decisions about how to instruct a group. The teachers were excited about her presentation and began to understand how individual assessment and new teaching techniques might work in tandem.

To build upon the enthusiasm generated in these sessions, Ruth converted the weekly mini-meetings from discussions about the workshops to hands-on sessions devoted to the new pedagogy. Through role playing (where teachers took the part of students and Hal and Ruth took turns playing the teacher), they rehearsed how teachers might incorporate the various strategies into their classroom practice. Ruth then followed the teachers into their classrooms. She counseled them individually as the new methods were tried. The principal would occasionally pop into classrooms at this point to show her interest as well. The teachers appreciated these efforts. Change in their pedagogy became evident when story charts, big books, and wall charts written by children started to appear in most of the primary classrooms.

Buoyed by these activities, in the early spring Ruth and Hal thought that the teachers were ready to turn their attention back to diagnostic technique and assessment of individual children's reading. In a workshop they were introduced to *running records*, a Reading Recovery assessment. This is a note-taking strategy in which a teacher learns to record both the successful reading and the specific miscues that a child makes during oral reading.

Alexander's teachers were not expected to master the running record based on a workshop demonstration. Rather, Hal suggested that Ruth be trained to use the assessment and that she then work individually with teachers on this important strategy. Following this in-service, the teacher and Ruth would jointly conduct a running record for a selected child. They would then analyze their results, compare notes, and decide the implications for the child's instruction. All of the teachers accepted Ruth's offer of assistance.

These assessments, which were conducted in May and June, proved that Ruth was now regarded as a teacher leader among her peers. Equally important, teachers knew that they had attained a new level of understanding about literacy teaching and learning and diagnostic pedagogy. Most of them had already had some successful experience with the new classroom teaching techniques. Now they were also able to administer and analyze a diagnostic, and use it to develop an individualized teaching plan. Appropriately, they felt a sense of accomplishment.

Taking Stock: First Reflections and Incipient Plans

The first year of Alexander's literacy initiative ended on a high note. An evaluation meeting convened by CSI suggested enthusiasm about the program and plans for the following year.

Teachers said that the new techniques introduced in the workshop helped them understand a new approach to teaching. These workshops engendered a desire among the faculty for further occasions for professional development. One teacher proposed that: "We need opportunities to observe in each other's classrooms and then come together and talk about what we saw and talk about what we think was good . . . just share things." Another teacher remarked:

> You know, teaching is a kind of isolating job. I've been teaching a long time. I just go into my classroom and I work with kids all day, and I never talk with adults. But the workshops this year have really brought us together. I feel focused, and I don't feel so isolated.

They requested more time to talk about teaching in faculty meetings the following year, and they asked for help in making the diagnostic techniques introduced in the workshops broadly applicable to their classrooms.

Teachers also talked about the changes they had made in their classroom practice. They said that the new teaching and assessment strategies introduced in the workshop created many exciting opportunities for children to learn, and turned teachers' attention from children's deficits to their knowledge and skills. Two classroom teachers reorganized their methods of instruction during the year. One, a kindergarten teacher, remarked at the meeting that she had stopped following the basal program's timetable and was now guided by the needs of individual children. She also spent more time reading books to her class and asking the children to read to her. She said, "When given the opportunity to read a lot they love it and they made more and faster progress." Similarly, a first-grade teacher chose to ignore the teacher's manual and use a more thematic approach to teaching. One of her new units included bringing an incubator to class and hatching chicken eggs. This science lesson was coupled with such stories as "Chicken Sunday" and "Little Red Hen." Students then wrote their own stories about chickens.

Other primary teachers were more cautious about moving away from the standard curriculum because they feared plummeting test scores and how their principal might react. Although they did not articulate their concerns at the meeting, Betty had been informed of them by both Ruth and Sara on several previous occasions. Betty used the meeting to announce that teachers did not have to administer every unit test in the basal. She said that the running records and other assessments that they were using from Reading Recovery were giving them more and better information than the basals did. She also used the meeting to congratulate teachers publicly for their work in the literacy initiative and to encourage their further efforts. She talked about "a job well done," and said, "I am proud of all of you . . . each of you." She went around the room, referring to each teacher by name and mentioning something new that she had observed them doing. For example, she commented on a particularly good story introduction with homemade puppets that she had seen in a first-grade classroom, and a beautiful wall chart in another class. Betty told the teachers that she saw more teachers reading to their children throughout the building, and that she liked the bulletin boards and other exhibits of children's writing that now complemented the artwork in the halls. The teachers blossomed in response to Betty's remarks.

The teachers did not take all of the credit, however. They called Ruth a "lifesaver," complained about the weight that they had gained from her coffeecake, and in front of us they asked their principal for assurance that she would be "really freed" to be literacy coordinator "full time" the following year. They wanted her to help them conduct running records on each of their new students in the fall; they wanted to use that information to place children in classrooms; and then they wanted to work with Ruth to create their instructional plans for the year. They asked us if they could have some refresher workshops on specific topics, and they wanted assurance that external support and training would continue to be accessible to them on a needs basis. The teachers also wanted to know if the literacy initiative was on schedule to extend to the intermediate and upper grades the following year. One teacher said: "I want the rest of the teachers to be able to do some of this stuff so that when my kids get into their classrooms they can keep learning like they did this year and having fun."

Ruth did not say anything at the meeting. In private, however, she told us:

> This had been the best year since I started teaching. I've done things that I didn't know I could do. I'm back at school for a master's, and I didn't think I could do that, and I'm literacy coordinator, too. I can't believe some of the things I've done. I'm so tired but I'm so excited and energized too. I don't know how I got it all done. I've always been so scared. This year, though, with Betty gone . . . I was good at things and I just can't believe it. I worked so hard and it all paid off for me. I'm proud of myself.

Finally, Betty announced her intention to attend CSI's residential summer institute for principals. Although we had encouraged her attendance for the past two summers, this was the first year that Betty could make the necessary child care arrangements. Ruth and the teachers were glad that she would have some time away from school for some rest and relaxation during the summer. We hoped it would be an opportunity for her to extend her support and professional network with principal colleagues from across the city. Betty surprised us, too, not only in her decision to attend the summer institute, but also by her discussion with the teachers about the basal tests. Although on the surface it was obvious that the teachers did not need to administer both the basal unit tests and the assessments from

Reading Recovery, at a deeper level Betty's decision suggested that she was trying to give the teachers more discretion over their own work. Her discussion of this issue seemed just as meaningful a political shift as did the teachers' public challenge to her about Ruth's time. It contrasted with her previous style of telling people what to do in private. It was as if Betty wanted her commitment to be on public record so that we might all help her stick to it.

Year Two of the Literacy Initiative: 1992–1993

The new school year started off on the same positive note, but there was a series of setbacks. Most of these were relatively easy to overcome, but one had lasting consequences, not only to the partnership between CSI and Alexander, but for the school's emergent professional community.

Inconsistent Support

One problem that fell into the former camp was Hal's resignation, which he announced just before the start of the school. His sudden departure was hard for Ruth and brought back some of her earlier feelings of insecurity. Ruth and Hal had established a trusting, collegial relationship, and the intensive assistance that he gave her had enabled her to provide a similar level of support to teachers.

We hired Guadalupe Hamersma, a respected former Chicago principal, to replace Hal. She and Ruth struck up a warm, personal relationship almost immediately, and her professional background and experience gave her instant credibility with Betty and the teachers. Guadalupe quickly stepped in to work with Ruth much as Hal had—first conferencing in private, and then receding into the background when Ruth felt competent to take over.

Difficulties of Recreating Roles and Norms

A more serious problem was the drop-off in activity at the primary level when Ruth turned her attention to the intermediate and upper-grade teachers. In theory, the phasing in of the initiative, and the expansion of her role in a school the size of Alexander, should not have been a problem for the primary teachers. In practice, it was.

When school began Ruth was unable to protect her time, especially because so many support staff that Betty had surrounded herself with over the years had such marginal skills. Ruth's personality was perhaps counterproductive, in that she found it impossible to see a problem in the school that went unattended and/or a job that was not well done. And though Betty may have fully intended to free Ruth at the time of her public declaration, she too found it difficult to break old habits of dependence and reliance on Ruth. Guadalupe began to refer to Ruth as the de facto principal, who had none of the authority but got too much of the responsibility and grief.

The problematic nature of Ruth's role, in combination with trying to expand the initiative to the intermediate and upper grades, meant that the work at the lower grades suffered. At first Ruth was baffled. She thought that the primary teachers should have been able to sustain the initiative better on their own because she knew that their technical skills and understanding were up to the tasks set out for them at the start of the year. What they seemed to miss, however, was Ruth's personal attention. They acted as if they resented her return (even part-time) to the second floor. Ruth felt frustrated by her inability to fix everything and do everything well. She expressed her resentment about the quandary that Betty had put her in. She told Guadalupe that she was:

> Being taken advantage of. It's like I've got so much to do I can't do anything right. And Betty knows that I won't say no to anything. She's my principal so I can't say no and keep my job, can I? Besides, she [Betty] knows that I don't know how [to say no].

The Fragile Nature of Trust

Because she had been teaching at this level before becoming literacy coordinator, Ruth expected that the second floor would be "like going home." She had not anticipated the erosion of trust, nor the resentment and suspicion of her former colleagues. One told her that "it felt like [she] had deserted them" the previous year, and that she "must have an attitude" now that she worked with "the university people." Although Ruth had taken great pains to ingratiate herself with the primary group, we had not adequately prepared her for the politics that awaited her homecoming. Ruth felt personally hurt, and she was concerned that the initiative would not get off to a good, fast start with this group if they did not trust her. She was disheartened, but she set herself the task of developing this social resource all over again.

Provoking a Family Crisis

The most serious setback took place in early November, when we shared a case study with Betty that we had written about the previous year's work at the school.

The case was developed from Hal's notes and was written as a self-evaluation report to the funders of the intervention project. We planned to share it first with the principal so that she might make corrections and comments. Although we wanted to be sure that we got the record straight, we also saw the document's potential to serve a second purpose and become a teaching case for the school. We hoped it might help us further our conversation with Betty, Ruth, and the primary faculty about their work and also how to improve ours.

Even before we gave Betty the case, however, we knew that it might make people at the school feel vulnerable. They had never seen a case before. To reduce potential problems, we decided that Sara would share it first with Betty, and then it would be up to Betty to keep it private or extend it to Ruth. Ruth, if she got it, would in turn help us decide if and how to share it with the primary teachers. We talked with Betty and Ruth about the case as it was being completed, and assured them that overall the case was flattering and positive about everyone. We warned them, however, that the case described points along the way where each of the principle players, including our staff, made mistakes.

A critical error was our underestimation of Betty's "fragile condition." We ignored our own protocol by giving the case to Betty when Sara was not available to read through it with her. Betty read nothing positive in our portrayal, and she felt that the case portrayed her as an over-controlling person. She said that we were insensitive to the context that she worked in, the difficulties that she had overcome when she first arrived at Alexander, and those that she still faced. Most important, she felt that the case described her as uncaring about her school community, when, in fact, "didn't we know that everyone thought of her as mom?"

Betty was especially sensitive to references about her absences. She wanted to know "who told us." She pointed the finger at Ruth and hinted that our portrayal of Ruth's development as literacy coordinator reflected badly on her: "If Ruth was *so* wonderful," she said, "then maybe I should leave and she can just take over! According to you guys, she already has!"

Betty did not keep the case private. Rather, she shared snippets with various members of her staff and said to them: "I'm not like this, am I?" Of course, they told her that she was not. Sara, and others on our staff whom Betty had gotten to know at the summer institute, extended many offers at this time to make amends. Sara told her that we thought the case was a positive and flattering story, because it showed such tremendous change and development on everyone's part. We asked if we might meet with her to learn what she thought was misrepresented, and how to correct it. Betty did eventually meet with us, but it was not until a month later, when she had sufficiently cooled down.

The story was rewritten, with sensitivity to Betty's comments, but the damage was irreparable. Ruth told Guadalupe that she was afraid to talk with anyone from CSI, and yet she wanted to. She said that although she trusted us to keep her confidence, Betty would accuse her of "being the one who talked" anyway.

Teachers were wary, too. They came to the workshops scheduled around this time, but they were quieter now. They milled around the back of the room at breaks, and they were reluctant to talk with us or the presenters from OSU, as had become their custom. Several teachers also confronted Sara and Guadalupe in private. They asked: "How could [we] do that to Betty? Didn't [we] know that she was fragile . . . that she had so much stress . . . that there were problems in her [biological] family? . . . that she was absent a lot?" Ruth and the teachers did not keep their distance for long. After a few weeks they seemed anxious to turn their attention back to the initiative, and it looked for a while as if the work might get back on track. Our hopes faltered, however, with further changes in Betty's behavior.

Betty began to attend the faculty meetings that Ruth would con-
vene—ostensibly to support her teachers' efforts—but their dialogue
died out whenever she walked in the room. She also moved her office
into Ruth's resource room when hers was being renovated, although
there were empty rooms on the first floor. Betty also stayed in the
resource room long after her office was finished, and this had the
effect that teachers stopped dropping in. Betty also stopped visiting
teachers' classrooms and showing an interest in their work. Several
complained to Guadalupe about her withholding behavior. They told
Guadalupe to tell the principal that they could not make progress
without her active support. This was also the time when, from Ruth's
point of view, Betty heaped even more extraneous duties on her, one
of which was teacher remediation. Ruth said that overall it felt like
she was "being punished for working with you the previous year. It's
insane. I was supposed to work with you. I was assigned to work
with you! I guess the problem was I did a good job." About the specific teacher remediation duty, Ruth said to Guadalupe:

> How can I do this? I'm not credentialed to do this! I don't
> want to do this! Mr. Jones shouldn't even be in a room with
> children! That's how bad he is! You've seen him! How can I
> do this to Mr. Jones and still tell other teachers that I'm in
> their classrooms to help? You guys tell her [Betty] to do it.
> You said I shouldn't do this kind of stuff. Tell her I just can't!

When Sara talked privately with Betty about the conflict between
remediation and support, and also the untenable role that Ruth was
in, Betty chuckled nervously and said, "Well, yeah, but you've seen
him teach and you know how bad he is. I've got to do something.
Maybe you could hire him over at the university and get him out of
here for me? That'll work. After all, he's working on his Nova Ph.D.!"

Understanding Patterns of School Organization: Applying a Family Lens

Perhaps the most important challenge that faces urban school
intervention work is how to understand and be helpful to the com-

munity of educators that has worked in isolation for decades in a context like Alexander's. As noted earlier, there is a history of top-down control in most urban districts. One intent of decentralization, be it Chicago's reform or site-based management strategies in other urban districts, is to break this pattern of control. Although there are many examples of schools both nationally and in Chicago that have been able to seize this opportunity to chart their own futures, we do not regard it as a robust strategy. We know of too many schools, like Alexander, that cannot imagine alternatives to their present condition. Moreover, they lack the social resources, behavioral norms, leadership capacities, and resident technical expertise to improve themselves. Alexander proved resilient to the multiyear efforts of an external support team, not because we did not try hard enough, but because we did not understand, except retrospectively, the fragile dynamics of the school community we were working in.

Much of the recent reform literature suggests that urban schools must move from bureaucratic control to professional community, and this is what we thought when we started our work, too. What we found in Alexander, however, was a different structure: a dysfunctional family where the faculty are described by their principal as "kids," and the teachers, in turn, refer to and protect their principal when she is ill as if she were their fragile "mom."

Although John Dewey likened "a good school to a family" decades ago, researchers are unaccustomed to applying this lens. When we began to look through the family lens to better understand our work at Alexander, however, our experiences, and especially the roadblocks that we encountered, began to cohere and make sense. Unfortunately, Alexander fit the pattern of a dysfunctional family rather than a healthy one, a place where the overcontrolling mom was unable to let her children grow up. Although Ruth felt proud and liberated by the growth that she experienced during the year that she worked with us, Betty was threatened by the same events.

The fact that elementary schools may be patterned like families, both functional and more problematic ones, puts an extra burden on external support organizations. It suggests that urban schools may need more than technical knowledge and even sustained support to recreate themselves into professional communities. Rather, in addition to these resources, the school community needs help to break deeply woven but problematic norms, individual insecurities about change, and, in Alexander's case, codependent relationships among the professional staff. Alexander seems to us an important case because it illuminates and, in fact, in its dysfunction exaggerates much of the depth and complexity of the change process that needs to occur before such schools can become professional communities, particularly in cases where there are strong leaders who have been in the school for a long time.

The work at Alexander points to some limits of even the most intensive approach to school intervention and support. Although we failed overall in our efforts to help this school, we saw growth and development in all of the teachers, and we were deeply impressed by the strides that Ruth made. In Chicago, local school communities have the power to select their principal, but where strong maternal (or paternal) patterns of control persist, the opportunities for genuine school-based professional community are limited in ways that cannot be addressed by breaking the bureaucratic routine.

6

Changing the Tire on a Moving Bus

Barriers to Professional

Community at Whitehead School

M . PEG LONNQUIST
JEAN A . KING

An Innovative Teacher-Led School

Organizationally, Whitehead Middle School[1] is among the most radically different schools in the United States. An inspirational speech that challenged educators to invent a school that would prepare students for the information age led to the creation of the school by an innovative superintendent. School designers, who were determined to break the mold and create a viable school for the future, developed a plan with an alternative vision, including a student-centered curriculum; individualized, project-based education; and the extensive use of cutting-edge technology. There was palpable excitement among designers, teachers, parents, students, and the community as this model school proudly opened in its temporary space in 1989.

133

Early in 1991, Whitehead Magnet School moved to a newly renovated physical facility in a large metropolitan downtown area. Most
visitors to Whitehead leave amazed by the facilities and the technology available to students, including a learning systems lab, two
computer labs, two classrooms equipped with discourse systems,
synthesizers in the music room, the latest video equipment, and
additional computers in the resource center and every classroom.
Whitehead staff are quick to point out, however, that technology at
the school is the means to an end, rather than an end in itself. The
school is "high tech, high-touch, and high-teach," and teachers work
hard to implement a student-centered curriculum.

The teams of consultants who designed the school applied an
educational philosophy based on the following notions:

1. the importance of student choice and involvement in the design of educational programs;
2. the need for individualization of student programs;
3. the need to eliminate conventional forms of assessment in favor of more complex demonstrations of student progress;
4. the incorporation of technology into every aspect of the instructional and learning process; and
5. the need to professionalize the role of the teachers to free them
   to carry out the school agenda.

To explain how the school operates, the school's information coordinator describes a boy with a real interest in aviation. Because of his
personal growth plan, the boy had opportunities to

> meet with aviators, and one of the nice things that has come
> from that is that he is also much more interested in mathe-
> matics and much better at mathematics because he has a real
> vested interest in becoming a good mathematician if he is
> indeed going to become a pilot.

The Center for School Organization and Restructuring reports
that an indicator of a restructured school is that the student or
teacher's experience is different from that of a student in a traditional
school (Newmann, 1991a, 1991b). Although a day at Whitehead has

a great deal in common with the comprehensive high school model (e.g., students change classes every period), several unique innovations and challenging contextual issues create a very different experience for teachers and students.

Student Experience

Whitehead School provides a different experience for students from the moment one approaches the door. For security reasons the front doors are locked and one cannot enter without being buzzed in by the school receptionist. The school's name is displayed only on a computerized paper banner inside the storm doors. Once inside the school, people notice the interesting interior design and the absolute absence of anything except paint on the walls. No student work, no announcements, and no posters are displayed. The receptionist sits behind a large oval counter, alone at his computer, because all the other staff offices are on the top floor. The cafeteria and gym, on the other hand, look like those at most schools. But as one tours the building, one sees that most classrooms are furnished with round tables, chairs with wheels, a TV monitor, and one or more computers. Three learning spaces house about 30 computers, and two classrooms look like small theaters equipped with interactive computer systems. All the visual messages communicate· This is different.

Whitehead's first set of students spanned grades four through six and numbered 160. The number of student applications was so high before the school opened that a waiting list had to be formed. Four years later, in 1992–1993, Whitehead serves 230 students, in mixed age and ability groups, from grades four through eight. More than 60% of the students are boys, presumably because of the perception that the school is technologically focused. About 50% of the students are children of color, and 15% are designated for special education, which reflects the district population. The population has changed dramatically over the years. Few of the original students remain. Whitehead is now serving many students who had a difficult time in other schools and did not choose Whitehead primarily for its philosophy.

Beyond the facility and the availability of technology, the student experience is unique in that the students have input into the selection of courses offered, and they are required to attend an advisory and an individualized computer lab session each day. Computers are not used for every class, but there is an attempt to integrate the use of technology in most subjects. Although not every student has a class off-site, many do leave the school several times a week for classes at the nearby art museum, the science museum, and the public library, or for a community service project. Additionally, the school is ungraded and students are grouped in courses based on their interests. As a result, learning takes place in mixed age and ability groups.

To promote individualized learning, teachers meet with each student and his or her parents/guardians each term to develop personalized growth plans. The personalized growth plans are intended to help students identify their cognitive, affective, and psychomotor skills, and their interests and needs, and to encourage students to be responsible for their own learning. As part of the plan, students identify resources they need to meet their goals and are responsible for describing their progress toward their goals at a conference at the end of each term. The personalized growth plans work well for motivated students with involved parents, which at the school's inception teachers estimated was about 90% of their population. However, parental attendance at conferences has dwindled to about 30%.

The student evaluation process was in continuous development during our study and was perceived by both teachers and outsiders as somewhat chaotic. Grades are not given and progress toward personal growth goals is measured by work examples and performances. The rhetoric was that students would leave Whitehead with personal portfolios containing what they felt was their best work from each class. That portfolio might include artwork, written reports, a computer disc with a program they designed, math work, and the like. Due to the overwhelming amount of work, teachers do not always supervise this process well, and some portfolios end up being quite impressive, though others are thin. Parents complain that they rarely see the items and have little to compare them to. The lead teachers indicate that it is the students' responsibility to maintain these portfolios anyway, because "students are responsible for their own learning." In addition to the portfolios, an exhibition/open house is held each term, at which students display their work on walls in the classrooms or in the meeting room, on computers, on videos, or through performances. These have been successful, cel-ebratory events with a high level of participation from students, teachers, and parents/guardians.

For students who are self-motivated the experience is generally wonderful. One student has invented computer games; another gained considerable expertise in creating videos, several of which aired on a local TV station; one learned all about the body and its changes in adolescence; and another became enthralled with the art of making museum exhibits. Students love having a high measure of control over what courses will be offered and on selecting the ones that they want to take, with only a few subjects required (math, writ-ing, and computer lab). Although not all the courses students re-quested are offered (e.g., hang gliding and skydiving were never offered), the teachers make every effort to offer any course requested by a significant number of students. This has caused teachers to argue over the benefits gained by students who chose independent studies related to fantasy war games, or about several other students who spent a good deal of their self-directed learning time playing cards or simply chatting. For the students who are not self-directed or who have not yet become self-directed, there is also a constant debate about whether they are falling through the cracks because the system needs to be changed or because "some students don't belong here."

Within the classroom, experiences vary widely. With little guid-ance on how to actualize the Whitehead idea in the classroom, many teachers resort to what they know how to do. Some teachers come to the school with backgrounds in experiential education, inquiry learn-ing, and open schools, and they teach using those methodologies. Many teachers are excellent at creating a classroom where critical thinking is evident. Others use fairly traditional teaching methods, modified only by the lack of textbooks and letter grades. Students seem to adapt regardless of the teaching style. One student, listing her favorite teachers, named some from each camp.

The fourth through eighth grade span makes after-school activi-ties a dilemma. Elementary schools are not known for after-school activities; however, some students told us they were going to transfer after sixth grade so they could be at a school with a track team. The school does sponsor a math team and a swim team. All other club type groups meet during the lunch activities half hour, including a chess club and a "Dungeons and Dragons" group. For the past 2 years, students could participate in a musical production as a course choice.

Teachers' Experience

Each year has brought vast changes to Whitehead, but the teachers have always experienced at Whitehead a different work life from that at traditional schools. To begin with, Whitehead's fame brings scores of visitors and researchers to the school, requiring school personnel and student tour guides to manage the flow (Louis & King, 1993) and creating the sense of always being in a fishbowl. As one student told us, "Sometimes I feel like a guinea pig [because there are so many visitors]."

One of the most enjoyable aspects of this restructured school cited by the general teachers is the freedom to be creative in course design and the opportunity to teach courses outside one's discipline. Each teacher polls his or her students near the end of the term and, based on their requests, new classes are designed. Some exciting classes are offered, for example: Aeronautics, HyperCard, Dinosaurs (at the science museum), Photography (at the art museum), Local Refugees (at the history museum), Africa (taught by a teacher who had just spent 6 months there), and Internet (by networking with students in Bosnia). However, this structure also creates a good deal of stress as every 9 weeks teachers scramble to create five or more new courses in a school that does not allow textbooks and encourages off-site learning.

The school opened with the four teachers on the leadership team, two educational assistants, a physical education instructor, four interns from a nearby college, one clerical staff, and money to purchase the services of consultants/specialists occasionally. From the beginning the school had the unusual privilege of recruiting and selecting its teachers. In the spirit of all-school involvement, staff are interviewed by a team of parents, students, and teachers from the school. The student population and staff number increased each year so that by year four there are 230 students and 21 full-time employees: four teachers on the leadership team, one physical education instructor, six general teachers, five educational assistants, five part-time specialists (including a video instructor), a part-time librarian, two clerical staff members, and no interns. Whitehead is also visited by several part-time professionals for speech therapy, nursing services, and special education needs.

Initially, the school year was extended to begin in September and last until mid-July. This calendar gave teachers 20 extra days to spend with students and parents on the student's personal growth plan each term and also allowed for additional staff development. However, due to the heavy curricular development demands, most staff development days became individual work days for lesson planning. At the end of the third year, the extra days were eliminated due to district-wide budget cuts, and the school was forced to conform to the district-wide calendar. Teachers continued with the personal growth plan process, but now they are scheduled on the teachers' own time in the afternoon and in the evenings.

The school layout is an unusual one compared to most schools. All of the teacher's offices are all located on the same floor. Each general teacher has an individual cublicle with a computer. Each of the four teacher leaders has a small office, also with a computer. The computers are networked and the teachers make significant use of E-mail. Teachers rotate through the classrooms located on the lower floors each period. The theory was that this system would promote the use of the different types of technology and encourage off-site learning.

Another major difference that teachers describe is the enormous number of meetings compared to other schools. Instructional staff members meet once a week before school. In addition, there are subject team meetings, meetings about difficult students, and various school committee meetings to attend. The school council meets once a month, and most of the teachers attend these meetings or one of their subcommittee meetings. As mentioned previously, every term teachers set up individual sessions with each student and his or her parents or guardians for 1 hour to discuss and revise the student's personal growth plan.

Whitehead has experimented with a few different class schedules. A change is proposed and, unlike the stereotype of "we tried that once," this group of teachers is quite ready to say, "let's try it." During the fourth year the school adopted an A/B schedule with five periods, an advisory time, lunch, and a shorter activity period/recess each day. A typical day for a general teacher begins with a meeting with one of the staff groups at 8:00 a.m. At 9:05 the teacher meets with an advisory group for a half hour. These are the students with whom they meet about personalized growth plans. Some teachers plan activities for their 15 to 22 advisees during this time, and others allow studying or free time. The advising process is complicated because advisers often have some advisees who are not taking any of their classes. At 9:30, the teacher facilitates the first class, at 10:30 the teacher moves to a different room with a new group of students for a different subject, or a morning class may meet off-site for 2 hours at the science, art, or history museum. At 11:30 the teacher takes his or her students to the cafeteria and supervises them while they eat. At 12:00 the teacher supervises a lunch activity, such as the chess club or computer lab. At 12:30, the third subject is taught in another classroom. At 1:30, there is an hour for preparation. At 2:30, it is time for subject number four. On an A/B day plan, the next day the teacher might have almost all different classes. For example, one teacher taught Science Fiction Reading, Typing, Spanish I, and Spanish II on A days, and on B days she taught State History with a consultant at the history museum, Geography, repeated Spanish I, and cotaught a Rivers class.

Training and evaluation of pedagogy are not given high priority at Whitehead. Though the four teacher leaders spent hours discussing teaching philosophy during the first year, new teachers are given little or no training about how to translate the Whitehead philosophy into their classrooms. Teachers told us they knew they were to use technology and the community for learning whenever possible, they were not to use textbooks, and that each student should end the term with a project suitable for his or her portfolio. They also knew that Whitehead students were supposed to "learn how to learn" on their own.

No mentoring system is in place and little cross-teaching occurs, except with outside agencies. Many new teachers expressed feeling shame when they asked for help from the leadership team and thus stopped doing so. Because teaching is an isolated act, much like it is in traditional schools, there is no sense of urgency to follow the "Whitehead way," and teachers proceed using the methods that seem comfortable to them. On the other hand, there are pockets of shared learning and support among the general teachers, especially those who teach similar subjects. No teacher mentioned experiencing an evaluation of teaching skills, and only when there was crisis did the school discuss the school's operational processes—the teacher leaders said there just was not time to do it any other way.

On top of the challenges of trying to teach differently, outside the classroom there is a great deal of tension related to the leadership structure and how it is implemented. The leadership model, consisting of a team of teachers (one head teacher and three teacher leaders) is among Whitehead's main experimental features. The team is responsible for most administrative, curricular, and instructional issues, along with a school site council that routinely discusses school matters. The school designers intended to empower and professionalize teachers at Whitehead through this structure. Their dream was that teachers, freed of old notions and administrative constraints, could create and manage an innovative school. An operating assumption was that teacher leadership would foster the growth of professional community, not only between Whitehead faculty and staff but also with the larger school community. Like Sirotnik (1989) they felt that the "ultimate power to change is and always has been— in the head, hands and hearts of the educators who work in our schools." However, battles between the teacher leaders and the general leaders led to enormous feelings of frustration and stress. General teachers often felt belittled rather than supported as they struggled with the emergent educational methods. A constant argument took place over discipline—who had responsibility for discipline, what appropriate disciplinary tactics were, whether "good" teachers had discipline problems, and, perhaps more fundamentally, if off-task students should even be disciplined. The original leadership team felt that students who are not on-task should be left alone, because then they will get bored and begin working. Teacher leaders told us "success stories" in which students tested the structure to see whether they would be compelled to work. After satisfying themselves that they were in fact responsible for their own learning, the students "buckle[d] down and get[got] to work." As the school's population shifted to include fewer self-motivated students and more teachers who disagreed with this position, a bigger disagreement developed.

General teachers have expressed anger throughout the study about their lack of influence. They feel their ideas for improving the school are continually ignored. Nearly all of the teachers explain how two of the teacher leaders created an atmosphere where people are afraid to question anything. A staff member recalls, "I have seen competent teachers shamed and reduced to tears for questioning a decision." Eventually the frustration grows to the point that the general teachers either withdraw into their classrooms and try to suppress their concerns about larger school issues, or leave Whitehead. According to two teachers:

> Again and again we [the general teachers] think this time we will be discussing real issues, real improvements. But when we get to the meeting, [one of the teacher leadership team] says, "We got together and decided to discuss this instead." Last week I finally decided to disengage from all the politics, and I have felt a lot less crazy.
>
> There is no shared decision making in the school . . . no mechanism for engaging staff in dialogue or sharing problems. Whitehead is not a community of learners for teachers.

Additionally, attempts by the general staff to make the climate more friendly during the years were greeted with some disdain, and several teacher leaders stated publicly that they would never socialize with the general staff members. The turnover rate of general staff members is astounding. In 3 years, 13 general teachers and more than 30 staff—about one third of the staff per year—left the school. Indeed, one of the principals said the school has been a "war zone with casualties."

The Teacher Leader Experience

The lead teachers describe their experiences quite differently from the general teachers. Their first year had been one of great excitement and extremely long hours as they tried to get a unique school up and running in the face of significant obstacles while at the same time teaching 160 students each day. They maintain that their focus is on their commitment to the vision of Whitehead and their responsibility for maintaining it. The teacher leaders feel over-whelmed with their responsibilities, explaining that they attend even more meetings than the general teachers, because they also meet to-gether weekly and sometimes with district committees. On the other hand, their class schedule appears a bit lighter than that of the general teachers, because it includes some classes where students primarily do independent work.

The teacher leaders also experience the tension in the school climate, but they look upon it as a problem of having selected teachers who did not fit with the philosophy.

> *Interviewer:* If the discipline committee were to propose what you saw as contrary to the core beliefs of the school—something like an in-house suspension room—would that get heard?

> *Teacher Leader:* It would get heard, but we're the keepers of the vision, and the response would be that is not aligned with the vision. We have different jobs and responsibilities and we would not let that sort of thing happen. Our job descriptions give us leadership responsibility. The general teachers' job descriptions are different. It is hard to get clear what the expectations are when hiring people during the job interview process. General teachers don't have the responsibility of developing program here and therefore they don't have a vote in developing program. But there is a forum where everyone's voice is heard. This is an opportunity to voice views that are aligned with the core views, but if it is not aligned, then, wait a minute, that is a different discussion.

The Development of
Professional Community at Whitehead

Although Whitehead is justifiably proud of a number of students[2] who flourished at the school, data suggest that school-wide professional community has, after 4 years, simply not developed at Whitehead. The problems with professional community at White-

head seem even more acute when compared with the high expectations everyone had for the school. However, if that is the dark cloud,
the silver lining is that we can learn a great deal from Whitehead's
initial lack of success in developing professional community.[3] The
most basic problem regarding professional community at Whitehead
appears on the surface to be the leadership team's failure to attend
to the work life of teachers, and notably their failure to purposefully
create a professional community. But the story is more complex than
that statement suggests. Some problems with professional community are inherent in a fairly turbulent context, some in the school's
structure, and some in the combination of personalities chosen to fill
the leadership team positions.

Turbulent Context

Contextual difficulties arose at Whitehead's inception and continue to plague the school. Throughout the first 3 years, it seemed at
times that just about everyone was either criticizing Whitehead or
applying pressure for change. There was pressure to be the "ideal
school of the future," and most people expected too much too soon.
The school board barely voted to establish Whitehead and they
watched with a critical eye to see how the school fared. The local
educational community was angered by what they saw as a gross
number of financial privileges, and Whitehead became the school
other teachers "loved to hate." Some district staff were hostile toward
the school for reasons that included staffing and budgeting snafus
that were covered by using district funds. Parents were upset about
discipline problems they perceived as being poorly handled. Parent
representatives on the school council felt they were not being listened
to, and pressed for responsiveness. "Sometimes I feel like a dachs-
hund nipping at the heels of an elephant," one council member
noted.

One newspaper reporter relentlessly aired any criticism that
could be mustered, reportedly because of a personal dislike for the
then superintendent. By hurting his "baby," the critiques were intended to attack the superintendent. One issue that the reporter high-
lighted was falling standardized test scores in some areas. Although
traditional assessments were never intended to be a part of White-

head's evaluation process, this nevertheless created pressure on a school still in its infancy. Ironically, there was a prevailing belief among the district office staff that Whitehead was a publicity grabber, unlike the other magnet programs that had been established without garnering press coverage.

Initially, the first four staff hired were to be given a year to continue working on the design before the school opened its doors. However, that idea was abandoned and the leadership team had less than 2 months to get everything in order before students arrived. Due to the rush to open, staff development on interpersonal skills and on the use of technology and new pedagogical techniques was put aside. The cost of this haste included professional community development, according to some staff members. One staff member observed:

> I think you need to develop the team, before you develop the school. . . . Teachers by nature are self-employed, and we are not taught how to be sharing, how to delegate, how to take criticism, how to give positive criticism, those kinds of things. I think those are things that if any school wants to do this kind of model where we really try to create a team of teachers, you need to have that team have a chance to create itself.

In the rush to open, there was little time to learn how to use the new state-of-the-art technology, and because the facility remodeling had not been finished, the school shared a site with another program for the first year and a half. All courses were prepared from scratch, according to a philosophy that included the refreshing idea of rejecting textbooks and using original sources. In addition, procedures and policies were being rethought and reinvented. Several interviewees used the metaphor that the Whitehead staff that year ended up trying to "change the tire on a moving bus." One of the principals described the scope of the task and the problems it created:

> How do you develop a dream—a vision of this brand-new, throw-out-everything, start-building-from-scratch program and at the same time develop interns, at the same time [as] teach 25 kids an hour? You can't really expect all that to hap-

pen. In the press of creating the school for students, the leadership team established the powerful precedent that immediate student concerns come first and that long-term organizational culture and climate issues came at best a distant or even nonexistent second.

The following years brought additional contextual dilemmas as the number of students grew and grades seven and eight were added to the mix. This brought the normal challenges of working with teenagers in the school, as well as questions about how to successfully teach classes containing students from age 9 to 14, from 4 feet tall to 6 feet tall.

In spite of the superintendent's enthusiasm for the school, the district office staff seemed to set up roadblocks so that the school would fail. These obstacles came from conceptual misjudgments and personal biases. Conceptually, the district supported the inspiring vision for a school of the future, but gave the staff little time and training about how to realize the dream. They set up a fascinating experiment in teacher management, and then asked all the leadership team to carry a full teaching load in addition. One administrator reflected that the district allowed the press to "beat up on the school with no response." A traditional principal was assigned to the school during years three and four, when several nontraditional school advocates were available. The school was intended to be site-base managed, which had budget implications, but the official decree to do so was not received for 3 years.

Other obstacles seemed to stem from personal reactions to the Whitehead experiment. Some middle-level district office staff were angered by the exceptions granted Whitehead and the extra work they caused, or perhaps, some speculated, they were just resistant to such a radical change from traditional schooling. Additionally, the word in the central office was that the leadership team felt that no one in the district office could understand or help them because Whitehead was unique. Regardless of its validity, this perception added to a measure of animosity that was not addressed. Whatever the reason, some central office staff did cause delays and difficulties for the school. Teachers speculate that Whitehead is intentionally assigned students by unsupportive district office staff who want the school to fail. Vacancies for teachers have not been filled in a timely manner. The district office reportedly showed even less support after the departure of the superintendent who first approved the project. Yet, it is also important to remember that the superintendent and several district staff members were tremendous fans of the school and provided Whitehead with unusual opportunities, including an external evaluation team to provide formative evaluations at the end of each of the first 3 years so that the school could reflect on its progress and enhance its organizational learning process.

Outside the immediate community, Whitehead School became famous almost immediately, and the leadership team appeared to enjoy their popularity as speakers at conferences and other schools around the country. Those moments in the spotlight, however, may have allowed them to further overlook the mounting problems at home.

Structural Problems

Structurally, the school sought to break the traditional mold, and designers presented the idea of four teacher leaders who would facilitate a site-based managed school. Although the designers were well intentioned, the structure reflected the espoused mission of teacher empowerment only on the surface and not in concrete, practical terms.

Though the spirit of the plan was to empower teachers, the structure gave just four teachers decision-making power, year-round contracts, and substantially higher pay. The designers had unwittingly created for Whitehead a hierarchy with more tiers than in most traditional schools: a half-time principal,[4] a head teacher, assistant teacher leaders, general teachers, specialists, paraprofessionals, interns, clerical staff, food workers, and janitors. In retrospect, it appears that little thought was given to how the leadership team layer of the hierarchy would affect power dynamics among teachers, and what might facilitate effective working relationships. An active parent council member observed:

> It is not real legitimate to have power over. . . . One of the biggest things that this school is working on, the most radical

and the most difficult, is shifting power around. They've said
the power doesn't all belong to the administration, it can rest
within the teachers to some degree. And they said the power
doesn't all reside in the textbook or whoever makes curriculum decisions for a school district, it can rest in the families,
it can rest in the student. . . . [But be careful of] the resentment
that people have when the power shifts.

The leadership team's roles were not well defined, and their responsibilities and goals became a persistent and heated discussion
topic between the leadership team and principals, between the leadership team and the general teachers, and between the leadership
team and parent members of the school council. As one teacher told
us: "They're called the leadership team, and they're supposed to lead,
but there's a lot of ambiguity as to what they are leading, and why
and where. In 3 years no one's given a clear answer to me, so it's clear
as mud to the new staff." The role of the half-time principal was even
less developed because it was not part of the initial design, and the
individual holding that position, appointed by the central office,
changed almost annually.

Failure to develop professional community at Whitehead was
also attributed to how the start-up structure was carried out. In the
original structure, the head teacher was supposed to carry a partial
teaching load, which would allow time for the administrative and
vision-tending duties. The plan was not executed that way. The other
teachers also felt they would have benefited from some extra time
built into the structure, at least during the start-up phase. Though
they were excited about creating whole new curriculums and thinking about the pedagogy one should use for citizens of the 21st century, that task alone was also overwhelming. Something had to fall
by the wayside:

I think it all goes back to the initial problem of time. We all
understood that there were these conflicts and they were im-
pacting on our work, but we also, especially the teachers, had
to get 250 evaluations done and had to create new curriculum and really this [the conflict] was down on the back
burner all the time. . . . Although having some of this friction

on the staff certainly impacts the students, it doesn't impact them as much as if we don't have curriculum for them, if we don't have PGPs [personal growth plans] for them, if we don't have technologies available and know how to use them. So there were always things that seemed to take more immediate priority. It's like I can shuffle through another day being a little bit hostile to X, but I can't shuffle through another day without having something to do in my chemistry class. And so it always was on the back burner.

Unfortunately, the structural idea of a leadership team of teachers, attempted in this turbulent context, seemed to reinforce hierarchical thinking and therefore constrained the development of a successful professional community. One staff member created a metaphor to express his views on the structure and operations, "I see it [Whitehead] as a Cadillac hauling peanuts: a beautiful opportunity with a wonderful vision, but it isn't being used well or for its intended purpose."

Staff members at Whitehead, however, were not disillusioned with the idea of a teacher leader structure, but rather felt that its translation into reality needed work. A general teacher who had left Whitehead reflected:

I really feel strongly about the school having a lead staff member—to lead the staff in decision-making processes, and then everybody else working in teams and groups to solve problems, and to research and to know what works and what doesn't work, and work around that—the kind of person who leads them into a decision-making process, in making collective decisions. I'm not really sure that the personalities that are there are personalities that allow people to be interjecting and making positive decisions.

The Teacher Leaders—Committed but Individualistic

There is no doubt that the context and the structure created a challenging environment for the leadership team, nor is there any doubt that the leadership team was dedicated. Principals, parents, and the community repeatedly emphasized that all the teachers were highly committed to students and to authentic student learning. Every interviewee stressed that the leadership team worked extremely long hours during the first years, using the know-how they had:

> There is one thing you cannot say about the leadership team and that is they're lazy. They have busted their buns this whole time. Really worked hard, and really put a lot of effort in to this and worked late into the night and early morning and everything.

However, it was not enough to be a good teacher who worked hard. These teachers' lack of clarity about their roles, the combination of their personalities, and their lack of leadership skills, most notably their lack of attention to consciously developing and nurturing a healthy organizational climate, combined to exacerbate an already overwhelming challenge. These factors resulted in the leadership team embracing a highly bureaucratic way of operating, with rigid notions of their roles. The bureaucratic style allowed the four teacher leaders on the leadership team to survive their stressful predicament by claiming that certain problems, especially the school climate, did not fall in their domain. One of the leadership team members explained: "The focus for leadership . . . was on the students and the program and not on the people. And we also really made a conscious decision not to focus on the people. . . . I think that we looked at that to be the role of the building administrator." In their division of responsibilities, some important tasks were overlooked, role boundaries were not well defined, and no system of checks and balances was in place. As a result, the leadership team would decide they had the power to veto one idea and yet let other issues fall through the cracks. Of course, the school culture that emerged under these conditions was not a model of professional community.

The leadership team that was hired, not unlike most teachers, had little experience in leadership or organization development. Additionally, these four personalities were more comfortable working alone and were often described as private and individualistic. According to the external evaluator,[5] from the beginning "the leadership team was not very communicative with each other or other staff as a whole. The leadership team had conflicting values and were unclear how they wanted to develop most of the school's structures, processes, and policies." Nevertheless, the foursome seemed to assume that this was "their school," because they had been the sole professionals during the first year. When several teachers were added the second year, along with another grade level of students, the conflict escalated. The new teachers felt the leadership team was entrenched in their positions, responded as if threatened when offered suggestions, and closed ranks against them. The leadership team, on the other hand, perceived that their endless efforts to create a school from scratch were not being appreciated. One staff member described the situation this way:

> Certain members of the leadership team have problems sharing anything any more because they don't want to hear this, "Why didn't you do it that way?" Their knee-jerk reaction is "You weren't here, how dare you say why didn't I, how dare you criticize?".... And so this barrier has gone up . . . there is a level of childishness on both sides.

This leadership team also felt uncomfortable with any identification of themselves as management. When consultants were brought in to defuse the mounting internal tensions and provide leadership training, the leadership team stated they really did not see themselves in leadership positions, and were sometimes outwardly hostile to the consultants. They told one of the principals that they saw themselves as curriculum leaders and as working to facilitate site-based management, but absolutely not as having responsibility to supervise or help other teachers. A teacher leader explained:

> There isn't any sort of real structured mechanism like a very highly organized site-based management system, where if someone were to say, if you wanted to make this decision you talk to this person or this committee. . . . I would say that there might be a certain amount of frustration for a person who might come and expect there to be some sort of formula.

And frustration there was. The anger among general teachers about their lack of voice and influence was extremely high throughout the study. General teachers described how they repeatedly saw their agendas dismissed, ignored, or, most often, postponed until a later date that they felt never arrived. The general teachers and parents felt that decisions were based on what the leadership team wanted to do. Several teachers indicated that in spite of rhetoric to the contrary, the leadership team only asked for teacher input to "create the illusion that they had a chance to contribute." One interviewee observed that, "The leadership staff are very bright and good with students, but their success has blinded them to the need for input from others. The *concept* of shared decision making persists . . . but it was never practiced."

Covert and overt tensions and conflicts among the leadership team, and also between the leadership team and the general teachers, eliminated the sense of trust and camaraderie that is critical to the development of community. Additionally, everyone reported that conflict was not dealt with adequately. However, one of the principals explained that he felt that avoidance of conflict may have finally been the correct choice at Whitehead: "Open conflict is okay when you are in a situation where we trust each other. And there is no trust at all here. So open conflict is either war, bloodletting, or it results in people leaving. Or you don't engage in it. It is kind of a win-lose situation."

In their defense, the leadership team was constantly under a great deal of pressure, and most of the people interviewed felt that they were either not aware of the damage their behavior was causing, or did not know how they might change it. One teacher leader said that it was the head teacher's responsibility and not the rest of the team's responsibility to take care of the school climate. One principal surmised that the leadership team became so "shell-shocked" that they had to shut down, no longer realizing how authoritarian they were being or how their style affected others. The sense of the team's functioning as a bureaucracy allowed the overwhelmed staff to reject the notion of a collective team of professionals responsible for the good of the entire organization.

Although Whitehead's leadership team showed concern for the *students* needs and choices, they made the mistake of not paying attention to the needs of their colleagues. They envisioned other teachers as self-sufficient professionals in private practice, with the notion of professional community simply not part of their conceptual framework. When this notion was challenged, they refused to engage in solving a problem that, for them, had no meaning.

A Year "On Hold"

In spring of 1992 there were indications at Whitehead that this story might take a positive turn. A budget conflict between the school and the financially strapped district at the close of the third school year galvanized a sense of school unity. The head teacher went on sabbatical, and a new head teacher was chosen from the ranks of the general teachers. The district brought in a new principal, and there was a genuine possibility for the new leaders to initiate changes and intentionally create a community of learning. But that possibility was not realized.

The crisis that created a temporary unity among teachers at the end of the third year quickly dissipated as the realities of a continuing lack of trust surfaced in the fall of year four. The new principal, who openly declared he was traditional and did not embrace the Whitehead philosophy, worked less than half-time hours. He quickly surmised that nothing could be done to change the dynamics, so he focused on removing the original leadership team members. The new head teacher—the potential hero from the "lower caste" of general teachers—had to learn about organization development on the job in a tension-filled environment. Although the new head teacher made an effort to begin building some sense of community, she had acclimated to the school culture that avoided conflict and was neither ready, nor given support, to bring the problems out in the open. In spite of some glimpses of increasing communication, socialization, and respect among the general teachers, the tensions continued to fester under the surface. The replacement head teacher was not warmly welcomed by the other three teacher leaders, and no sense of a supportive team with common goals emerged. If that weren't enough to worry about, the new head teacher was teaching seven-eighths time and had all of the school's discipline problems dumped in her lap:

[The new head teacher] is limited to some degree because there is resentment from some leadership team members. She is really being divided between the principal and the teacher leaders. And so we are back into that little game. . . . She is hampered now by being the head teacher, by having the political conflicts that are going on, by simply not having enough time.

Clearly, Whitehead School has yet to develop a professional community. However, hope springs eternal. The development of professional community may yet occur in this restructured school. This school does offer the potential for a community of learning built upon a vision and rhetoric that are inspiring. In the spring of 1993, the principal abolished the leadership team structure, with the support of the superintendent and the school board, and a new structure was introduced several months later. The original leadership team, hardworking—yet viewed as dictatorial by the staff—all received involuntary transfers at the end of the school year and thus did not return to the school. The school continues with the basic instructional philosophy and hopes that instituting a new leadership structure and recruiting more than 50% new teachers can stop the war and bring peace into the lives of teachers. Perhaps teachers will focus on tapping into each student's unique potential in an atmosphere of trust and support, and the new leadership can begin laying the groundwork for the creation of a true professional community.

Epilogue, Year Five

In spite of a shaky start in year five, at the close of the school year the Whitehead staff finally appears well on its way to developing a healthy, active professional community. This has occurred in spite of the fact that half of the teachers are first-year teachers, the half-time principal does not support the philosophy and has taken a back seat throughout the year, an English as a Second Language program was added to the building, and the school year began with two substitute teachers (out of eight full-time classroom teachers) who were not replaced until November.

The new leadership structure maintains the half-time principal position, joined by one head teacher who teaches half-time. This head teacher, a former general teacher who is dedicated to the Whitehead vision, spent an enormous amount of her own time in the summer preparing for the opening of school. Her plan was to continue the experiment and in addition, motivated partially by this study, work to create a collegial environment. During opening week she invited as speakers some of the people who still treasure the Whitehead dream. Their talks provided some inspiration and words of wisdom to the new and returning staff. The teachers were divided into teams, hoping to promote both deprivatization of practice and reflective dialogue. Some structural conditions of the school were changed. Teams moved to shared office spaces on the same floors as their class-rooms, and common prep times were arranged. Although she was not able to get an extended staff orientation period, and therefore teachers had to have time during the week for the preparation of their courses, the head teacher was able to include team-building exercises and open discussions about preferred methods of working together.

Most important of all, the new head teacher professed and then modeled a leadership style that was open to suggestions, and encour-aged teachers to share responsibility for shaping the school's culture. Observations of staff meetings revealed a new era. All the teachers paid attention during staff meetings, unlike other years where many corrected papers, organized their day, or wrote notes back and forth. Teachers challenged each other respectfully and without fear of re-percussions. Teachers even publicly praised one another at meetings. By the end of the year, the teachers were engaged in a group process to redesign the school after reviewing articles about other innovative school change efforts. In the middle of the third year at Whitehead, one of the researchers wrote: "A common ideology about education does not guarantee a sense of community. Community requires be-havioral expectations about mutual assistance and responsibility for the day-to-day enactment of the work, and the diffusion of a collec-tive sense of responsibility for long-term development throughout the school." Though Whitehead has not yet completely achieved this collective sense of responsibility for long-term development, observ-ing the changes in the last year might give Whitehead supporters great hope.

When I ask returning staff about the differences they note this year, invariably they mention the school climate. A telling moment regarding the climate change happened during one of the in-service days. All of the teachers were down on the floor, jointly and harmoniously problem solving to make the proposed schedule work smoothly. When the head teacher recounted this story, tears came to her eyes. Even the students noticed. One veteran student told me that this year the teachers hang out together in the lobby, talking and laughing after the buses leave.

An incident that occurred at the beginning of the year showed the head teacher's leadership style and how she gained trust and support from both students and staff. The head teacher envisioned just two teams of teachers and students, and staff orientation proceeded under this assumption. However, when school began, several returning students felt the new structure vastly limited their choices. The head teacher met with the staff and together they came up with a plan for three teams that allowed for three different pedagogical models. She then asked the teachers to choose which model/team they would like. The following week, the head teacher called all of the returning students down to the meeting rooms and gave them the option of choosing one of the new teams, or a team structured like the one they had participated in during the previous year. Although a bit chaotic, the action expressed respect for the students, a high desire for teacher participation in the school design, and unusual flexibility in an institutional setting. Most important, it set the base for developing serious discussion of pedagogy—a first for Whitehead.

Many of the innovations remained, yet there were also some significant changes. A major difference for the students was an increase in the teachers' shared norms about discipline. This group of teachers agreed to become more traditional in that area. To begin with, they changed from having the students use their first names to using the formal titles of Mr., Ms., and Mrs. A discipline plan was developed that includes a passcard each day for students, where teachers can write positive or negative remarks. The accumulation of negative remarks carries the consequence of spending time in an after-school detention program. In addition, other norms are continually being discussed and defined more concretely than they were with the original visionary language about the school.

Other indicators of professional community appear to be increasing, though they are not at levels that the head teacher or any of the other teachers would consider ideal. Staff are more willing to share knowledge, and indications of collaboration have increased greatly. For example, the swimming instructor developed a list of terms used in his class and the English as a Second Language teachers taught them to their students. At one of the staff meetings where faculty were discussing the difficulties of working with teen students, a teacher described and praised some methods used by another teacher. Collegial relationships and collaboration increased because of the team structure, though some teams did not find their team matches made in heaven. The head teacher, always the optimist, notes however that they did not have enough time to do the proper amount of professional development on working in teams. This was especially critical, given that there were so many novice teachers, and the Whitehead teaching philosophy is demanding even for experienced teachers.

To improve the context, throughout the year the new head teacher worked with the parent council to woo the school board. Among other things, she showed them several of the most impressive student portfolios and continued to keep them informed about the school's successes throughout the year. As the board shows increasing support for the Whitehead experiment, some of the district office staff seem to be slowly coming around to a more supportive stance toward the school—or at least to a less negative attitude.

Though the development of professional community seems to be improving, the dream of a revolutionary school of the future is hanging by a thin thread. In some ways the school has become less innovative over the years. Certainly the detention room is at odds with the original vision of self-motivated, responsible student learners. The pedagogy used by teachers today is closer to traditional than that used by the original teachers. The use of technology has decreased, because this group of predominantly green teachers has had even less time to pursue how to integrate its use. The team structure introduced a traditional self-contained classroom model from elementary schools, though it does span from fourth through sixth grade. They added that option because of their experience that some kids seemed to be lost and burned out by changing rooms so much, to the teachers' way of thinking because they need one adult in their school life most of the day, and perhaps the same kids around as well. The new leadership structure is not as revolutionary as the former leadership team idea, and next year the school will get a full-time principal. The thin thread that truly could connect the school's future with its past rests primarily with the former head teacher, the only influential keeper of the vision within the school. If she leaves or is run over by the new principal, even those innovations that remain could vanish.

What's Next?

Next year at Whitehead may bring more changes. The school is expanding to serve kindergarten through third grade and has just hired its first full-time principal, who has spent the past 10 years in the corporate world. The head teacher will continue to work at the school and is hopeful about the new principal, who seems enthusiastic about the Whitehead vision. The question remains, however, as to whether Whitehead can at last achieve the dream of a viable school of the future operated within a healthy learning organization.

Notes

1. Certain identifying details about the case have been changed in order to ensure the anonymity promised to the school community. We have not, however, altered features critical to the case description or analysis.

2. It is interesting to note that the former Whitehead evaluator has talked to teachers this year who were severe critics of Whitehead but are now teaching Whitehead graduates: "The teachers say that the students are different. They are definitely more technologically literate, they seem to have more resources at their disposal, they are more independent learners, they seem very calm, and they know where they are going."

3. In describing the problems experienced by this school, we faced uncomfortable decisions about reporting harsh judgments regarding hardworking people we have come to know and respect. We have tried to be fair in our presentation of the situations and have given the main players an opportunity to give feedback on this chapter. Ultimately, our intention is to prevent others from creating similar situations that are damaging for all the staff involved and, as another consequence, less than ideal for students.

4. In the first year a half-time principal was added to the design because of the principals' union requests.

5. To maintain the promise of confidentiality, we are not able to cite the evaluator's work in this chapter. We can only apologize to the evaluator for this and state that we appreciate the work that was done.

7

Dewey Middle School

Getting Past the First

Stages of Restructuring[1]

DANIEL A. WEISS
KAREN SEASHORE LOUIS
JEREMY HOPKINS

Dewey Middle School is an experimental effort initiated 7 years ago in a medium-sized city located on the East Coast. It opened with considerable fanfare as an alternative to the traditional junior high schools in the district. However, the development of Dewey as a place where teachers could work together to create innovative experiential education programs for inner-city youths never materialized as either its designers or its teachers hoped. Teachers in the school have worked hard to make Dewey a special place for students, but are increasingly puzzled by questions about why it is not working as well as they had planned—both for the students and for themselves. One reason for Dewey's lack of success is the unwillingness of the staff to compromise the individual freedoms of the teachers, which has resulted in a lack of coherent, consistent policies and academic focus. The staff failed to develop the professional community needed for Dewey to realize its vision.

History and Characteristics of Dewey

Dewey Middle School was initiated by Rick Hally, a prominent business leader, who wanted to make a personal contribution to the inner-city educational system through which he had sent his children. Increasingly concerned that the system was not providing a high-quality education, he held several informal discussions in 1988 with business community and local educational leaders, including the president of the district teachers' union. These individuals were united in the belief that the city had a need to improve the quality of middle school education. Hally commented, "The city has a good school system, but we feel it could be even better."

Relying on the model of how architectural firms compete for real estate designs, their discussions culminated in an open design competition to create a new public school for the city. A formal request for proposals announced the competition, and the planning group ultimately received more than 50 proposals. Five semifinalists were paid $1,000 each to elaborate their models, and the winning proposal, with features of the four other proposals, was deemed ready for immediate implementation.

Hally promised to raise $300,000 to $400,000 in private sector money to help cover the start-up costs. The teachers' union also pledged its support. "We felt it was important to be partners from the beginning," said the president of the local teachers' union. "We pledged that the union would alter the rules or regulations or contract language that got in the way of making it happen." The promise of private funds and the strong lobby from the union caused the school board to unanimously approve the Dewey proposal.

Once the planning group had completed the model for Dewey, teachers and a principal were hired to attempt to bring the design to life. The exact working out of the new school was left to the teachers and students. Some planning committee members wanted to continue the planning process and delay opening the school until the fall of 1990. However, the increasing student population and the district's need to place those students created pressure to open immediately. Unfortunately, Hally was only able to raise part of the funds he promised to deliver from the business community; the school had to survive within the per capita allotment of the local district, just like any other middle school, with no additional start-up or training budget. Because the school was planned by external experts and was supposed to get additional resources from the private sector, Dewey got limited support from the district superintendent and school board. This added to the pressure of getting the school operating.

The first year at Dewey passed in a whirlwind of activity as teachers tried to carry out plans that, ultimately, were more conceptual than practical. As one teacher put it, "We need time to sort out roles, expectations, and communication. . . . Options are not always considered, and good decisions aren't made. The staff can't see the forest from [sic] the trees." The planning process, which included Hally and the authors of the model—a retired principal and a retired teacher—was a year long. Due to an oversight on their part, the planning did not include any of the individuals who would eventually be responsible for carrying out the plan. The idealistic vision of a community-based school that generated the official Dewey model did not translate easily into practice.

The original vision for Dewey, which still plays a prominent role in its brochures and promotional videos, is principally based on an ideal of community education. Students are bussed daily to various sites to use the city as an integral part of the curriculum. In so doing, students are expected to better grasp the ecological, governmental, and architectural complexities of their urban environment as the school attempts to promote understandings primarily through hands-on encounters with the workings of the city. These facets of the urban environment were expected to take care of the natural scientific, social scientific, and aesthetic domains, respectively, of a middle school education. This vision had the promise of commanding a unified school culture that would focus on educating students for a rapidly changing society where issues of an ecological, governmental, and aesthetic nature are perpetually held in an uneasy tension. At least this was the theoretical basis for the school's vision.

A Taste of Dewey

Dewey Middle School serves approximately 190[2] students in grades six through eight. Students work together in mixed-aged groupings. The school is divided into three disciplinary teams or sites—art, social studies, and science. The sites are scattered around the city in order to increase the diversity of community involvement. The home base or main school building is located in a former parochial school.

Students meet in the main building in the morning for homeroom and math. The teachers originally tried to integrate math into the three teams, but a vocal math teacher felt that math was being neglected. Thus, a more traditional math program was adopted. As a consequence, math is taught for one period after homeroom. After math, students go to one of three sites to which they rotate every 3 months. The arts site, which includes drama, fine arts, the language arts, and P.E., is also located in the old parochial school building. For science and environmental education, students are bussed to a local university, where they use a set of classrooms and labs. The social studies site is in a downtown business complex owned by the school's business partner, a local financial firm.

Students begin and end each day at the home base site except on Fridays, when they spend the whole day at the home base site. The rationale behind this structural arrangement is to provide students with community experiences where "the larger community collaborates to provide expertise and resources." A community curriculum coordinator attempts to simplify this by setting up students with mentors (university graduate students) and educational excursions into the city to better understand the workings of the urban, political, and business worlds.

Dewey serves a diverse student population (approximately 40% are students of color) and is known in the school district, unofficially, as an alternative school that has the potential for handling those students who have failed in more traditional settings. An alternative environment is the goal of the school. Thus, students are often viewed as intelligent, but at risk of becoming educational failures. This means that many either had or have behavior or learning problems. The need to reinforce the open, child-centered focus of the school's philosophy while maintaining reasonable order has remained a source of unresolved tension, often manifesting itself in teacher stress and occasional friction among staff and between staff and parents.

There are eight core teachers[3] who are responsible for the delivery of what Dewey calls the urban curriculum. These teachers also act as home base teachers and, as mentioned earlier, are teamed in terms of the three curriculum areas.[4] Besides these teachers, there are one P.E. teacher, two prep teachers, and one part-time "student advocate" who serves as a counselor.[5] Other professional staff include a social worker, a nurse, one part-time community coordinator, and a part-time principal.[6]

A typical day for a Dewey teacher formally starts at around 8:30 a.m., at the old parochial school site. This turn-of-the-century building, in varying states of decay, serves as the administration center for the school and houses all of the home base classrooms, one of which doubles as an art room. The facility is large enough to contain all of the students—and indeed this is the location where they all begin and end their day. The school shares the facility with an independent drug abuse program for adolescents and also some offices of the local police department. The Dewey home base site consists of nine classrooms; three small, interconnected offices (one used by the principal, one used by the secretary, and one housing the school photocopying machine); and three other small offices, housing the school nurse, the student counselor and a social worker, respectively. The nurse's office, which manages to squeeze in a daybed, a desk, a file cabinet as well as a couple of tables and chairs, also doubles as a place for staff to eat their lunch or drink coffee. However, being a very cramped space lacking any soft chairs and often filled with one or two student patients, as well as possessing the only staff bathroom in the entire building, it is usually avoided by staff. The one communal area that regularly gets most of the staff flowing through it is the office housing the photocopying machine, in addition to one Macintosh computer and laser printer, and the mailboxes. However, this area is connected closely to the secretary's office and is often so busy and that it's perhaps the most public space in the whole school, making even moderately confidential discussion impossible.

Entering the school in the morning, perhaps the most striking impression that you receive is the school's particular brand of informality. Coming in through the front entrance, up a flight of stone steps, you immediately face the main corridor and an annex containing abandoned tables and desks, along with a couple of tired stand-up bulletin boards. The old enamel-tiled walls are peppered with the dwarfed offerings of fading student artwork, with little or no explanation of their content or theme, which serves as one illustration of the lack of academic focus at Dewey. Turning right down the wide corridor eventually takes you to the secretary's and principal's office. The door is permanently open, and greeting you is the secretary's desk in full frontal. Surrounding the desk are three or four easy chairs, the only ones in the building, and a coffee table holding a selection of well-thumbed fashion magazines. Louise herself is a hive of activity, answering the phone; talking with parents, students, and staff who almost incessantly mill around her desk, advising them on anything from bus schedules and paychecks to the likes and dislikes of individual students; and apparently bringing some kind of "waiting room" order to the frequently mixed array of persons who use the comfy chairs. Such individuals may be students cooling off from some classroom disruption, overflow from the medical room, freshly suspended students, or simply students (perhaps the majority) who need/want to get out of the classroom for a bit.

The Reality of Dewey

Dewey allows its staff to command an unusually high degree of autonomy vis-à-vis the development of curriculum content and participation in school policy making. It is a site-based managed school with a part-time principal, Dr. Booth, who is also in charge of two other elementary schools. She deliberately takes a backseat role in the school policy-making process and actively supports and encourages her staff to take the reins. Her belief in the importance of teacher empowerment was a main reason why she was initially chosen from several interested applicants. Her style has been to facilitate and support teachers in what they are trying to do, but not to do the initiating herself.[7] This is due to her personal philosophy and the time constraints placed on her by having the responsibility of three schools.

The staff, as a whole, thinks of themselves as progressive. However, there is some uncertainty as to what that means. As one teacher put it, "I see us as such individuals to a fault sometimes because we come from such different angles to things. And yet, I do think we share what I would say is a progressive teaching style, and yet that's not always true either."

Dewey teachers have often shown themselves as readily giving much extra time to improve their school culture and self-made curricula. Despite all of this, things invariably go wrong at Dewey. The educational visions of individuals remains precisely that: individual visions. The school culture (to the extent that it exists) is not community driven, and what coherence there is in the school is largely received rather than created. This insight is not altogether lost on the teachers. As one teacher put it: "This is an experimental school—but what does that mean? It's hard to know if people have the same vision. And that's perhaps one of the biggest problems with Dewey."

The school staff suffers from having at its disposal a few expert systems and traditions around which to organize their efforts. However, they lack the experiences in educational design and curriculum theory that would provide the means for cooperatively finding their direction. Despite the best intentions of the professional staff at Dewey, many conditions, constraints, and other variables have prevented the implementation of its original vision. Rather than being an effective, innovative community, Dewey remains a collection of independent pedagogues. The faculty's inability to act collectively makes the implementation of its purported vision both incoherent and unrealizable.

There are several reasons behind Dewey's lack of coherence. The organization, the structure, and the values of the school inhibit the development of professional community. Examples of how these affect the school are found in the staff meetings, curriculum and instruction, school logistics, and discipline.

Values

Individual freedom is a strong value at Dewey. This is exemplified by the staff's inability to establish coherent policies. There is an unwillingness to impose rules or policies upon the whole staff; thus, exceptions are constantly being made for both the staff and students.

When the staff tried to develop a home base curriculum, this behavior was clearly in effect. The afternoon home base is set aside for such items as AIDS awareness, nutrition, and other aspects of health and sex education, and also with helping students develop their reading, writing, and studying skills. Some of this curriculum is established by the district and state, but the rest is up to the individual teachers. The result of this has been that in each classroom students are generally doing different things. Some teachers try to use that time at the end of the day as a cooling-off period, when the students can read, write, or do homework. Other teachers have activities to keep the students on-task. During one staff development day, an attempt was made to coordinate the home base curriculum. One teacher who did not want to give up the activities she planned for her students vehemently opposed this suggestion. Several staff acknowledged similar sentiments, and the issue was dropped. This left the home base curriculum unchanged and still uncoordinated, which further left a void in any collective academic focus and reinforced the climate of individuality.

Staff Meetings

The lack of accountability encourages the individual freedom at Dewey. The school was designed so that the teachers would run the school, but instead of becoming interdependent, they have become independent. A main reason for this is that the teachers do not hold one another accountable. This is evident in the staff meetings.

On Tuesdays, all staff are expected to attend the weekly staff meeting in the resource room on the second floor. This surprisingly light and spacious room, formerly a classroom, contains a long boardroom-style table and all, or as many as can, sit around it. Many of the staff, including the principal, arrive late to the meeting, and one teacher rarely attends. The culture of the school seems to condone this kind of behavior: Topics will be restated for those who are tardy, or a vote will be postponed until all of the members are present, but there is little or no discussion about the need for promptness.

The agenda for the meeting comes from the teachers themselves. Either they have seen the principal that morning or earlier, and the items are collected and printed by her, or as is the case more recently, a previously assigned facilitator takes charge of this duty. Whatever the system, however, the prioritizing of items is often very ad hoc. It is common for discussions to be abandoned midstream as the participants realize, after some exchange, that they do not possess necessary background information and/or the ramifications of an issue are far too deep for the allotted meeting time to provide an acceptable solution. When agenda items are differentiated, it is usually on the grounds of whether they involve issues relating to immediate practical arrangements that affect everyone. These items tend not to be different from the items that are dealt with at "corridor meetings." The teachers are aware of the inefficiency of their staff meetings, as the following quote indicates: "It doesn't matter if we need to buy a roll of toilet paper or there needs to be a major decision, we'll just talk about it endlessly then put off making a decision." Another teacher noted: "We seem to just talk and talk and talk. Too much talking, nothing seems to come from it."

Not surprisingly then, it was realized at the beginning of Dewey's third year that such nuts-and-bolts agendas, as one teacher put it, were necessary but didn't fulfill what many felt was the frustrating inability of the staff to tackle issues of a more philosophical and educational nature. Student achievement and student learning are rarely addressed, but when they are, the discussion tends to be centered around an abstract philosophical debate that does not directly relate to Dewey's student body. One particularly vocal new teacher decided to remedy this by inaugurating an additional Wednesday biweekly morning meeting, which would specifically address some of the deeper, more vision-related issues of the school. After about five such meetings, the idea was abandoned, principally because of the inability of the group to come to productive focus, and the failure to agree on how such an agenda ought to be prioritized.

Aside from the inability of the faculty to use staff meetings to reach decisions, their interactions in this context reveal much about the nature of the administrative structure that pervades the school. The principal has access to information and insight into some of the hidden, or otherwise, agendas of the school office, which sometimes gives her an edge over what teachers can know. However, unlike traditionally hierarchical structures, her style of leadership is typically not one where such a position is used to enforce her authority: She sees her role as a support to staff, and a person whose role is to encourage rather than direct. This sometimes puts her in the uncomfortable position of supporting her staff's efforts to take full responsibility for school decisions, but at the same time fearing to intervene decisively to help them align their work with the district's dictates and/or agendas in ways that would advance the interests of the school. This is brought out in the following comments made concerning the way a particular staff meeting went:

> Sometimes they [the teachers] don't realize what's going on with the [district] office. Mick would like to have things stay the same—I see his point but it's not as simple as that. Students are money and we can't afford to turn our back on the opportunity of increasing our enrollment. Our credibility with the office is thin . . . sometimes I think . . . they [Jeff and others who wished to keep the school population down] need a reality check.

Nevertheless, most of the staff appreciate the principal's policy of encouraging open discussion and democratic decision making and tend to see it as part of their understanding of professionalism:

> Yes, this is what a teacher should be able to do. I like it here because its not often that you find a school where you can really make a difference to how things go.
> I suppose what we do is just like what a lot of schools are now doing . . . having teachers take on more responsibility.

However, the problems of having an inexperienced staff take charge of school-wide decisions did not go unnoticed by some faculty: "I've come out of this meeting and I think, what have we achieved? We can't even agree on what we need to agree on!" Inefficient use of time is often displayed at staff meetings because neither the principal, nor anyone else, was willing to point out the need to keep discussion focused and away from the anecdotal, despite complaints about the "waste of time" that occurred outside the meetings.

Despite the fact that the responsibility for facilitating staff meetings was always supposedly delegated to a specific individual, no one appeared invested with enough legitimate authority to focus the staff. The effort of the staff member who sought to create a "reflective" meeting that was distinct from the "business" meeting was a brave one, but he lacked the necessary expertise/authority to drive it forward. Perhaps because of lack of experience, teachers failed to take the trouble to effectively research the possible configurations of options for any given issue on the table, so meetings were often devoted to working out the options in relatively brief committee-of-the-whole settings. Finally, the group often lacked a taskmaster to keep the discussion focused on the realm of the possible. The principal understood this problem in the school's process, but because of her commitment to staff empowerment, felt unable to intervene. Once again, it is not that the staff did not care or was not committed, they simply did not have the understanding or the expertise to collectively organize themselves in an efficient manner that would produce concrete results.

Staff Coordination: Logistics and Time

Another example of Dewey's disjointed behavior can be found in the semiformal *corridor meetings*, which take place every morning except Tuesday and involve the whole staff, usually minus part-time teachers and assistants. Gathering at one end of the ground floor corridor, the meetings last for about 15 minutes and begin at 8:30 a.m. All participants have to stand up, and have an equal chance of suggesting agenda items by merely announcing them. The main point of such meetings is generally understood to be the clearing up of immediate planning and possible logistical conflicts or issues in order to facilitate the smoother running of the day. Because Dewey relies so heavily on busing students to a variety of sites and locations, these corridor meetings are often frenetic and intense, with individuals sometimes walking away at the point when they believe that no more business pertains to them. Occasionally, a discipline issue will be brought up for discussion, but again the point is more to inform on how an individual has been or will be managed, rather than to explore the merits or otherwise of a given policy.

Because the school has no P.A. or intercom system, one staff member suggested that every morning the staff have a "hot sheet" to help coordinate administrative announcements and logistics. The idea was that a staff member would put the hot sheet together before the morning meeting and then it would be read as announcements in homeroom. This way, there would be a consistency in communication between the students and staff. This policy was met with some resistance. One teacher felt that reading the announcements in homeroom would take away time from other activities. He was also concerned that "it would just end up being one more piece of paper on [his] desk." Other teachers were concerned about who was going to take the daily responsibility for writing and printing it. Subsequently, the idea never got off the ground. Thus, the lack of a coordinated system of communication further adds to the confusion at Dewey.

The Students' Day and the Use of Time and Space

The day-to-day reality of teaching at Dewey begins abruptly when it is announced, usually before the corridor meeting has been concluded, that the first busloads of students have arrived and teachers make their way to their classrooms. Typically, this is around 9:20 a.m., though school officially starts at 9:30 a.m.

One of the most striking things about Dewey is the movement of its students throughout any given day. Though this was not the case in its first 2 years, currently all students are expected to report to the central site each morning. Anywhere between 10:40 and 10:55 a.m., though often preparation has begun around 10:30, one third of the students are bused to the university site where they work with mentors on some science-based project, and similarly another third are bused to the downtown site within the business complex, and the remainder spend the day at the main site for art-related activities, namely, English, fine arts, and drama. Typically, somewhere between 1:30 and 1:50 p.m., the students are back in their home bases, with their home base teacher, and have afternoon homeroom until it is time to board the bus at 4:20 p.m.

The logistical problems of moving students around don't end here. Once at one of the outside sites, students are typically split up into smaller groups and allocated to either mentors or an assistant teacher to take them to the downtown public library, or an assistant teacher to take them to an exhibition or other field trip. All of this has to be coordinated in such a way that full-time teachers receive their contiguous 55 minutes of afternoon prep time. Not surprisingly, teachers are often unable to take prep time together, and anyway might find themselves in locations other than their home base classroom. One of the implications of this is that teachers find it impossible to create time for planning curriculum within the official school prep provision. A comment by a new teacher is representative of this: "One of the problems with this school is that we never have a chance to really sit down and talk about what we're going to do. I hardly ever see Mick or the others [the social science team members] except at the morning meetings."

The school day for a Dewey student is broadly partitioned into three segments: home base, one of three curriculum sites, and home base once again. Within the curriculum site, students are invariably split up into smaller groups for mentoring, some mini-field trip, or a library visit. When they return to their home base, which they do en masse, they might also receive some site-based curriculum teaching from one of two prep teachers, or a P.E. lesson in the great hall at the top of the building. Thus, the students' final home base time is itself segmented. Adding up all the time to move students to different locations, it can take up to 20 minutes of busing time to transport students from the parochial site to the university site alone. Add to this the time it takes to get the students settled down, get them equipped for their various excursions, walk to the appropriate bus, brief them on arrival, attempt to divide them up for different activities, plus the time to debrief them, reassemble them, and get them back on the bus and then into the appropriate homeroom—the whole process literally takes hours. None of the traveling time is used for study and the students regard it as free time to chat and while away the time, often by listening to personal stereos or playing mini video games. If one also factors in the constants of student lunch and one other recess, the result is a day that is easily open to much student abuse. Some of the students are aware of the dangers of so much looseness:

> Now this is a school built for someone who can be very self-controlling and can decide what they think is right and can take it upon themselves to do work and set their own deadlines, and it's something a lot of kids can't handle—setting their own deadlines, you know.

And according to another student:

> Some students, you know, will just use that power to be able
> to just goof off and not go out of their way to learn anything,
> not go out of their way to be helpful, and they'll take that
> power and use it to, you know, to cut classes and, um, do
> things that disrupt the other students' learning, you know,
> because they have more choice here and the teachers let kids
> get by with that more because it's their choice.

Though this particular time issue has rarely been an agenda item,
and when it has it isn't perceived as a particularly major problem, it
is clear that many staff members feel a little uneasy about the situation. Some see it as an inevitable and necessary evil of having such
a radical community education program, though others, despite the
Dewey mission, would wish to deemphasize this aspect altogether.

The time issue is an example of how a structural constraint of
moving students around various sites has limited Dewey's educational potential by decreasing the amount of time students spend
on-task. As mentioned earlier, the daily schedule does not permit the
teachers time to meet in teams or other groups. This constant sepa-
ration of teachers and students over the course of the day detracts
from the building of community within the school.

School Climate and the Use of Space

The home base site comprises a basically traditional, turn-of-the-
century school building. Each classroom has one door, typically at
the end of the room, thus making it impossible to observe the whole
space unless one is beyond the threshold. This allows most of the
classrooms to operate in a completely self-contained manner, invis-
ible to anyone who is not inside the room, which enhances the ability
of the teachers to act independently.

On the ground floor, where most of the classrooms are situated,
there is no attempt to utilize some of the wide corridor spaces for
learning purposes. In fact, when the whole school is in session, the
corridors are merely places where students meet, illicitly or otherwise, and/or drink from the water fountain. Female students have

to journey to the basement to use the bathroom, and because four other classrooms are located downstairs, the stairwell often becomes another student meeting place. Consequently, these spaces have the potential to become rather hostile areas, or at least spaces antithetical to a learning environment. Furthermore, teachers are sometimes seen to be ineffective in controlling students once they have established themselves in such places in small numbers. Students running up and down the stairs, raising their voices excitedly, and using such space to enhance their cliques can be witnessed daily in these areas. Some teachers, in exasperation, ask students what business they have in being outside their classrooms and repeatedly ask them to go back to their home base, but other staff turn a blind eye to those situations. For the most part, staff tend to keep themselves restricted to their own classrooms—concentrating on maintaining the atmosphere within while simultaneously controlling the frequency and number of students who take themselves out. There is a system of hall passes, but teachers have had difficulty in maintaining a consistent policy. In the following, Jim, the Dewey "student advocate," is addressing the whole staff about what he perceives as the importance of establishing and enforcing a consistent policy with regard to student movement:

> I'm a firm believer in boundaries. . . . I know many of us have a hard time with this. But kids need boundaries. . . . If a student is wandering the corridors, then this has to be for a legitimate purpose. They must have a pass with your [the teachers'] signature on it.

At a later date, Jim expressed his frustration that there was no one uniform pass design that everyone used, that is, that there was no enforcement of policy through uniformity of system and procedure. A number of other teachers have also expressed similar thoughts at one time or another; but so far, little has been done concerning the uniformity of passes, and teachers manage the movement of students as they see fit.

Perhaps it is ironic that because corridors are perceived to be potential places of anarchy, where students' movements have to be carefully controlled, they are not the places where staff are very visible—at least when school is in session. One reason for this might be that teachers often feel, quite sensibly, that they must limit themselves to only those domains in which control is achievable and/or that leaving the classroom is too risky. At any rate, because corridors are basically perceived as open to anarchic behavior, and because the physical design of the classrooms is so confining, there is no structured provision for systematic observation of staff practice, and the teachers have little or no sense of accountability to one another, there is little likelihood for achieving any kind of deprivatization of teacher practice.

School Climate and Discipline

Managing potentially disruptive or violent behavior seems to be the single most frequently visited topic of discussion among staff and, listening to the conversations, one gets the feeling that managing behavior is thought to be essentially either prior to or the precondition for curricula and pedagogic concerns: "If only we could get some control with the more disturbed students, then we could get on more with the business of good teaching," as one teacher remarked. And, more despairingly, following a particularly disruptive lesson where a student, apparently unprovoked, began yelling and dancing on the tables and refused to leave the room, "And we're supposed to teach in this!"

In Dewey, student behavior is rewarded or punished through a system of blue and orange slips. Getting three orange slips in any one week results in automatic detention, getting four warrants detention and a call home, and five warrants a 3-day home suspension. Alternatively, blue slips allow the student to enter the blue slip lottery, where the prizes range from free pizzas to submarine sandwiches, as well as guarantee the student some free-choice time on Friday afternoons. Though there is a range in the way teachers utilize this extrinsic motivational system, most of the discussions at staff meetings reveal that notions of unacceptable behavior are rarely understood to include poor academic activity. For most teachers and, by implication, for most students, negative behavior tends to be thought of exclusively as antisocial behavior. This is further reinforced by the role of the student advocate or mediator, whose management of students' problems is primarily focused on their social needs, as distinct from academic pursuits. In this his role is probably rather typical, but it does further underline the lack of academic focus in the school.

The delicate balance between student empowerment and acceptable conduct is one that many teachers struggle with and is a common theme in staff meeting agendas. Some of the student behavior observed during instructional time includes heating pizzas or popcorn in microwaves (which are in every classroom), wearing and sometimes playing personal stereos, wearing and using pacifiers and baby bottles, and an almost continuous consumption of candy, chips, and soft drinks. Often, such freedoms are uncomfortably condoned by the teachers, who are torn between wishing to keep on the good side of students and maintaining reasonable order. From time to time, staff edicts will announce that a specified activity or item is banned, but for the most part acceptable conduct is, at least for the more troubled portion of the student population, whatever the students can get away with.

The discomfort of this situation was somewhat confounded by the soft discipline approach of Dr. Booth. As one teacher commented, looking back at the time when she was the principal:

> You felt guilty if you suggested a student ought to be suspended. It was like a mark of your failure if that happened. She [the principal] would keep students at all costs. She'd have them work for her in the office and you'd probably get some worthless letter of apology from the kid. . . . Kids loved being sent to her because she would indulge them so much. The kids were laughing at us [the teachers].[8]

The Curriculum and Student Learning

As we have already noted, Dewey was created around a vision of facilitating an urban and community curriculum. As such, teachers have always been at liberty to develop their curricula around their interpretation of the Dewey vision and make use of the opportunities coming from the surrounding community and urban environment to enhance their curricular goals.

The initial group of teachers at Dewey was committed to the concept of experiential education. Few among the professional staff had any experience or training in what it meant, nor did the minimal budget and rapid start-up time demanded by the implementation schedule permit anyone to learn more about the research base for the school's plan. Once the school had opened, the effort required to prepare a curriculum whose content and mode of delivery were totally different from their previous experiences overwhelmed the teachers, while the principal was busy trying to organize a site council, as well as taking care of two other small schools that were within her administrative portfolio. In addition, none of the original team of teachers was experienced in coordinating curriculum development.

Another complication was that the original teaming design for the school had each teacher responsible for a mixed-age class covering three grades. As a result, any effective curriculum that was developed could only be implemented in a 3-year cycle. Thus, a teacher who agreed to work at Dewey knew that the first 3 years would involve a new curricular demand for each day. By the end of the second year it was agreed that this constant demand for development was not working, and the policy changed so that students would move in groups among the three sites, which would repeat a curriculum module three times over the course of the year.

Despite this change, the pressures of curriculum development on the staff were still severe. By the end of the third year, only two staff members were left from the initial group, and most who left claimed that they simply could not sustain the demands of the curriculum development process. As one teacher commented, "I still don't know what we're supposed to be teaching. It doesn't seem concrete to me."

The position of community coordinator was established specifically to have someone access the available resources in the community that could assist in generating a meaningful experiential education encounter and pass on the information to the rest of the staff. One consequence of this, particularly for the social science team, is that curricula tend to be formed in rather ad hoc ways, according to whatever is available. Many of the teachers interviewed did not think this was a particularly serious implication—"the flexible curriculum is the beauty of Dewey," as one teacher remarked—but some of its ramifications were not lost on the community coordinator herself:

> I get very frustrated sometimes. I feel that the staff don't appreciate the time and trouble that I spend in organizing trips . . . it takes a lot of phone calls. . . . I don't think they realize what I do but they wouldn't have the time to do it. . . . I hardly ever get invited to meetings so I never know what's going on. I can't plan if I don't know what the projects are . . . it takes time to organize these things.

In other words, the community coordinator provided the regular teachers with a modest relief of pressure, but because of the incessant development needs of the school, there was never time to try to fully utilize her in a collective development of experiential education.

There is a great deal of potential for Dewey teachers to plan and tailor curricula to suit their own tastes and students' needs. As mentioned earlier, the group process and decision-making skills of the staff are very poor. Most teachers tend to be preoccupied with surviving from day to day. Thus, much of the curriculum is both individually developed and of a poor quality. One teacher noted: "Let's face it, we don't have a curriculum here." When asked about developing one, he replied: "I don't have time. I'm just managing a crisis most of the time . . . it's always been the problem with Dewey. They want us to develop curriculum but they don't give us time to do it. There are people who get paid to do this."

An example of the kinds of problems in the curriculum can be found in a typical assignment from a well-established social studies teacher. The assignment consisted of asking the students to collect 100 names of any persons who made a significant impact in the United States. Following this, students then had to select one person who particularly interested them and write a 200-word report in 1 week. Little classroom reflection was given to the criteria that might govern the meaning of "significant impact." There was virtually no guidance for either the selection of the theme or the quality of the product, no attempt to focus on the writing process, no modeling from any of the social science teachers to demonstrate ways of extrapolating information from texts and organizing ideas, no encouraging students to act as additional audiences for the writing of others, and no provision for formally publishing final pieces. The absence of all these things and the gimmicky nature of many of the assignments typified much of the work done in this curriculum area.

Whether student learning is taking place is in question. This is due to many of the issues described earlier, such as discipline problems and limited time on-task. However, even when the students are on-task, it does not necessarily mean learning is taking place. Another example of this can be found in a project initiated by an art teacher, regarding one African tribe's method of communicating emotions to one another through various colors in little flags or tapestries. She explained what the colors and some of the symbols meant to the tribe and told the students to make a flag. Instead of engaging the students in a conversation regarding what the colors might mean to them, or why people chose to use specific symbols or patterns to convey specific messages, the remaining discussion revolved around what materials they could or could not use. The time on-task in this case turned out to be more of an exercise in coloring than in student learning. Unfortunately, these types of activities seem to fill much of Dewey's curriculum.

The Curriculum and the Teams

The core teachers at Dewey are teamed by discipline. The intention of the team is to provide a vehicle for improving not only curriculum focus but also the teachers' relationship with a smaller group of students. One of the ways in which this works is that teams supervise the transportation of students to the various sites and/or field trip locations. Typically, they also share the responsibility for dividing up the students for their various activities. However, once the students are divided (e.g., some might be taken to the library), the teachers that comprise the teams will deliver their lessons individually.

One of the teams' responsibilities is the development of curriculum. Typically, team meetings are suppose to take place on teacher days and in the teachers' own time, often just before school starts. Apart from the teacher days, when the principal usually creates some time for teams to meet, there is no other formal provision for meeting. Such constraints clearly impede what can be achieved by teams, and consequently, little of this was observed in the way of interdependent teaching roles. When asked what some of the negative aspects of Dewey are, one of the science teachers replied:

> Lack of time. If we had 30% of our contact time to spend on preparation and staff communication, it would be so much better. We could then begin to develop a real community. In fact, Jeff and I are getting together and forming a sort of subcommittee in order to find ways of establishing more of a community here.

Even when time was made available to the staff in a teacher planning day, the teachers tended to share what they individually did in their classrooms. The conversations tended to be more of a comparison of different teaching methods as opposed to a collaboration of team curriculum, as they were intended to be.

In addition to the time problem, one team in particular was further hampered by the uncooperativeness of one of its members. Ironically, one of the only teachers who gained across-the-board professional admiration for the way she conducted her class, and also gained the respect and loyalty of her students, happened to be a very poor team player. As one teacher admirer put it: "Pam was brilliant. She knew what she was about [as a teacher] and her kids adored her. But they were difficult to teach by anyone else. Yet, she made them feel special and almost apart from the rest of the school."

Not only did Pam not have much time for the real or apparent ideology of the school, but she also followed teachers' union rules to the point that she would literally walk out of meetings if they went over official time. Not surprisingly, her arrogance was not appreciated and she did much to undermine the confidence and sense of efficacy of the team she worked with. The principal worked very hard at encouraging her to leave Dewey. She finally transferred just prior to Christmas of last year.

Structuring the teams by discipline creates another problem. There is no mechanism for cross-team meetings. This translates into very little or no interdisciplinary collaboration by the teachers and is contradictory to the school's objective of having an interdisciplinary curriculum.

Problems With Knowledge Use and Expertise

The rhetoric concerning the quality of the Dewey community and what the school purports to stand for is fairly well known among the staff as well as the students. The community coordinator does a very effective job at selling the school and promoting its image. However, what Dewey sells itself as and what it is are two different things. Such ambiguity does not seem to be lost on students either. Here is a typical comment by a student who was asked to characterize the school: "Dewey is a school that it is very easy to learn in, plus it's very easy to get swept away with not learning because it gives students so much more power than other schools which I've been in. There's so much more choice." The same student went on to talk about what he perceived were the high goals of Dewey:

> A lot of them are fairly reasonable. The students will have some idea of what they are, but some of them are obscure and I couldn't name them right now, but I've been reading this pamphlet which explains it a little bit. It sounds sort of odd. It was one that they gave to the parents, I think when I first came here, and it just gave us an idea of what Dewey was like. Yeah. It struck me as being, you know, the goals were a little high. They were all good goals, but there were some of them seemed like they were something that the middle school kids couldn't really accomplish.

The rhetoric and the reality often seem to be at odds. Is Dewey a school that is "very easy to learn in," or is it a school where it's "easy to get swept away with not learning"? Opinions from staff conflict, even from the same individual. However, the environment at Dewey is a rather chaotic one, where the abuse of student freedoms is more common than its opposite. Perhaps most significantly, in the teacher prep week before the beginning of the new academic year, a number of teachers openly confessed their anxiety regarding their worth as professional educators. The tenor and intensity of the discussion were rare. Here are some excerpts from a discussion preceding a team meeting on developing social science curriculum goals: "I don't just want to manage the chaos again." Another teacher added:

> I'm going to sleep better tonight if I have a clearer idea about what I'm supposed to be teaching, to me that's what it's all about. Knowing what you're doing. Now I'll have something to say to parents [i.e., projecting into the future—when the goals have been established]

With many of the teachers there is a feeling of uncertainty and an anxiety concerning the educational efficacy of Dewey. How intense such anxiety is for the rest of the staff is difficult to say at this point, but there is certainly an openness to new curricular and pedagogical models, as attested to by the staff's unanimous interest in developing whole language.

Dewey invited a whole language specialist into the school to better facilitate this approach within the Dewey curriculum. On a staff development day, the presenter gave an introduction to the philosophy of whole language and the methods surrounding it. To give the staff a sense of how it could be implemented in the classroom, he provided several examples. The specialist admitted that his presentations were not training but just an introduction to whole language. Yet, some of the staff felt that they were adequately trained and were now using whole language—when in reality, they only had a limited understanding of the methods and philosophy.

Conclusion

Dewey's chaotic start-up clearly affected the degree to which teachers were able to work together to enact their hopes for the new school. As the description has indicated, there are other critical issues that might not have been resolved with more planning time. First, the structural problems of the school that were fundamental to its design created problems with the effective use of time and space and also made it extremely difficult for teachers to work together in any sustained way. Second, the school's teachers were expected to be empowered and to run the school, but they had little experience in basic administrative and leadership roles, such as prioritizing and analyzing problems, running meetings, planning, and so on. Because the principal was reluctant to intervene, there was much floundering.

The teachers lacked the expertise to do what was asked of them. Although they knew that the curriculum had not evolved as well as it should, and were aware of learning problems, such as poor reading skills, that needed to be addressed, they had great difficulty grappling with educational ideas. Even when they reached out for help, as in the case of inviting in the whole language consultant, they did not get what they wanted: a chance to discuss and work with the more fundamental ideas of education that had motivated the effort to bring Dewey into being.

As Dewey began its fifth year, neither any of the original teachers nor the original principal were left. One teacher likened Dewey to a middle-grade student—"still unsure of themselves and at such a critical stage in their development." Yet, little was done to change the school. Some teachers were willing to talk in private about the failure of the school to achieve its goals, but the conversations in meetings and in the hall remained at the superficial level of getting through the day. Subsequently, the organizational and physical structures of Dewey, as well as the culture that was created, have hindered the development of any form of professional community.

Notes

1. Jean King and Richard Flor provided field notes for the early phases of Dewey's development.

2. The enrollment in 1993–1994 increased to 220 students.

3. At least this was the case in the academic year 1992–1993. In 1993–1994 there were nine such teachers due to increased enrollment.

4. Last year the configuration consisted of three teams consisting of three, three, and two members for science, social science, and art, respectively. This year, each curriculum area has three teachers comprising a team.

5. At least this was the case in the academic year 1992–1993. In 1993–1994, he was full-time.

6. Most significantly, the school this year has a new full-time principal.

7. The role of the principal is described in more detail in Louis and King (1993).

8. Dr. Booth transferred to another school after the end of Dewey's fourth year. The policy of the new principal, who had been in the school for less than a year at the time this chapter was drafted, is tougher, and the staff seem to appreciate this.

PART THREE
REFLECTIONS ON PROFESSIONAL
COMMUNITY IN URBAN SCHOOLS

8

Developing Professional

Community in New and

Restructuring Urban Schools

SHARON D. KRUSE
KAREN SEASHORE LOUIS

In Part I we laid out the theoretical dimensions of teachers' professional community, and illustrated them in Part II by presenting individual cases of urban schools that have struggled to develop it. These cases suggest that the issues facing schools in a transformation process are as varied and complex as the schools themselves. This chapter considers the lessons that can be learned from the cases of these five city schools. Through the relative success and failure of these schools to develop professional community, we draw insights and conclusions about the structural and social and human resource conditions that may have an impact on the generation of a school-wide focus on professional success. The chapter first compares the five schools, using descriptive categories that capture the different phases of the school's development. These phases, which range from a mature professional community to a static professional community, help to provide the organizing structure for the remaining sections of the chapter that compare the schools, considering the specific structural and social characteristics of professional community. Finally, conclusions are offered that consider the conditions relative to one another and the overall theoretical framework.

Dimensions of Professional Community

Because each school is at a different developmental level related to its restructuring effort and attainment of professional community, the schools are first described individually and then later contrasted. Both discussions provide us with a unique snapshot of the school(s). The first allows us to identify the school in relation to a constant nominal ranking, according to the presence or absence of each dimension (e.g., reflective dialogue, deprivatization, focus on student learning, collaboration, and shared values) and its relation to school norms and values. The second provides us with the opportunity to contrast the schools and to analyze the link between structural and social and human resource conditions and the realization of professional community.

We used Miles and Huberman's (1994) recommended procedures for cross-case analysis to generate a comparison of the five schools on each of the five dimensions of professional community (Appendix C, Table 1). Besides using the matrix to summarize our data about each school's development, we also chose to rank them using a 4-point scale. The highest ranking (1) was identified as present when the dimension was consistently observed in the school and could be considered a defining factor of the school. The dimension is thus socially normative, providing a foundation for continuous school improvement efforts and the generation of mature professional community among staff.

We used a medium-high ranking (2) to distinguish schools that invested in the development of conditions and structures supportive of the development of professional community but had not, for a variety of reasons, fully used them to achieve this end. A critical mass of the faculty may have adopted the practices fully, but all faculty may not yet have had the opportunity to use the innovation. Thus, professional community in these schools is nascent, but has not yet reached the promise their structural or social conditions hold.

A medium ranking (3) was applied when a particular dimension was inconsistently present. The dimension might not have yet become normative in either the full faculty or for a critical mass of faculty, or might exist only as a by-product of other practice. Thus, it is not viewed as important in itself by most teachers.

Finally, we assigned a low ranking (4) when the dimension was minimally present or absent. The dimension may have been undefined or unclear in relation to school goals and practice. Low rankings may imply that the school was still developing its normative structures. Low rankings may also indicate a school in which conflicts remained unresolved or conversations were mired in indecision.

Considered together, the five dimensions provide a composite that allows us to describe the schools as either a mature, developing, fragmented, or static professional community. In each case the character and climate of these schools differ in both practice and theory, providing us with the ability to separate their stories and briefly present each as a unique case of the development of professional communities in schools.

Mature Community

Metro Academy, located in one of our largest cities, is a high school dedicated to an inquiry-based instructional program. All of Metro's faculty participate in decisions about instructional offerings and flexible scheduling options for those courses; students, through consultation with the teaching faculty, can also provide their opinions as to course offerings and schedules. Just as inquiry into learning is the school's instructional theme, inquiry into teaching is the faculty's professional theme. Teachers are provided numerous avenues—mentors, team teaching relationships, faculty meetings dedicated to reflection upon instructional and curricular issues—with which to access the instructional expertise of fellow colleagues.

The use of time within the school day and the physical proximity of teachers' office space provide ongoing opportunities to address issues and concerns in depth, scrutinizing assumptions that are basic to school philosophy and values. Faculty exchanges center on issues of instructional pedagogy and content, student social and personal development, and future curricular issues. These conversations are not only persistent but public, and provide strong possibilities for interdisciplinary collaboration. The hall talk and meetings reinforce rapport, trust, and respect among teachers for their skills with students and instruction. Metro is home to a mature professional community. It is a community in which faculty continues to refine their instructional and curricular ideals by highlighting immediate issues and concerns of students and staff, by tying them to enduring tensions in producing high-quality educational experiences. All members of the faculty jointly share and participate in the focus activities, commitment to the inquiry method of instruction, and curriculum planning. At Metro, all faculty and staff have a clear sense of both the traditions from which the school has sprung and its future mission.

Developing Community

Thomas Paine High School and Professional Development School provides a particularly good example of a community in the early stages of development, and helps us to understand better the roots from which Metro's mature community may have sprung. Paine's developing community is marked by an ongoing commitment by teachers to creating an educational environment focused on student learning and academic success. Paine's status as a Professional Development School has helped the teachers to converge around issues of student learning and to sustain conversation centered around curriculum and instruction. Teacher talk runs high at Paine and occurs in a variety of contexts that provide unique and challenging opportunities for engagement with their teaching colleagues. Brown bag lunches led by university faculty and teachers at Paine provide an uncommon informal forum for teachers to ponder their craft and to consider new ideas. Thus, informal and formal settings provide the opportunity for all teachers to participate in a continuum of teacher development activities.

Creating time for teachers to talk spills over into other arenas of the school community. Conversations, be they at lunch or in team meetings, center on issues of student achievement, which has stimulated teachers to interact regularly on many issues related to student learning. Whether they are discussions about curriculum or discipline, the focusing questions at Paine ask, "What good is this to students and how will you put it into place?" By creating spaces in the school where teachers can come together around issues of practice, whatever their level of expertise, faculty take advantage of the unique team structure, physical setting, and support for innovation provided by the administration. The principal, though remaining largely in the background, continues to emphasize the need to enhance student learning and academic success.

What differentiates Paine from Metro is that the faculty is still striving to speak in a common voice, with a commonly held set of convictions about students and instruction. The seeds have been planted and it remains the task of the teachers and the administration to make normative that which has been developed.

Fragmented Community

When we look at two of the distinctly different settings from among our cases—Alexander and Whitehead—we see conditions that lead us to conclude that serious reform efforts may still result in fragmented professional communities. We define a fragmented community as one in which there is only partial participation among the faculty, which may include competitive subgroups or simply a contrast between an apathetic majority and an involved minority. In either instance, our cases show that fragmented communities, where they persist over long periods, can create serious problems for restructuring efforts. To illustrate the conditions that allow the formation of fragmented professional communities, we need to look at two distinctly different settings: a traditional school that became involved in serious reform, and a new school of choice.

Alexander provides an example of an emerging community hampered by fragmentation. Alexander is an elementary school in a large, troubled city. Serving a poor, minority population, Alexander's history is one of unrest and crisis. Following the assignment of a new principal 10 years ago, the school regained its reputation as a safe place for teachers and students. Teachers, many of whom had served in the system for more than 20 years, felt the changes were positive, and a renewed sense of hope filled Alexander's halls. However, although the school returned to being a physically safe environment, instructional practice did not progress. Teachers lacked, both individually and collectively, basic teaching skills and understanding of quality instruction. Without this foundation, teachers could not improve their instruction without external help.

Following a legislatively mandated, city-wide school improvement initiative, staff of a university-based research and development center were invited into the school to provide in-service and instruction in literacy models for the primary teachers on the staff. The introduction and subsequent adoption of the techniques served briefly to bond the primary-level faculty by providing a shared belief structure and the time, vocabulary, and support needed to carry out essential changes. Levels of trust and respect among the primary faculty grew as the initiative gained hold in the school, providing further support for reflection and collaboration among the faculty. These faculty were in the initial stages of creating needed structural and social and human resources, as well as attempting to institutionalize the instructional changes already begun. However, for a variety of reasons community and its commitment did not extend to other faculty in the school, who were suspicious of the changes occurring in the lower grades. Thus, Alexander is considered to have a fragmented professional community.

Fragmented professional communities are fragile because their base of support is weak and, as the principal at Alexander withdrew support for the fledgling efforts of the staff, the community began to falter. Therefore, the experiences of the primary faculty at Alexander are instructive as we consider school-based efforts to build community in restructuring schools. Providing intensive outside technical assistance and support created the opportunity for tentative growth of community at Alexander, which was further nurtured by the development of leadership among the teachers. However, without clear support from the principal, the faculty could not sustain the growth toward community.

In contrast to the partial development seen at Alexander, Whitehead Middle School exhibits many conditions that support a strong community, yet the staff lacks professional cohesion at any level. Whitehead School, designed to be "high-tech, high-touch and high-teach" (Louis & King, 1993), began with total commitment from a small group of teachers that was not sustained as the faculty grew with the size of the school. Pockets of expertise exist within the staff and there is a strong contingent of extremely gifted and talented teachers at Whitehead; but the school lacks the ability to use the structures it has at its disposal for the creation of school-wide community.

Thus, although some teachers talk regularly, the conversation occurs outside the school or in small groups, and rarely addresses issues of concern to the entire staff. Expertise is not shared schoolwide. In a pattern begun by the lead teachers, as they labored to create an entire break-the-mold curriculum as they taught it, the school's development efforts are divided between staff and rarely involve joint work. Each member is left to decide how best to use the technology and instructional resources that are available.

These structures were designed to provide autonomous working conditions for teachers and the opportunity for collaboration and reflection. However, due to a core of leaders who felt threatened when teachers questioned the school's progress toward its goals, they have had the opposite effect: Teachers have felt isolated, unsupported, and even abandoned in their efforts to provide quality instruction for students. Although the staff members who have been there since the school opened share a sense of what the school is about, those who keep the vision cannot objectively discuss it with the newer staff. Thus, Whitehead is a school with low levels of trust and respect, which results in a diminution of reflective exchange and collaboration throughout the staff. Its community is segmented between the initial group of teacher leaders and those hired later, and is consequently unable to tap the resources that exist among its members.

Static Community

In comparison, Dewey Middle School is a school longing to find a base of expertise and to begin a desired professional exchange, but unable to take the first steps. Dewey, an innovative middle school focused around the notion of experiential learning for students, opened its doors as a new magnet school in 1989. Located in a midsize city, Dewey attracted many students who were looking for educational experiences based in the community rather than in a classroom using textbooks. Schooling occurred in three locations about the city—one was in the basement of a local church, a second at a nearby university, and the third within a downtown business complex. The ideal was to provide an experientially based educational program, intimately involving students in their own learning and their city.

However, in practice the staff lacked a clear understanding of what experiential learning entailed and, by virtue of being scattered throughout the city, teachers lacked the ability to constructively help each other in its definition. Without an adequate cognitive base or skill base, it became impossible for the staff to individually reflect upon or collectively discuss issues of teaching or student learning. Both a common vocabulary for such discussion and the ability to ground discussion in important issues were absent. The small faculty of 11 had a strong desire to improve and several times sought the assistance of district in-service personnel and outside consultants. However, consultants did not present them with the rich array of ideas and tools that they desperately wanted. The faculty has continued to experience many false starts and aborted attempts as they struggled to make sense of their mission. Thus, Dewey is a school with a static community. It wants to change, yet cannot quite find its way; thus, it finds itself stuck and unable to remedy its problems.

Dimensions Supporting the Development of Community—Cross-Case Analysis

Individually, the portraits of the schools provide benchmarks that permit us to identify both barriers and facilitators to the formation of professional community. Metro Academy has managed to integrate reflection throughout its approach to education. Reflective debate is a hallmark of an inquiry-based method of instruction, and the staff has incorporated this focus as a central strategy in its daily creation of climate and culture at Metro. By creating a climate in which inquiry is valued, the staff has managed both to continue the growth process related to instruction and to continue the process of refining what it means to be a restructuring school. The establishment of a communicative system that provides a framework for classroom pedagogy, and serves as a tool to analyze and resolve problems within the school, has empowered staff to probe the school philosophy deeply and regularly. When confronted by a teacher's concerns about the quality of his students' written material, the staff joined to study how the process of analysis might best be taught. With this support, the frustrated teacher brought student papers to a subsequent staff meeting to elicit guidance in teaching a difficult topic. Thus, the staff collectively engaged in a joint process of learning about their practice. In doing so, the teacher and the rest of the staff made public both the difficulties of teaching within the inquiry model and the frustrations of making concrete the practice in the classroom. Broaching issues central to the philosophical heart of the school allows teachers to contribute to the collective intellectual understanding of practice and underscores a collaborative focus on student learning. Thus, by modeling the theory and practice of inquiry, the staff continues to grow and gain maturity as a collective group of professionals working toward a shared set of goals and values. Metro's experience suggests that a foundation of open, reflective dialogue can reinforce the normative structures present in the school, creating an environment conducive to public practice and collaboration.

The grounding of Metro's professional community in this type of reflective discussion points to the importance of shared norms concerning what and how students are to learn.

Paine provides an equally important lesson about the necessity of a shared public focus around which teachers can intellectually gather. Before the sustained conversation that began when the Professional Development School was initiated, Paine teachers floundered, adopting uncoordinated innovations in search of a quick fix for the educational woes of inner-city students. As the dialogue at Paine emerged, teachers did not coalesce around a single instructional focus but adopted several themes designed to harmonize with a highly varied student population. By placing instruction designed around student needs at the heart of their efforts, however, teachers could thoughtfully adopt a variety of innovations and still engage in common conversations about instruction. The value of new practices was assessed, based on shared teacher experience with the students at Paine and discussions of what good practice meant in their specific context.

Although discussions have greatly improved teacher instruction at Paine, they have not occurred without a struggle. At this time the staff still lacks the cohesion generated by a widely shared cognitive and skill base. Thus, teachers share a commitment to student learning, but they do not share a well-defined vocabulary with which to discuss this topic to the same extent as does Metro. This is a result, in part, of the size and diversity of the school, but also of the embryonic stage of community development at Paine. However, Paine's teachers are growing more aware of these issues and are now working together and with local university faculty to address them.

In a fashion similar to Paine's, Alexander's primary teachers could start developing a fledgling community only after the school adopted a curriculum initiative that focused on improving literacy instruction. Alexander's experience is instructive. Without a shared curriculum and pedagogical framework, individual staff were unable to locate themselves in relation to the larger school community. Once the literacy initiative took hold and grew within Alexander, teachers could value the school as more than simply a safe place within a volatile city; additionally, the school became a place to learn. Their collective efforts to understand and engage in the teaching/learning process, based upon a commonly held notion of what good literacy instruction would look like, allowed the staff to open its doors to both colleagues and collaboration. As the staff further developed its understanding of the initiative, their collective normative sense of community within the school also grew, as did increasing levels of collaboration and public practice. Thus, it can be inferred that the development of the larger community requires the focused development of the individuals.

Notable in the Metro, Paine, and Alexander cases is the focus on student learning as central to the school's restructuring efforts. Whitehead also offers an instructive lesson concerning a collective focus on student learning. The school was designed to provide maximum independence for students in the selection of courses and projects within their course work. Additionally, the faculty was to offer integrated approaches to subject matter, combining writing across the curriculum with a strong base of technology to support student efforts. Although shared, the staff's values remained poorly focused. Student-centered learning proved too difficult a construct to operationalize without the establishment of the dimensions of reflection upon practice and a shared normative base. Whitehead had a vague vision of what it expected students to accomplish; however, the teachers lacked sufficient skills and trust within the community to translate a difficult concept into concrete instructional practices. Although many strong teachers held faculty positions at Whitehead, the normative and cultural climate of the school did not allow for questioning of methods or techniques that addressed the focus. Instead, efforts to scrutinize the philosophy and to grow collectively or collaboratively were discouraged in favor of an individualistic model that allowed some members to succeed while others faltered. Thus, teachers within the school became increasingly private in their practice, unable to force a serious collective examination of the school's instructional model. The Whitehead experience suggests that a focus on student learning is not sufficient for the creation of community, although it is an important construct of professional community.

Dewey's experience supports a conclusion that the dimensions of school-wide professional community identified in Chapter 2 are interactive and cumulative as supports for school reform. The staff at Dewey has, like Whitehead's, an espoused statement concerning the kind of experiences they wanted to provide to students, and the conditions for learning they wanted to create. However, it is inadequately specific to support the growth of strong professional community. Although the teaching staff meets regularly, there is consistent confusion about what the content of those meetings ought to include, and also problems in reaching decisions.

The many inconclusive discussions have contributed to the absence of a shared language and set of ideas that might help to frame discussions of instruction or curriculum. The lack of a common vocabulary further impedes the staff's ability to collectively reflect on and discuss practice. Thus, attempted efforts at collaboration—inservice offerings, integrated curriculum workshops—have failed due to a scarcity of shared norms concerning instruction and curriculum, rather than a deprivation of desire or talent among the faculty. The community remains static—waiting for a focus that will create the exchanges in which they are longing to participate.

We posit that an academic and instructional focus for staff activity is a precondition for the growth of mature community within schools. After examining these cases we also believe that the school's instructional focus must be based in norms and values, as it was in the primary faculty at Alexander and the full faculties at Metro and Paine, to provide sufficient support for other dimensions of community. Once a normative base is present, a staff can begin the task of reflection and discussion of practice. Conversation can focus around the philosophical notions on which the school is based, as Metro Academy illustrates, or around issues related directly to pedagogy, as in the conversation at Alexander. Our data suggest that once the dialogue becomes institutionalized, greater opportunity for collaboration and deprivatized practice exist. As the cases of Dewey and Whitehead show, suggestions of community can occur even in settings without a strong normative base. Those fragments are not, however, sufficient to sustain or create the larger community.[1]

Structural Conditions Related
to the Formation of Professional Community

Several structural conditions are necessary to support the creation of strong professional communities. The design of the school as a work setting can create an environment that supports collaborative, rather than parallel but unconnected, strategies for teaching and learning. Structural conditions that create interdependent work practice nourish interdependence elsewhere, creating stronger interpersonal connections between teachers that, in turn, reinforce collective goals. Working in concert, the structural conditions of (a) time to meet and talk, (b) physical proximity, (c) interdependent teaching roles, (d) communication structures and networks, and (e) teacher empowerment and school autonomy can create the needed foundation for professional community to emerge (Chapter 2).

Our data (summarized in Appendix C, Tables C.2 and C.2a) suggest three main conclusions relating to supportive structural conditions: (a) the absence of structural supports impedes the growth of professional community; (b) the presence of supportive structures is not sufficient to sustain the growth of professional community; and

(c) the creation of professional community is not an automatic consequence of teacher empowerment or school autonomy; other factors, including time and physical proximity, are of equal or greater importance.

Fragmented and Static Communities

From its inception Whitehead School enjoyed many structural features that made other teachers in the relatively affluent school district jealous. The school calendar was developed with 20 additional days to provide teachers with time throughout the school year to meet, plan, talk, and develop curriculum. Faculty offices and classrooms were designed to provide optimal private space, but with public meeting areas. Computer networks linked, via E-mail, all teachers who didn't have common preparation periods. Furthermore, the instructional design of the school encouraged integrated curriculum and teaching roles. However, in spite of these advantages, factors unrelated to structure caused Whitehead to fail at developing more than a fragmented community.

In contrast, because of its design, Dewey lacked most of the structural conditions that we have suggested may be necessary for the creation of community. Although empowered to create a magnet school devoted to experiential learning, the staff did not have the focused time and physical proximity necessary to develop a productive curriculum. The state and district supported the creation of Dewey with waivers to excuse the school from existing curriculum and instructional mandates, giving the faculty the authority to create radical change. However, with a lack of necessary cognitive and skill bases, a scarcity of time, and the physical isolation of the faculty, there was no capacity to make full use of the formal empowerment. Therefore, the staff became frustrated in its efforts and fruitlessly struggled to create a forum in which it could address its developing and varied concerns.

Similarly, Alexander initially had few of the necessary structural conditions related to supporting the growth of community. Insufficient resources had hindered the school's growth toward community, creating instead a school of unconnected teachers and classrooms. Before the literacy initiative the school lacked a unifying theme and, like Dewey, could not realize the opportunity given them by the state-mandated reform effort. The literacy initiative provided such a theme for the primary faculty and, through enhancing human and social resources, for a while stimulated the rearrangement of structural resources to facilitate the teachers' improvement process. Only by putting in place clearly articulated goals and values was the primary staff able to create structures that support community. Where time did not exist during the school day to focus teacher efforts upon student learning, it was created in pockets of well-attended morning meetings and Saturday workshops. The meetings enhanced communication; and more teachers began to gather for focused conversations about processes related to the teaching and learning of reading. Thus, conditions that the staff could not easily affect, such as the physical proximity of classes and the lack of interdependent teaching roles, were relieved. Although the development of community at Alexander faltered, the first year of the case illustrates the potency of teacher efforts to make use of conditions and structures that support their goals when they receive external assistance.

Developing and Mature Communities

Metro, like Whitehead, was specifically designed to provide maximum structural supports for teaching and change efforts, although it lacked the extensive technical and monetary resources of the latter. Staff meetings are frequent and memos are a regular part of school communication structures; both provide ongoing methods to converse and pose new issues and problems related to teaching and learning at Metro. Faculty office space clusters in a large room that provides maximum contact between teachers who work together toward the development of courses and teaching roles. New teachers apprentice beside more seasoned veterans of the inquiry process, coteaching and learning the methodology of instruction at Metro. Class schedules are flexible, allowing lab courses to meet in blocks and lectures/discussion groups to meet for 75 to 90 minutes when necessary. Thus, structure supports a strong normative and social and human resource base, and results in a mature community that can create needed change as necessary to support school goals.

Paine's case permits a snapshot of a comprehensive high school struggling to create the necessary structural conditions for reform and professional community. Unlike Alexander's effort, which was stalled before it was fully implemented, Paine's teachers worked together to meet the immediate needs of both teachers and the students throughout the school. The creation of a team structure that centered on the needs of diverse groups of students is paralleled by efforts to create a more collective community of thought through the Professional Development School. Working in concert with the team structure, the Professional Development School allows teachers to continue to work with one another even if they do not share a similar team assignment. Thus, teachers who are on some teams enjoy the close physical proximity of classrooms and meeting areas, both individual and team planning periods, and autonomy within the classroom to act in the beat interests of their students. Teachers who do not share team assignments can maintain contact by the brown bag lunches, which keep teachers in informal contact with each other and also provide a forum for planning and mentoring. However popular the lunches have been for the faculty, they do not provide enough communication for the large staff at Paine. Because the school lacks E-mail to link teachers to the large amounts of information generated on a daily basis in a high school, the staff is continuing to worry about the communication problems fostered in large comprehensive high schools.

The Thomas Paine and Metro experiences suggest that communication structures need to exist on two levels: first, they must meet the daily needs of students and faculty, and second, they must contribute to visioning for new ideas and planning for future developments. In both schools, communication structures were a key component in the successful generation of community.

Summary

From these data we posit that although the absence of structural conditions can impede the growth of professional community, their presence cannot ensure it. In particular, structure alone cannot mitigate the political dynamic that can impede the growth of community.

Instead, structure appears to act in tandem with other dimensions and social and human resource factors, helping the creation of communities of learning.

Our data suggest that the structural conditions consist of preconditions and intervening factors. Preconditions necessary for community to develop include both teacher empowerment/school autonomy and time to meet and talk. Intervening factors include physical proximity, communication structures and networks, and interdependent teaching roles.[2] We suggest that there are two conclusions: (a) structural changes in schools must occur in combination to support the development of professional communities (i.e., the creation of an array of communication networks or curriculum based in interdependent teaching roles requires the support of both time and teacher empowerment for the development of professional community to occur); and (b) when established, preconditions discussed here help to create an environment in which teachers can take advantage of other intervening structural conditions and factors. In other words, there is no "magic bullet" among the many recommendations by the current pundits of school reform.

Social and Human Resource Conditions
Related to the Formation of Professional Community

Our data suggest that the development of professional community requires several preconditions related to social and human resources. School-based community offers faculty the opportunity to grow and develop, creating a workplace that is supportive of both people and the process of school change. The social and human resource conditions supportive of the development of community include openness to improvement, trust and respect, shared expertise, a sense of efficacy, leadership, and socialization mechanisms. According to our analysis, the social and human resource supports most central to the growth of school communities are (a) teacher expertise related to cognitive and skill outcomes for classroom practice; and (b) leadership supportive of teacher efforts, inclusive of cognitive and skill acquisition.[3]

Fragmented and Static Communities

Basic to the formation of rapport, trust, and respect within restructuring and new schools is the ability to use the available expertise and skill base. Neither Alexander nor Whitehead nor Dewey could establish a level of rapport between teachers that would encourage the development of a shared cognitive and skill base. In both cases, the inability to foster (Dewey) or share (Alexander, Whitehead) cognitive and skill-based expertise were directly influenced by the leadership present within the school.

The barriers preventing the creation of instructional skills and cognitive knowledge differed in each school. Whitehead had many talented teachers who delivered authentic instruction and engaged students in academic tasks. Yet, the leadership team actively discouraged the staff from raising serious questions about teaching, favoring instead a reliance upon individual judgment over group expertise. Dependence upon individual expertise not only left the staff open to uneven instruction across subject areas, but also undermined the interdisciplinary curriculum that was to have been a banner of the school. It also resulted in an implicit tension between those who were experienced and successful and those who were still learning and faltering. The consequence was a decrease in the level of trust among faculty, reinforced by a leadership group that ignored the need of the staff to discuss the effects of uneven experiences on students. In summary, Whitehead's leadership did not support collectively defined knowledge and skills and did not attend to the social and emotional needs of staff who were struggling with difficult pedagogical questions.

The teachers at Dewey, in contrast, received positive responses from the principal for their support of the school's students. The principal created a climate in which efforts related to the school's agenda were reinforced, although such efforts were not always grounded in thorough analysis of instruction or cognitive needs. Because the first years of the school's existence were so demanding, it became taboo for staff to discuss issues of skill or success in teaching for fear of disrupting this fragile positive climate. The absence of serious questions worked to undermine trust and a sense of efficacy among staff, because many members suspected conversation about whether the school was successful for all students was needed, but none felt comfortable broaching the subject. Additionally, the absence of discussions about needed cognitive and instructional skills detracted from the staff's ability to use outside resources. The offerings often did not fit well with the needs of the staff and were not cumulative in their impact. Thus, from this case, we suggest that strong social support alone is not sufficient for the creation of professionally based community structures.

At Alexander the leadership came from the developing position of the school-based literacy coordinator. Chosen from the teaching ranks, she worked to develop an instructional climate superimposed on the family-like culture that had previously characterized the school. In fact, when "the principal-as-mom" began to question the authority of the literacy coordinator, levels of trust decreased among faculty, inhibiting further growth.

At Alexander the development of an emergent community was grounded in an initiative created to improve instruction. As primary teachers gained expertise in the use of new literacy techniques and methods, they also gained trust in the process and the people related to the process. Community was built out of shared instructional and cognitive needs identified by the school itself. Thus, the development of a strong cognitive base, paired with a supportive social and instructional leader in the literacy coordinator, prepared these teachers to trust one another as they learned to trust their own growing skills. However, these gains were enjoyed by only a minority of the faculty. Alexander's fragmented progression, coupled with muted power struggles within the administration of the school, underscore the importance of school-wide community and a supportive leadership core if change is to be sustained.

Developing and Mature Communities

The data from Paine and Metro paint a different picture. These schools placed cognitive knowledge and instructional skills at the forefront of their restructuring efforts and focused teaching efforts around communal goals and expectations for practice. Both had leaders who encouraged instructional improvement and supported further questioning and analysis of practice. Yet, the stories of these schools are very different. At Metro the leadership emerged from the directors of the school. Acting as facilitators of learning, these leaders worked with the staff in the creation of school climate and culture. The climate at Metro consistently stressed growth and inquiry into practice. Through meetings, mentorships, and collaborative work, the faculty were regularly expected to be open to improvement. Because all inquiry was viewed as beneficial, any faculty member, no matter how inexperienced, could present an individual or collective problem for resolution. By creating norms of valuing content and action research for faculty as well as students, the staff could build on previous success and discovery and mature together.

At Paine, the principal provided the initial pressure necessary to begin a massive school change initiative. Instead of supplying the instructional focus and modeling the practice of a particular style of teaching, the administration encourages teachers to develop different programs designed around specific and varied student needs. Continued openness to improvement is valued at Paine, yet it remains less directed from the center and more focused on semi-autonomous groups of teachers. Coupled with an action research component, such practices foster growing levels of trust and respect among faculty as they individually and jointly search for new skills and ideas related to quality pedagogy.

Summary

We conclude that a strong cognitive and skill base is necessary for teachers to focus their efforts upon school-based communities. This base provides three direct benefits for the developing school community: (a) it undergirds the development of trust and respect among staff, which in turn leads to both (b) a sense of efficacy and increased openness to improvement, and (c) the emergence of mechanisms to socialize other teachers—both newly recruited and those who have been less involved—to the professional culture and practices.

Cognitive expertise is not enough, however, to focus a school's professional community and move it toward maturity in the absence of supportive leadership. The influential teachers and administrators of the school are responsible for three distinct contributions to the development of professional community: (a) reinforcing trust and respect as efforts for the improvement of instruction are developed and refined; (b) creating an environment open to improvement effort and success; and (c) recognizing efforts that improve instruction and increase student learning, which results in an increased sense of efficacy.

In summary, the development of a social and human resource support system for schools must be based on the creation of shared cognitive and skill bases that are understood and valued by both teachers and school leaders. Supportive leadership and shared competencies establish the foundation for teachers to develop necessary social ties, rapport, trust, and respect for community to mature.[4]

Conclusion

The creation of strong professional communities holds several potential advantages for schools. Among them are the development of teachers' collective responsibility for the achievement of students and the instructional performance of teachers; increased personal commitment of professionals to their work; the establishment of values, norms, and belief structures as the instrumental control mechanism for school achievement, rather than a traditional normative control mechanism based on rules, roles, and regulations; and the establishment of flexible boundaries that lead to greater organizational learning. The creation of professional community can also militate against the teacher isolation and lack of external reward the profession offers (Chapter 2).

However, creating professional communities within schools is a complex process. In contrasting the creation of community in the five schools, we found a great deal of variability in the growth and development of community, ranging from static to mature. Our analysis suggests that, among the five dimensions of community, a shared normative and value base paired with reflective dialogue provide the most essential foundational support for professional community. In turn, these characteristics of the school's structure help create a focus on student learning, collaborative structures, and deprivatized teaching within schools that enrich the development of community structures and the quality of teachers' commitment to their work. Our analysis of both structural and social and human resource conditions necessary for the creation of community further suggests that four conditions—time, teacher empowerment/school autonomy, cognitive and skill bases, and supportive leadership—are necessary, although not solely sufficient, for the creation of strong, mature, professional communities.

Considering the cases presented Part II, we suggest that the creation of communities within schools is a difficult but obtainable goal for urban schools. The ideal professional community is one in which the collective forces of professional skill and knowledge are interconnected and complementary to school structures and social and human relationships between staff members. The cases suggest that we much view school community as integral to, rather than distinct from, school structure and culture. Rather than being an end in itself, the formation and development of mature communities become both a positive outcome for schools involved in improvement and a facilitator for stabilizing and expanding school-based reform.

Notes

1. Figure D.1 suggests strong interactions among the dimensions of professional community. See Appendix D, Figure D.1.

2. The relationships between these conditions are illustrated in Appendix D, Figure 2, which indicates linkages between structural conditions and the subsequent formation of school-based community.

3. See Appendix C, Tables C.3 and C.3a.

4. The relationships between these conditions are displayed in Appendix D, Figure 3.

9

Getting There

Promoting Professional Community

in Urban Schools

KAREN SEASHORE LOUIS
SHARON D. KRUSE

The cases presented in Part II demonstrate that professional community is possible in urban schools, but difficult to achieve. The schools in our sample were chosen because they appeared, to knowledgeable outsiders, as promising settings for the improvement of teachers' work life: They focused on empowering teachers, they had additional resources to provide external assistance from agencies that wanted to improve urban schools, and they gave evidence of interesting structural and curricular efforts that seemed to promise the possibility of liberating teachers from the stereotypical "egg carton" models of schooling, where individual teachers labor with their pupils in isolated classrooms. Yet, as we saw in Chapter 8, only two schools stand out as either mature or developing professional communities. A third, initially promising effort, withered due to both inconsistent leadership and difficulty in moving the new forms of interaction from the initial group of teachers to the whole school. A fourth failed to develop professional community during its first 5 years of effort but shows signs of living up to the promise that it initially held. The final case is a "stuck" school that shows no movement toward community. Overall, not even an optimist would claim that the results are more than a half-full cup.

We can, however, learn from these cases—not only about what not to do, but also about some promising approaches. Our case presentations have focused primarily on the daily life of schools, and the evolution of professional community. In this chapter we range beyond the cases and use additional data that bear on the roles of administrators and policymakers in urban districts. We address one critical question: What can they do to make professional community a more achievable reality? This chapter is divided into two main sections: lessons for principals or other school-based leaders, and those for educators or other key constituencies outside the schools.

Reshaping School Leadership

When the authors of the case chapters in Part II began to discuss the implications of their data, an initial reaction was that the relative success or failure in each school was largely conditioned by how well the formal leaders enacted their role. As we delved further into our data, we realized that leadership was only one aspect of the story of how school-wide professional community emerges, as we have illustrated in Chapter 8. However, in none of our cases is the leadership story an unimportant one. Our interest in elaborating the way in which school leaders can promote professional community does not, therefore, emerge from a desire to reify the role of the principal. Rather, whatever their title or formal role definition, it is clear that principals or other designated leaders continue to be best positioned to help guide faculty toward new forms of effective schooling.

A recent review of existing literature and new data examining the changing role of leadership in restructuring schools identifies several patterns that are particularly relevant to the development of professional community (Murphy & Louis, 1994):

- Effective leadership must emerge from the center of the school, rather than from the top.
- Supporting teacher success in the classroom should be the major focus of leadership.
- Change management is an integral part of the leadership role rather than an add-on task.
- Both vision and attention to detail are important.
- Providing intellectual leadership to support teachers' change efforts is critical.
- Managing school culture is as important as making the buses run on time.
- Micro-politics are central to effective restructuring and are largely managed by the school leadership.

None of the above points is novel, but they are not fully developed in the literature on school reform. Our cases elaborate on them and suggest, in addition, some new ones:

- School leaders must play a very significant role in expansion of professional community within a school.
- Even in teacher-run schools, those in formal leadership positions retain the greatest influence over the quality of professional community.

We will not treat all points separately in the discussion that follows, but we will integrate them in ways that reflect the behavior of the school leaders in our cases. In addition, although the role of change management is clearly an important subtheme in each case, we will not explore it in detail in this chapter, which will focus on the development of professional community rather than the broader topic of restructuring.

Leading From the Center:
The Role of Leaders in Teacher-Run Schools

This topic has been most extensively covered in previous research (Murphy, 1994), and our work confirms much of what has been previously said. We add to the existing findings about the need to delegate, to develop collaborative decision-making processes, and to step back from being the problem solver in a school, by linking these roles more explicitly to the development of community.

The formal titles and the role definitions of the individuals who served as school leaders in our cases varied from the traditional (at Alexander and Thomas Paine) to the decidedly avant-garde (Whitehead). Yet, in each case we also see that the formal definition of leadership was less important than the way in which it was enacted. In the more successful schools, the individual(s) in leadership positions clearly defined themselves as at the center of the school's staff rather than at the top. For example, at Metro the two directors didn't have a separate office but had desks in the common teachers' room. One of the directors was viewed as the school's master teacher, and regularly gave demonstration lessons for other faculty. Thus, the directors were regarded as leaders by the faculty, but they appear to have been viewed primarily as first among equals because of their expertise.

At Thomas Paine, the first principal who began the change program was relatively traditional in her management style and clearly occupied an authoritative position. The current principal, however, has eschewed this role, preferring instead to give leadership to others and to guide by example and by indirectly inducing thoughtfulness, rather than by making direct suggestions. For example, when problems are raised in faculty meetings, his contribution is likely to include a story that serves as a parable suggesting some choices that could be made but that requires interpretation by the faculty. Faculty, who were initially bemused by this strategy, have subsequently engaged eagerly in the discussions that ensue.

The leadership picture at Alexander, like the outcomes of its efforts to develop professional community, is mixed. The principal was the warm yet firm "mom"—one traditional role for elementary principals. In her absence, however, the literacy coordinator developed a style that was distinctly from the center, by using her position largely to bring teachers together to work through the new instructional strategies for teaching reading. Again, she physically located her office in a central location and made it an inviting gathering place devoted to professional conversation. Rather than convening formal faculty meetings as the unofficial principal, she arranged informal occasions that stimulated teacher discussion. In each instance, her role as a coordinator was played down and her role as a source of support and assistance was emphasized.

In contrast, the teacher leadership team at Whitehead clearly communicated its superior status and responsibilities to other teachers. The team had self-contained offices, as contrasted with well-equipped carrels for the others. The team ran all the meetings, determined agendas, and also persistently reminded other teachers that the team had the responsibility for deciding whether proposed actions were consistent with the school's philosophy. Thus, although they were not principals, their role was enacted from the top.

At Dewey, on the other hand, the principal declined to play even a coordinating role: Rather than leading from the top or from the center, she sat on the sidelines in the expectation that teachers would take charge, as they were supposed to under the school's design. The fact that she was frequently out of the main school building, due to her responsibilities as a principal in two other schools and meetings in the district office, distanced her even more from the life of teachers. She was, of course, not visible to most teachers and students who spent much of their time out of the building.

In summary, these cases suggest several important conclusions that relate the behavior of leaders to professional community. First, *leading from the center means being at the center.* In some cases this meant a physical presence, including a change of office; in others, being present in the classrooms and halls. Accessibility characterized all three of the schools that made the most progress toward professional community. Second, it means *giving up some typical behavior expected of leaders,* such as running meetings, being authoritative, and spending time solving problems rather than working on helping people to solve problems. The issue is not delegation of authority, and it does not mean detachment from a strong presence as a stimulus for change, as we will discuss further below. Third, it means using every opportunity to stimulate discussion: Being at the center of a professional community means *creating the networks of conversation that tie faculty together* around common issues of instruction and teaching.

Supporting Teachers in the Classroom

We have asserted in Chapter 2 and Chapter 8 that professional community is intimately tied to increased cognitive understanding of instruction and learning, and to a more sophisticated repertoire of teaching skills. This contention suggests that individual learning provides the foundation for the development of the group. Community can reinforce individual learning, but it may not be a sufficient stimulus.

Our cases suggest that focusing attention on the needs of individual teachers—that is, providing instructional leadership—is a critical aspect of the community development process. It is ironic that at least some reports about the impact of restructuring on the principal's role suggest that they find that new principal responsibilities associated with school-based management, teacher empowerment, and general change management have reduced the time devoted to issues of instruction (Murphy, 1994). These pressures are clearly present in our case studies. Given the complex nature of change in these schools, what did the leaders do to help individual teachers?

The answers are varied, but point to a simple conclusion: In all three of our more successful schools, roles were differentiated so that there were additional people available to provide support to individual teachers. In Metro, for example, there were two directors. One covered administrative tasks outside the school and filled needed professional and political liaison functions with other agencies and groups. The other stayed at the school and focused on teaching and support to teachers. Given the small size of Metro's staff—only 11 full-time teachers and 16 staff in total, of which 2 were in the director positions—the potential was high for reaching all teachers when they needed help. In addition, the school's strong tradition of bringing individual pedagogical problems to be solved through group discussion provided additional support for individual teacher growth, while simultaneously reinforcing community responsibility for teaching. In this school, responsibility for supporting improved instruction was a leadership function shared by all, although it was orchestrated by the directors.

At Thomas Paine, support for individual teachers was not provided directly by the principal. Instead, much of the support for this large school comes from three external sources: (a) university faculty associated with the Professional Development School; (b) the district's Professional Development Plan process, supported by a staff member from the district office who works with individual teachers; and (c) the mentorship program, funded by the state, which pairs mentor teachers with less experienced colleagues. Although none of these is a substitute for the intense, direct intervention provided at Metro, in a large school such support does have the advantage of being person-independent (when faculty from the university cycle in and out, or the district's Professional Development Plan specialist turns over, the support system does not come to a halt) and flexible in meeting the needs of a staff that is far more diverse than Metro's in terms of experience and expertise.

Alexander, with its exceptional needs for individual development, combines the internal and external support models seen in Metro and Paine. Outside experts are the source of training and follow-up support for faculty, and the combination of the literacy coordinator (who is trusted to visit classrooms and work with individual teachers on instruction) and an external liaison (who helps the literacy coordinator) provided enough individual attention to help the teachers in the lower grades. This level of support, though far more generous than is available to most schools, proved inadequate when the program was expanded to the upper four grades, and the principal failed to back the restructuring efforts.

A close reading of the cases should make it clear that, although individual support is needed in all contexts, the amount varies with the level of skill and expertise among the staff. Metro had as much as it needed with the regular attention of a teaching director; Alexander required two full-time people attached to the site, and intensive training from an array of experts, in order to meet the needs of the initial target group of the primary faculty. The resources that worked well at Paine were more than those at Metro, but far less than at Alexander, matching the characteristics of the staff, which varied from expert teacher to novice.

In neither Whitehead nor Dewey did the leaders pay attention to helping individual teachers improve their classroom skills. Although Whitehead organized several teaching teams that paired experienced and inexperienced teachers, in the classrooms that we observed no feedback was given to inexperienced teachers even when their instructional strategies were clearly poor. Although the physical layout of the building provided easy opportunity for teachers and teacher leaders to observe one another (all classrooms either had large walls of glass or were open spaces), teachers rarely sought or gave assistance to one another.

At Dewey, where the level of teacher skills in experiential education was poor, teachers were not offered any opportunities for individual consultation or feedback. In both schools, the low skill level of some teachers was one of the undiscussible issues facing the school. In other words, because instruction was hard to discuss with peers who were known to be ineffective teachers, the development of community focused on teaching and learning was obviously inhibited.

The main points of this discussion are that (a) leaders need to provide attention to *individual teacher development* in their particular classrooms; (b) they do not need to do so directly but can *rely on others within and outside the school* as long as they ensure that support is actually available; and (c) for teachers to feel comfortable asking for and receiving assistance as individuals, the school needs to foster *a climate where instruction is viewed as problematic* and is often discussed.

Focusing Change: Visions of Professional Community

Principals and other school leaders help in keeping the staff focused on the big picture and making sure that the resources are in place daily to support teachers' professional community. The leadership of the school sets the tone for the larger school culture, and the emergent school community takes its cue from the leadership model the school employs. It is important that school leaders be aware of the differing patterns and forms of community relationships that can develop. In the cases included in Part II, we saw two distinct forms of vision for community: democratic and autocratic. Although community can be developed using autocratic leadership styles, it will, according to most writers, be a different kind of community. Simply stated, democratic communities are marked by a fair process that assures the equitable treatment of members of the community (Bryk, Lee, & Holland, 1993; Bull, Fruehling, & Chattergy, 1992; Kymlicka, 1991). A democracy is more than a form of government; it is primarily a mode of associated living through communicated experience. The process of communicating ideas, ideals, shared concerns, and interests forms the foundation of democratic practice.

In contrast, the autocratic community is marked by a lack of a concern for the process by which decision making occurs and the subsequent treatment of individuals for which those decisions have import (Crowley, 1987; Gutman, 1987; Kymlicka, 1990; Mann, 1986). Autocratic leaders hold all the cards; their power is unlimited and domineering. The leader decides, perhaps with the help of a few trusted confidants, the policy and practice for others of the community. Thus, school climate and culture are marked by set notions, unquestioned policies, and a sense of the status quo as all there is or could be.

Access to influence, determination of topics that are priorities for discussion, who gets what information and when, and how decisions are made are all influenced by the style of leadership employed within the school. The style of leadership, be it democratic, autocratic, or somewhere in between, influences the probability that communal ties, rather than associative ties, will emerge. Figure 9.1, based on the work of Sargent and Miller (1971, p. 245) and Ball (1987), contrasts the behavior of autocratic and democratic leaders.

The democratic group, exemplified by Metro and Paine, permits dissent between members, and the result is increased learning for all members of the organization rather than just a few individuals. Tradition is not blindly preserved, rather it is challenged, discussed, and used to hone the common underlying principles on which the community rests. The autocratic community, exemplified to some extent by Alexander and to a greater extent by Whitehead, may be efficient and even exciting on the surface (remember that Whitehead demonstrated excellence in teaching and overwhelmed its many visitors with the overt manifestations of its alternative approach to schooling), but it cannot sustain the professional dialogue and growth that we have been discussing in this book.

We conclude that school leaders in our more effective schools held not only an emergent vision of schooling, but also an emergent vision of professional community. Even when this was not explicitly articulated, *the ability of the leadership to effect changes within the school depended to a great extent on its vision of a democratically based professional community.* This proved, particularly in the case of Paine, to be more

	Autocratic Community	Democratic Community
Access to Influence	Group involvement is defined by those in power.	Each group member is given opportunity for influence.
Goals	Group goals are defined by power leaders.	Alternative goals are discussed.
Parameters of Discussion	Discussion is limited to the party line.	Novel approaches to the status quo are explored.
Facilitative Roles	Efforts are made to control interactions of members.	Efforts are made to stimulate new ideas.
Information Flow	Inner circle controls knowledge of the organization.	Members are given all available information.
Decision Making	Decisions are made quickly.	Group consensus is preferable; time is taken to reach decisions.
Group Cohesion	Cohesion is measured by adherence to values set by the power elite.	Cohesion is formed by affirmation of opposing viewpoints and relationships.

Figure 9.1. Visions of Autocratic and Democratic Community

important than the compelling nature of its ideas about the education of students.

Managing Culture:
Providing Intellectual Leadership

Mohrman and Cummings (1989) put acquiring and grappling with knowledge at the top of their list of the foundational characteristics of self-designing, high-performance organizations. Consistent with this, the culture of emergent professional communities in our cases is a decidedly intellectual one. Teachers at Metro, as we have noted, struggle with problems of practice at a conceptual as well as a practical level because they are committed to inquiry; teachers at Alexander attended workshops and discussed their homework because they were engaged with new ideas. At Thomas Paine, many teachers were involved in brown bag lunches (occasionally with university faculty), where they discussed new conceptual approaches to teaching as well as how these practices would apply to Paine.

Leaders in these more successful schools were very active in supporting a culture of inquiry and the use of ideas, particularly ideas brought in from outside the school. Conspicuously absent was the "not invented here" attitude that prevents teachers from thinking about alternative practices and educational approaches designed elsewhere.

However, in general, individual teachers in these schools did not operate as autonomous intellectuals who actively sought and incorporated ideas from research and other practice settings into their work. Instead, we saw school leaders playing the most active role in foraging outside the school for ideas and people to help teachers increase their skills and their active inquiry into their practices. This role for leaders was clearest at Metro, where a director served as the active liaison between the school and a network of educators involved in alternative education. Although all Metro teachers frequently searched for information and resources to carry out school projects, and to attach students to their settings in inquiry learning, it was the director who brought in information about new ideas, strategies, and practices that were being developed elsewhere. At Alexander, this role was delegated in part by the principal to university-based support groups. However, the success of this partnership was dependent on the principal's championing of it. Initially, the principal worked with teachers to convince them of the value of working with outside groups and the new ideas that they brought in to help students. The importance of a principal's championing an effort is illustrated by the decline in effectiveness of the outside groups when the principal withdrew support.

Paine is the exception to this generalization because, with the support of the Professional Development School effort, teachers are coming to see their role as brokers of knowledge from both inside and outside. Even at Paine, however, the principal actively reinforced the need for information and data, sometimes generated inside and sometimes externally acquired, to decide "What is working and how do we know?" Teachers independently bring new ideas to the teams with the principal's blessing. By promoting action research in the school, he has promoted the role of teachers as both generators and consumers of knowledge.

In sum, in these deprived and dispirited urban schools with no history of informal exchanges with universities or research and development on teaching, it strikes us as highly unlikely that we would have observed the emergence of conceptual thinking had this not also been a priority for the principal.

A striking characteristic of Whitehead and Dewey is their relative lack of access to the ideas about school reform and instructional practices that are readily available in professional literature, and their inability to generate information about their own practices within the school. Although both were designed by people who were well connected to networks of reformers around the country, the leaders in the schools did not play an active role in stimulating the teachers to get access to and make use of them. Teachers in these two schools, left to their own initiative, appeared to have neither experience with nor personal connections to sources of knowledge and ideas. This is most profoundly apparent at Dewey, where the widely available expertise on experiential education was never tapped by teachers, either individually or collectively, until a staff member associated with this research project connected them to a conference on the subject. At Dewey, the absence of new ideas from outside the school appears to have been at least part of the reason why efforts to coordinate and discuss big educational ideas were frustrated.

We conclude that teachers need sustained discussion of important ideas and mutual support for finding new practices developed elsewhere to enhance professional community, but this will be more likely to occur *if principals are active in either personally building bridges to the world of research and development outside the school*, or actively pushing the role of external assistance that can do so. Even the hand-picked faculties of Whitehead and Metro, which included many exceptionally able teachers, needed a leadership initiative to sustain a culture of intellectual ferment.

Micro-Politics and Professional Community

Reform efforts in urban schools are highly susceptible to failure induced from outside. Managing relationships with external groups so that teachers feel more empowered is critical to successful improvement (Louis & Miles, 1990). Beck (1994) asserts that a key emerging role for principals in restructuring schools involves managing the internal conflicts that are inevitably associated with change. Our analysis of school-wide professional community, which emphasizes commonality, collegiality, and cooperation, should not be interpreted as excluding conflict. Good communities encourage debate, and debates engender the potential for division. Without some conflict, the professional communities would become completely unified in their approach to teaching and learning, and become even more likely than fragmented schools to resist ideas that challenge their consensus. Argyris and Schön (1978) have argued persuasively that in order for organizations to be genuinely reflective, they must challenge their own values—a process that inevitably induces conflict.

When we look at our cases, it is apparent that in the most successful professional communities—Metro and Thomas Paine—the management of conflict was largely embedded within the activities of the professional community. Principals, by and large, do not personally resolve conflicts but provide a supportive environment and structures in which teachers resolve them through discussion and debate. Conflict resolution is not judicial in style, but in most cases involves incremental and persistent efforts to confront disagreements. By providing many forums for discussion and debate, teachers frequently appear to arrive at an agreement about action that did not avoid differences but adjudicated them in an apparently seamless way. An outside observer might question whether Metro, at least during the time that we observed it, engaged in serious discussion of its basic values, and whether the unquestioned consensus about inquiry learning may have created an environment that prevented consideration of alternatives to the school's vision. It is hard, for example, to imagine a Metro teacher telling his or her colleagues that the inquiry method was not suitable for all of the children enrolled in the school.

This was clearly not true with Paine, where teachers in the different teams needed to justify their choices to each other and, at least in some meetings, confronted each other in ways that caused a reassessment of decisions and actions. The case notes that these debates were more likely to occur in small meetings, where people had more time to explain their positions, and more attention was paid to "hard listening." Teachers who did not wish to play a part in these tougher discussions were not, however, forced to do so. This means that Paine's management of the micro-politics of the school operated at two levels: One is open and largely positive, where people argued and reached positions reflecting the views of multiple teachers but still respected the positions of others; but the other is the traditional mode of simply ignoring conflict. As Paine demonstrates, it is the former activity that leads to community, but the latter results in a persistence of autonomous naysayers. The conflict management strategy at Paine is deeply influenced by the leadership style of the principal, whose willingness to live with ambiguity and tolerance for diversity among the staff is also coupled with a preference for incremental approaches to conflict resolution. The effectiveness of the strategies for conflict management at Paine is likely to be put to a more severe test in the coming year, as faculty confront issues of multiculturalism in the school and curriculum; but at least there is a solid foundation of experience in effectively resolving hard issues within the faculty.

Patterns of conflict management at Alexander and Whitehead are sadly similar. In both cases the faculty were aware of conflicts, but generally avoided discussing them because of overt or covert discouragement by the school leadership. Many of the conflicts appeared to quickly devolve into issues of power and control, rather than staying centered on ideas and the development of strong justifications for educational action. These schools are classic cases of micro-politics as described by Blase (1992), in which community interest is ultimately subordinated to perceived self-interest.

We conclude that effective school leaders manage conflicts that arise within professional communities by (a) *encouraging forums that are safe, and hard listening settings* for teachers to discuss differences of opinion; (b) *constantly reinforcing community values and effectiveness, rather than self-interest, as the criteria against which differences should be adjudicated;* and (c) *being willing to live with ambiguity* as data are used to assess and resolve differences. By doing so, conflict management reinforces rather than fragments community.

Extending Professional Community

Professional community is like most other major innovations in education: The problem is typically not to find enthusiasts to begin the hard work of change, but to move change beyond the initial implementers to include all or most faculty. Without the movement beyond the enthusiasts, however, community will remain, at best, fragmented. This is an issue primarily for existing schools whose faculty have long been used to individualism and autonomy in the classroom. In many new schools of choice, on the other hand, teachers can be recruited because of their interest in whatever curricular or instructional vision has been chosen as the focus, and they thus in reality share some common perspective; Metro is a case in point. However, as is clear from the case of Whitehead, the problem of extending community throughout the staff may also affect other new schools designed to grow in stages.

At Paine, the initial phase of community development was headed toward fragmentation. Community was easily achieved within the initial International Baccalaureate team and subsequently within the other small teams (Essentials and Open). But the question of how to get teachers involved across teams, and especially to integrate the diffuse Comprehensive team and the special education SPREAD team into the conversations was confronted directly by the teachers, though it is not yet fully resolved. Although the teams reflected natural groupings of teachers, external stimulus from the linkage with the University in a Professional Development School and the state-mandated Outcomes Assessment provided a framework for cross-team discussions that kept the issue of school-wide professional community on the agenda.

At Alexander and Whitehead, the problem of extending community was neither fully anticipated nor resolved. In both schools, the development of community within the initial group—the primary teachers at Alexander, and the lead teachers at Whitehead—was observable. At Alexander, however, intermediate and upper-grade teachers, who were not involved in the first year of the literacy program, were unreceptive and showed little interest in participating as newcomers in the discussions and changes in teaching. The teachers recruited to Whitehead after the opening year felt not only left out of the discussions about the school's purpose and curriculum but also excluded from the cohesive teacher leader group that believed itself to be the "keepers of the vision."

The role of leaders at these schools in the process of making community inclusive is clear. At Paine, the current principal is very sensitive to issues of inclusion and has focused much of his attention on identifying issues that cross all teams—such as the upcoming focus for the 1994–1995 school year on multiculturalism and the support for the university linkage. These efforts have increased school-wide community, although they have not eliminated the basic problem of enlarging cohesiveness beyond the teams. Most teachers acknowledge that it is still difficult to get everyone working on a school-wide agenda. However, the fact that many teachers recognize this as an issue that they and the principal must deal with is a sign that he has effectively instilled the belief that school-wide community is an important goal.

At Alexander and Whitehead, on the other hand, leaders seemed ambivalent about fostering school-wide professional community, as distinct from their commitment to promoting solid instructional practices. At Alexander, the principal praised individual teachers whose classroom instruction improved but did not consistently support teachers' collective dialogue. At Whitehead, the teacher leaders, who simply didn't understand that newcomers would not share their understanding of the school, viewed discordant ideas as personally threatening. Efforts by other teachers to create opportunities for informal discussion (as in the pizza nights), were ignored by the teacher leaders, although their opinions and values would in all likelihood have carried a great deal of weight in this context. At neither Alexander nor Whitehead, however, would we view the inattention to spreading professional community exclusively in terms of a need to preserve power relationships within in school, although this may have been an element. Rather, interviews with the leaders suggest that they simply did not understand that creating community is a difficult task, which requires inventing activities to pull many faculty together to achieve a specific common goal. Here the example of Metro is instructive: Although Metro had a small, handpicked faculty, the significance of the all-school fall project as a way of annually reinforcing the interdependent nature of their work should not be overlooked.

In summary, our cases suggest that expansion of emerging professional communities is a key issue for schools who are restructuring, and that leaders play a key role in fostering this process. Among these, the most important is *creating meaningful opportunities for teachers to come together across subgroups* to work on issues of concern to all. Because teachers tend to be focused on the immediate work of their own groups or teams, and have less access to the outside resources that may help to catalyze opportunities for all-school activity, this is unlikely to occur without administrative foresight and involvement.

Implications for Policy

The above discussion identifies the concrete actions of leaders in urban schools that promote school-wide professional community. We do not have direct information in the cases about policy setting outside the school that can have a similar effect, but we can draw on other data not presented here to develop several inferences about what may need to be done in districts (and, by implication, some states) to enhance results.

Providing Support for School-Based Management

Most urban districts have, by now, instituted some policy that supports school-based management, even if they are located in a state that does not officially espouse this as a policy directive. However, the gap between policy and support is wide. Let us here examine Whitehead and Dewey, both located in cities with a reputation for progressive, excellent education. In both instances the districts had either a district-wide or an optional program for school-based management; both Dewey and Whitehead were among those so classified. But what did this mean in practice?

In general, we find that these two schools, like others reviewed in Louis and Murphy (1994), received ambiguous signals about their march down their own road to school reform. Whitehead was besieged by negative publicity surrounding standardized testing scores. Rather than insulating the new school from this district requirement for a period, to allow them to develop their own portfolio assessments, the superintendent demanded that they increase scores in a 1-year period, or face curtailment of their experiment. Not surprisingly, teacher discussions focused more on standardized tests than on improving portfolio assessment. At Dewey, the district negotiated extremely expensive space for the home base that was not only inadequate but also made the implementation of the community-based program more difficult. The school was given no leeway to find its own facilities, where the physical plant might have been more conducive to both the teaching and the teacher development programs. The point is not that either district was malevolent, but that their own short-term needs distracted them from a focus on a more democratic form of decentralized management, which would have allowed each school to control key aspects of their program—assessment and location/space.

Although principals/school leaders in all of our cases worked hard to buffer their schools against district decisions that may have been rational from a system perspective, but were decidedly irrational when viewed from a school perspective, teachers' professional community suffered. Where teachers do not believe that the system understands them—whether the system is the district office, the teachers' union, or organized constituencies in the business community—it becomes easier to complain and harder to focus on the hard work of dialogue, development, and change. In our view, even moderately sized urban districts are more prone to this than smaller districts, where top-level central administrators are more likely to be in touch with schools and understand how they vary. In Dewey's district there were 60 schools; in Whitehead's, approximately 45. Both these numbers are too large to ensure intimate knowledge of buildings without a strong priority on doing so.

Policies to Ensure Effective School Leadership

Our discussion above highlights the significant role of building-level leadership in the development of professional community. Yet, in only two of our cases was building leadership up to the task of understanding and promoting professional community. Without any data other than access to both unpublished and published materials from other researchers, we would venture the guess that our two-out-of-five finding is not very far off the mark for the general population of schools; and it corresponds closely to the findings for Chicago Elementary Schools reported by Bryk et al. (1993). We observe, in addition, that most districts have weak or entirely inadequate systems of recruiting and supporting building-level leadership (Louis, 1994). When principals retire, it is rare to recruit a replacement with much attention to the specific match between the capacities of the applicant and the needs of the school. Nor do systems pay much attention to principal assessment. Dewey's sidelines principal for its first 4 years was rewarded for her difficult job by a promotion to a regular school; Paine's acquisition of the talented James Hissop was more likely due to his race than to thoughtful attention to his skills in that setting, and although he had limited administrative experience and was put in charge of "the worst in the city," he received no special support or training. The problems with the teacher leaders at Whitehead were known to the district office after a formative evaluation report was delivered in the second year, but there was little intervention to develop the skills and consensus that might have allowed them to succeed. Whitehead had a titular half-time principal, who might have provided assistance of this kind, but there were three occupants of this position in 5 years, one of whom was on a phased retirement, and another of whom was a self-proclaimed traditional educator who was not in favor of the educational approach espoused at Whitehead. Alexander's case suggests that community control will be no panacea: A community with limited social capital, grateful for the principal's work in creating a safe haven for kids, would not have the skills to assess whether the match between the principal's style and the school improvement effort was appropriate.

Policies to Link Schools
With Information and Assistance

Only one school in our study—Whitehead—could be assessed as advantaged in terms of formal resources (budget and facilities). All of the others survive, like most urban schools, on a shoestring. Yet they varied enormously in terms of their ability to get access to and make use of resources that are readily available if one knows how to and believes it is important to seek them. In all three cases where schools were effectively linked to outside assistance and information, it was largely outside district policy. The only exception to this was Paine's use of the district's Professional Development Plan consultant. As we noted in Chapter 1, the socioeconomic and organizational conditions of urban schools tend to make them more isolated. Unless districts intervene to help, reform efforts will be dependent on a talented school leader who is serendipitously linked to useful sources of assistance, or a chance encounter that creates an interest in a particular school by a prospective supplier of ideas.

Providing Leadership to Direct Community
Attention to Teachers' Needs in Restructuring

As was discussed in Chapter 1, urban schools often exist in settings where the goals and means for educating children are even more contested than in other communities. Unfortunately, there is a tendency for education, because it consumes most of the local tax dollars, to become a political football, tossed between the proponents of community control, the central bureaucracy, and various players in the political establishment. In only a few cities have leaders crafted a common language to describe the needs and the focus of schools. In even fewer does this common focus include attention to the needs of teachers, in addition to students and learning. The cities in which our schools were located are generally supportive of education, and state legislatures have proven willing (albeit in a grumbling fashion) to allocate additional resources to meet the special needs of the urban centers. Yet the politics of control being played out in district offices, city councils, and school boards continue to consume enormous amounts of energy on the part of school-based authorities, distracting them from the needs of professional community. It is clear (at least to us) that education needs more powerful voices for community— community that includes professional needs and also incorporates the broader parental community, a topic not discussed in this volume. Schools will continue to struggle toward better educational alternatives for the increasingly disparate range of students who enter their doors, but for them to succeed, they deserve far more consistent intellectual leadership from the top.

Draft Outline

Longitudinal Case Studies

I. Description of the School
   A. Staffing/Key Staff
   B. Structure
      1. Organizational Chart
      2. Formal Communication Structures/Procedures
   C. Key Restructuring Activities
      1. Student Experiences
      2. Teachers' Professional Work
      3. Leadership and Governance
      4. Relationships With Parents/Community/External Resources
   D. District Context
   E. Physical Plant
   F. Distinctive Features of Organizational Culture
   G. Other Important Features

II. Historical Overview—How Did the School Get the Way It Is?
   A. Role of Current Teachers and Administrators
   B. District Role
   C. Other Key Actors
   D. Chronology of Key Events
   E. Appendices (List)

III. Decision Making
   A. Key Decision Domains Being Tracked (Brief Description)
   B. For Each Domain:
      1. How did the domain get to the top of the priority list: Who decided?
      2. Who has a part to play in decision making—what are the roles of various actors?
      3. What are the "rules" or norms governing decision making?
      4. What communication channels are used during the decision process?
      5. Provide a chronology of key events/decisions.
   C. How Do Power and Politics Work in the School Context?
   D. How Do Organizational Environment, Leadership, Structures (Including the Authority and Communication Structures), and Climate Affect the Decision-Making Process?
   E. What Are the Implications for Teachers' Roles in Restructuring?

IV. Professional Communities
   A. What Do Teachers Talk About When They Get Together Informally? At Staff Meetings?
      1. Is there any evidence of a shared language?
      2. Are dialogues consistent across groups?
      3. To what degree does "teacher talk" involve exchanging/using knowledge?
      4. Where does reflective dialogue occur?
   B. What Are the Patterns of Groups and Networks for Exchange of Professional Knowledge and Ideas?
   C. How Is Professionalism Defined by Teachers and Others? (Implicit Definitions Are Okay Right Now.)
   D. How Is Community Defined by Teachers and Others? What Type of Community Do Teachers See Themselves as Belonging to?
   E. How Does Staff Development Relate to the Development of Professional Community?

    F. What Evidence Exists That Relationships in the School Exhibit:
       1. Trust
       2. Community
       3. Professionalism?
    G. How Do Organizational Environment, Leadership, Structures, and Climate Affect the Decision-Making Process?
    H. What Are the Implications for Teachers' Roles in Restructuring?

V. Organizational Learning
    A. How Does the School Go About Getting Information From External Sources?
       1. What external sources are used, and for what purposes?
       2. How often/how deeply does the school use external sources?
    B. How Does the School Go About Getting Information From Internal Sources?
       1. What kinds of internal information are collected and for what purposes? (curriculum, student performance, parent satisfaction, etc.)
       2. How is internally generated information used?
    C. How Does the School Process Information (Interpretation, Distribution, Memory)?
       1. What does the school do with information that challenges the assumptions of what is being done?
       2. What does the school do with information that supports what is being done?
       3. How often, and under what circumstances, does reflective dialogue seem to occur?
       4. What evidence, if any, exists that points to organizational learning disabilities? (paradigm peddling/politics, fruitless cycling in-and-out of ideas, etc.)
    D. How Do Organizational Environment, Leadership, Structures, and Climate Affect the Decision-Making Process?

E. What Are the Implications for Teachers' Roles in Restructuring?

VI. What Are the Facilitators and Barriers to Long-Term Restructuring?
   A. What Are the Current Problems and Issues Facing the School? (These May Include Human Resources, Structure, Power and Politics, Environment, etc.)
      1. To what extent do these affect teachers' work?
      2. To what extent do these affect student experiences?
   B. What Process Is Used to Address These Problems/Issues?
   C. What Are the Facilitators That Support the Staff in Addressing Problems/Issues?

Outline of the Elements
of a Professional Community

I. Professionalism and Community
   A. Professionalization emphasizes:
      1. A technical knowledge base shared among all members of the profession.
      2. Membership control over entry to the profession.
      3. The norm of client-orientation (putting client needs before personal interest and treating all clients as equally deserving of professional attention).
   B. Community emphasizes:
      1. The importance of broadly shared values and norms of behavior.
      2. The importance of a sense of responsibility for the collective good.
      3. The need for an extended relationship of caring between individuals.
   C. Professional community and organizational community:
      1. The professional community model emphasizes the universally applicable knowledge base, values, and so on. Identification is with the discipline/profession.
      2. The organizational community literature emphasizes the values, caring relationships, climate, and the like as factors affecting organizational performance.

Knowledge of the organizational setting is assumed to improve performance.

3. A school-based model of professional community focuses on integrating 1 and 2.

II. School-Based Professional Community: Why Would We Want It?
   A. Increased collective responsibility (across individuals/departments) for performance (performance may be defined more broadly than increased student achievement).
   B. Increased personal commitment of professionals to their work; increased willingness to work hard for the goals of the school.
   C. Empowerment of teachers, which may reinforce A and B.

III. School-Based Professional Community: What Are Its Specific Characteristics?
   A. Reflective Dialogue: conversations about serious educational issues or problems that involve the application of new knowledge in a sustained manner. Reflective dialogue frequently results in implications for changed behavior.
   B. Deprivatization of Practice: frequent examination of individual teaching behaviors, through both observation and case analysis that is rooted in the desire to improve.
   C. Collective Focus on Student Learning (as opposed to teaching strategies or techniques).
   D. Collaboration: involvement of professional staff in developmental activities that have consequences for more than one person. Collaboration must go beyond collegiality, which may involve superficial exchanges of help, support, or assistance.
   E. Shared Norms/Values:
      1. Professional staff must share a commitment to both the outcomes of professional community (II.A-II.D) and the central features of professional community (III.A-III.B).

2. Additional values observed in restructuring schools include (a) all students can learn; (b) all students are of equal value; (c) expanded responsibility of professional staff for student development that goes beyond academic achievement; (d) a sense of obligation to keep learning about the craft of teaching; and (e) shared beliefs about how to treat students in and out of class, for example, how to deal with student behavior.

IV. What Conditions Support the Development of School-Based Professional Community?
   A. Structural Conditions:
      1. Time to meet and talk.
      2. Small size.
      3. Physical proximity.
      4. Interdependent formal teaching roles (team teaching, etc.).
      5. Communication structures/networks (E-mail, regular meetings, etc.).
      6. School autonomy, teacher empowerment (SBM/SDM).
      7. Control over membership (ability to select teachers and administrators; some ability to encourage nonsupportive staff to leave).
   B. Social and Human Resources:
      1. Openness to improvement/willingness to accept feedback.
      2. Trust and respect from relevant colleagues and the district.
      3. Adequate cognitive and skill base; understanding of the knowledge base for effective teaching and learning.
      4. Supportive leadership (postheroic leaders who do not view themselves as the architects of school effectiveness).
      5. Relatively intensive socialization processes.

Comparisons of Schools in the Study

Table C.1 Schools Ranked by Dimensions

	Dewey	**Metro**	**Whitehead**	**Paine**	**Alexander***
Reflective Dialogue	4	1	3	2	2 / 4
Depriva-tization of Practice	4	1	4	2	2 / 4
Focus on Student Learning	4	1	2	2	2 / 4
Collaboration	3	1	3	1	2 / 4
Shared Norms and Values	3	1	3	2	2 / 4

Ranking Scale
1. Dimension is consistently present, a defining factor of the school; is structurally and socially normative.
2. Dimension is consistently present, yet is not consistently utilized by the full faculty in an ongoing manner.
3. Dimension is inconsistently present, a secondary by-product of other school factors and/or dimensions; not structurally or socially normative.
4. Dimension lacks presence, undefined or unclear in relation to school goals.
NOTE: *Number above the line refers to the first year of the change effort, below refers to the decline during the second year.

Table C.2 Structural Conditions—Ranked Schools

	Dewey	Metro	Whitehead	Paine	Alexander
Time to Meet and Talk	4	1	3	1	3
Physical Proximity	4	1	3	1	4
Inter-dependent Teaching Roles	4	1	4	2	4
Communication Structures and Networks	2	1	3	4	4
Teacher Empowerment and School Autonomy	3	1	3	1	4

Ranking Scale
1. Present and serves as a facilitator to the formation of professional community.
2. Present and serves as a facilitator toward the formation of professional community in portions of the faculty.
3. Present but is not utilized in ways that facilitate formation of professional community.
4. Absence of structure impedes the formation of professional community.

Table C.2a Structural Conditions/Supporting Data

	Dewey	Metro	Whitehead	Paine	Alexander
Time to Meet and Talk	• Off-site classes and disparate schedules impede the ability of staff to create time-planning instruction.	• Staff meetings organized to provide feedback concerning issues of teaching and learning.	• School calendar designed to have formal weekly meetings and 20 developmental days.	• Teams have joint planning time. • Forums and brown bag lunches provide opportunity for larger groups to discuss issues of teaching and learning.	• Closed campus inhibits creation of time during the school day. • Optional morning meetings serve to begin building partial community.
Physical Proximity	• School design and philosophy hinder the formation of professional community as off-site classes keep staff separate.	• Faculty offices grouped to provide maximum contact as classes are spread throughout another school building.	• Faculty offices are situated for maximum personal and technological contact.	• Administrators try to place team members in rooms near each other.	• Traditional classroom structures, scheduling, and school norms inhibited creative use of physically close rooms.
Interdependent Teaching Roles	• Lack of physical proximity and time obstructs staff efforts to create interdependence.	• Cotaught labs. • New teacher apprentice relationships. • External contact.	• Opportunity existed for teachers and students to design and implement inter- and intradisciplinary classes.	• Some teams work toward shared interdisciplinary planning and interdependence.	• Traditional structures, norms, and schedules did not encourage interdependence.

(continued)

Table C.2a (Continued)

	Dewey	Metro	Whitehead	Paine	Alexander
Communication Structures and Networks	• Extensive traditional meeting structures exist although staff lacks cognitive base to create needed dialogue.	• Formal staff meetings for curriculum and informal regular memos from directors.	• Extensive traditional and electronic mail structures exist yet were not utilized in deep or meaningful ways.	• Extensive formal and informal meetings provide teachers time to jointly plan. • School-wide communication weak, lacking multiple structures for full group discussion.	• Hierarchical administrative structures patterned communication as linear and nondialectic.
Teacher Empowerment and School Autonomy	• Waivers and magnet program status allow staff to plan instruction and curriculum within stated philosophy and goals.	• Courses designed and planned around teacher identified issues. • Mini-school status.	• Students and teachers developed individualized learning plans and courses for maximum student engagement.	• Multiple structures promote teacher-led initiatives. • Collective focus on improvement of practice is normative.	• Introduction of cognitive and affective skill bases created readiness among staff for expanded roles.

Table C.3 Social and Human Resource Conditions—
Ranked Schools

	Dewey	Metro	Whitehead	Paine	Alexander
Openness to Improve- ment	2	1	4	1	2
Trust and Respect	4	1	4	1	2
Cognitive and Skill Base	4	1	3	2	2
Supportive Leadership	4	1	4	1	2
Socialization	3	1	4	3	2
Sense of Efficacy	4	1	3	3	2

Ranking Scale
1. Present and serves as a facilitator to formation of professional community.
2. Present and serves as a facilitator toward the formation of professional community in portions of the faculty.
3. Present but is not utilized in ways that facilitate formation of professional community.
4. Absence of structure impedes the formation of professional community.

Table C.3a Social and Human Resource Conditions—Supporting Data

	Dewey	Metro	Whitehead	Paine	Alexander
Openness to Improvement	• Staff remains eager for new curricula and pedagogical models, yet lacks the abilities to obtain useful developmental activities.	• Teaching/learning experiences designed around inquiry and seminar-style instruction. • Mentorships and team models of teaching normative.	• Leadership actively discourages the introduction of new ideas, favoring instead a dependence upon individual rather than group expertise.	• Outcomes accreditation, commitment to research, and PDS status focuses on continual improvement. • Leadership actively encourages initiatives focused to increase student achievement and success.	• Unclear at leadership levels. • Primary teachers actively seek new instructional and pedagogical skills in literacy.
Trust and Respect	• Norms related to conflict avoidance hinder the staff's ability to create a social basis for trust and respect.	• Strong levels of freedom exist in relation to planning of curriculum. • As a result of good teaching, trust and respect are created.	• Poor climate, in part, a product of the leadership hierarchy, inhibits the ability to build trust and respect.	• Strong levels of trust and respect for teacher effort and initiative exist.	• Efforts to build trust and respect prove effective as primary teachers attend mini-meetings and developmental activities.
Cognitive and Skill Base	• Poor resource base related to school philosophy and goals inhibits the rise of expertise.	• Expertise is developed through meetings, mentorships, and collaborative work.	• Individual teachers have distinct cognitive and instructional skill bases, yet these are unevenly distributed and shared.	• Growing numbers of faculty exhibit strong trust and respect for teachers' skill levels. • PDS status focuses on the creation of knowledge about and respect for others' work.	• Literacy initiative and mentorship roles create a cognitive and skill base in reading for primary faculty.

	Dewey	Metro	Whitehead	Paine	Alexander
Supportive Leadership	• Strong socioemotional leadership exists, although intellectual- and discipline-based leadership are lacking.	• Facilitative, transformational leadership style is favored over more traditional models.	• External pressures and creation of a layered hierarchy and individualistic personalities impede the development of professional community.	• Long-term supportive leadership continued for school change efforts. • Teacher ownership in programs and practices encouraged through teacher leadership positions.	• Principal's return following illness mediated against formation of professional community. • Literacy coordinator provided support for instructional goals.
Socialization	• Teams serve as a basis for integration but rarely focus on professional community.	• Immersion in experience through modeling and mentoring is normative.	• School climate impedes socialization as staff lack handbooks and training/development opportunities.	• School size and varied team foci impede strong faculty-wide socialization. • Teacher teams model instructional innovations for members.	• Within the literacy effort, socialization to instructional and cognitive skills is high.
Sense of Efficacy	• Lacking needed cognitive skills and leadership, teachers do not feel successful in their efforts.	• Success is experienced in relation to strong teaching/learning practices. • Shared moral obligation to teaching creates efficacy.	• School climate hindered widespread feelings of success among faculty.	• Previous history and extensive problems within the student population hinder teachers' efforts within the classroom.	• Teachers involved in the literacy efforts gained success related to teaching efforts.

Frameworks for Studying

Professional Communities

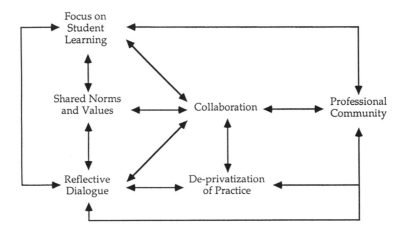

Figure D.1. Relationships Between Dimensions of Community

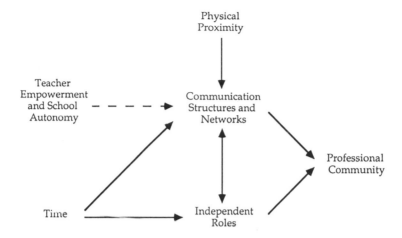

Figure D.2. Relationships Between Structural Conditions of Community

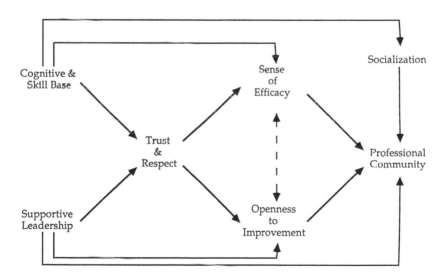

Figure D.3. Relationships Between Social and Human Resource Conditions of Community

References

Abbott, A. (1991). The order of professionalization: An empirical analysis. *Work and Occupations*, 355-384.

Angle, H. L., & Perry, J. L. (1983). Organizational commitment: Individual and organizational influences. *Work and Occupations, 10,* 123-146.

Apple, M. (1985). Teaching and "women's work": A comparative historical and ideological analysis. *Teachers College Record, 86,* 445-473.

Argyris, C., & Schön, D. (1978). *Organizational learning.* Reading, MA: Addison-Wesley.

Avineri, S., & De-Shalit, A. (Eds.). (1992). *Communitarianism and individualism.* New York: Oxford University Press.

Ball, S. J. (1987). *The micro-politics of the school: Towards a theory of school organization.* London: Methuen.

Beck, L. G. (1992). Meeting the challenge of the future: The place of a caring ethic in educational administration. *American Journal of Education, 100,* 454-496.

Beck, L. G. (1994). Cultivating a caring school community: One principal's story. In J. Murphy & K. S. Louis (Eds.), *Reshaping the principalship: Insights for transformational reform efforts* (pp. 177-202). Thousand Oaks, CA: Corwin.

Bellah, R. M., Madsen, R., Sullivan, W. M., Swidler, A., & Tipton, S. M. (1985). *Habits of the heart: Individualism and commitment in American life.* New York: Perennial Library.

Bellah, R. M., Madsen, R., Sullivan, W. M., Swidler, A., & Tipton, S. M. (1991). *The good society.* New York: Knopf.

Benveniste, G. (1988). *Professionalizing the organization.* San Francisco: Jossey-Bass.

Blase, J. (1992). *The micropolitics of effective school-based leadership: Teachers' perspectives.* Paper presented at the annual meetings of the American Educational Research Association, San Francisco.

Brief, A. P., & Motowidlo, S. J. (1986). Prosocial organizational behaviors. *Academy of Management Review, 11,* 710-725.

Brown, J. S., & Duguid, P. (1991). Organizational learning and communities of practice: Toward a unified view of working, learning, and innovation. *Organizational Science, 2,* 40-57.

Bryk, A. S. (1992). *A two year proposal to the Chicago community trust to support the center for school improvement.* Chicago: Center for School Improvement.

Bryk, A. S., & Driscoll, M. E. (1988). *The school as community: Theoretical foundations, contextual influences, and consequences for students and teachers.* Madison: Center for Effective Secondary Schools, University of Wisconsin.

Bryk, A. S., Easton, J. Q., Kerbow, D., Rollow, S. G., & Sebring, P. A. (1993). *A view from the elementary school: The state of reform in Chicago.* Chicago: Consortium on Chicago School Research.

Bryk, A. S., Lee, V., & Holland, P. (1993). *Catholic schools and the common good.* Cambridge, MA: Harvard University Press.

Bryk, A. S., & Rollow, S. G. (1992). *The Chicago experiment: Enhanced democratic participation as a lever for school improvement.* Madison: Center for the Organization and Restructuring of Schools, University of Wisconsin.

Bryk, A. S., & Rollow, S. G. (1993). *Restructuring school governance: The Chicago experience* (Issue Report No. 3). Madison: Center for the Organization and Restructuring of Schools, University of Wisconsin.

Bucher, R., & Stelling, J. (1969). Characteristics of professional organizations. *Journal of Health and Social Behavior, 10,* 3-15.

Bull, B. L., Fruehling, R. T., & Chattergy, V. (1992). *The ethics of multicultural and bilingual education.* New York: Teachers College Press.

Caldwell, B. J., & Spinks, J. M. (1992). *Leading the self-managed school.* New York: Falmer.

Carnegie Foundation for the Advancement of Teaching. (1988). *An imperiled generation: Saving urban schools.* Princeton, NJ: Author.

Center for Research on the Context of Secondary School Teaching (CRC). (1991). *Report of survey findings to Horizons high school, Wyoming, Michigan, March, 1991.* Unpublished report supplied by Dan Diedrich, director of Horizons High School.

Chicago School Reform, Public Act 85-1418. (1989). Springfield: General Assembly of the State of Illinois.

Cibulka, J. (1992). Urban education as a field of study: Problems of knowledge and power. In J. Cibulka, R. Reed, & K. Wong (Eds.), *The politics of education in the United States.* Washington, DC: Falmer.

Cibulka, J., Reed, R., & Wong, K. (Eds.). *The politics of education in the United States.* Washington, DC: Falmer.

Clift, R. T., Houston, W. R., & Pugach, M. C. (Eds.) (1990). *Encouraging reflective practice in education: An analysis of issues and programs.* New York: Teachers College Press.

Cohen, D. K. (1988). Knowledge of teaching: Plus que ça change . . . In P. W. Jackson (Ed.), *Contributing to educational change* (pp. 27-84). Berkeley, CA: McCutcheon.

Cohn, M. M., Kottkamp, R. B., McCloskey, G. N., & Provenzo, E. F. (1987). *Teachers' perspective on the problems of their profession: Implications for policymakers and practitioners.* Unpublished manuscript.

Coleman, J., & Hoffer, T. (1987) *Public and private high schools: The impact of communities.* New York: Basic Books.

Congressional Record. (1994, January 25). Message from the president of the United States (House Document 103-177). Washington, DC: Government Printing Office.

Cook, A. (1991). The high school inquiry classroom. In K. Jervis & C. Montag (Eds.), *Progressive education for 1992: Transforming practice* (pp. 149-151). New York: Teachers College Press.

Corcoran, T., Walker, L., & White, J. L. (1988). *Working in urban schools.* Washington, DC: Institute for Educational Leadership.

Corwin, R., & Louis, K. S. (1982). Organizational barriers to the utilization of research. *Administrative Science Quarterly, 27,* 623-640.

Crandall, D. P., Eiseman, J. W., & Louis, K. S. (1986). Strategic planning issues that bear in the success of school improvement efforts. *Educational Administration Quarterly, 22,* 21-53.

Crowley, B. L. (1987). *The self, the individual and the community.* Oxford, UK: Clarendon.

Darling-Hammond, L. (1984). *Beyond the commission reports: The coming crises in teaching.* Santa Monica, CA: RAND.

Darling-Hammond, L. (1987). The over-regulated curriculum and the press for teacher professionalism. *NASSP Bulletin, 71,* 22-29.

Darling-Hammond, L., & Goodwin, A. L. (1993). Progress towards professionalism in teaching. In G. Cawelti (Ed.), *Challenges and achievements of American education: The 1993 ASCD yearbook* (pp. 19-52). Alexandria, VA: Association for Supervision and Curriculum Development.

Darling-Hammond, L., & Snyder, J. (1992). Framing accountability: Creating learner-centered schools. In A. Lieberman (Ed.), *The changing contexts of teaching* (91st yearbook, pp. 11-36). New York: Teachers College Press.

Dewey, J. (1944). *Democracy and education.* New York: Free Press. (Original work published 1915)

Driscoll, M. E. (1989). *The school as community.* Unpublished doctoral dissertation, University of Chicago.

Dworkin, R. (1977). *Taking rights seriously.* Cambridge, MA: Harvard University Press.

Dworkin, R. (1989). Liberal community. *California Law Review, 77,* 479-504.

Easton, J. Q., Bryk, A. S., Driscoll, M. E., Kotsakis, J. G., Sebring, P. A., & van der Ploeg, A. J. (1991). *Charting reform: The teachers' turn.* Chicago: Consortium on Chicago School Research.

Englert, R. (1993). Understanding the urban context and conditions of practice of school administration. In P. Forsyth & M. Tallerico (Eds.), *City schools: Leading the way.* Newbury Park, CA: Corwin.

Etzioni, A. (1991). *A responsive society.* San Francisco: Jossey-Bass.

Etzioni, A. (1993). *The spirit of community: Rights, responsibilities, and the communitarian agenda.* New York: Crown.

Feldman, L. B. (1982). Sex roles and family dynamics. In F. Walsh (Ed.), *Normal family processes.* New York: Guilford Press.

Firestone, W. A., & Rosenblum, S. (1988). Building commitment in urban high schools. *Educational Evaluation and Policy Analysis, 93,* 285-299.

Ford, D. (1991). *The school principal and Chicago school reform: Principal's early perceptions of reform initiatives.* Chicago: Chicago Panel on Public School Policy and Finance.

Forsyth, P. B., & Danisiewicz, P. B. (1985). Toward a theory of professionalization. *Work and Occupations, 12,* 59-76.

Fullan, M. (1992). *Successful school improvement.* Buckingham, Philadelphia: Open University Press.

Garner, C., & Raudenbush, S. (1991). Neighborhood effects of educational attainment: A multilevel analysis. *Sociology of Education, 64,* 251-262.

Giroux, H. (1988). *Schooling and the struggle for private life.* Minneapolis: University of Minnesota Press.

Goodlad, J. (1984). *A place called school.* New York: McGraw-Hill.

Green, T. F. (1985). The formation of conscience in an age of technology. *American Journal of Education, 94,* 1-32.

Grimmett, P. P., & Crehan, E. P. (1992). The nature of collegiality in teacher development: The case of clinical supervision. In M. Fullan & A. Hargreaves (Eds.), *Teacher development and educational change* (pp. 56-85). London: Falmer.

Gutman, A. (1987). *Democratic education.* Princeton, NJ: Princeton University Press.

Hargreaves, A. (1992). *Restructuring restructuring: Postmodernity and the prospects for educational change.* Unpublished manuscript.

Hargreaves, A., & Dawe, R. (1990). Paths of professional development: Contrived collegiality, collaborative culture, and the case of peer coaching. *Teaching and Teacher Education, 6,* 227-241.

Hess, G. A. (1991). *School restructuring, Chicago style.* Newbury Park, CA: Corwin.

Hill, P., Wise, A., & Shapiro, L. (1989). *Educational progress. Cities mobilize to improve their schools.* Santa Monica, CA: RAND.

Hord, S. M., Rutherford, W. L., Huling-Austin, L., & Hall, G. E. (1987). *Taking charge of change.* Alexandria, VA: Association for Supervision and Curriculum Development.

Johnson, S. M. (1990). *Teachers at work: Achieving success in our schools.* New York: Basic Books.

Kanter, R. M. (1983). *The change masters: Innovation for productivity in the American corporation.* New York: Simon & Schuster.

Kymlicka, W. (1991). *Contemporary political philosophy: An introduction.* Oxford, UK: Clarendon.

Lee, V., Dedrick, R., & Smith, J. (1991). The effect of social organization on teachers' efficacy and satisfaction. *Sociology of Education, 64,* 190-208.

Lee, V., & Smith, J. (1993). Effects of school restructuring on the achievement and engagement of middle school students. *Sociology of Education, 66,* 164-187.

Leithwood, K. (1993, October). *Transformational leadership and organizational change.* Invited address before the University Council of Educational Administration, Houston.

Lieberman, A., Saxl, E. R., & Miles, M. B. (1988). Teacher leadership: Ideology and practice. In A. Lieberman (Ed.), *Building a professional culture in schools* (pp. 148-166). New York: Teachers College Press.

Liebowitz, S. E. (1991). *On becoming a reflective practitioner.* Paper presented at the annual meeting of the American Association for Adult and Continuing Education, Montreal.

Little, J. W. (1990). The persistence of privacy: Autonomy and initiative in teachers' professional relations. *Teachers College Record, 91,* 509-536.

Litwak, E. (1961). Models of bureaucracy which permit conflict. *American Journal of Sociology, 67,* 177-185.

Lortie, D. C. (1975). *Schoolteacher: A sociological study.* Chicago: University of Chicago Press.

Louis, K. S. (1991a). Social and community values and the quality of teachers' work life. In M. McLaughlin, J. Talbert, & N. Bascia (Eds.), *The context of teachers' work in secondary schools.* New York: Teachers College Press.

Louis, K. S. (1991b). *Teacher commitment, sense of efficacy and quality of work life: Results from a survey.* Paper delivered at the annual meeting of the American Educational Research Association, San Francisco.

Louis, K. S. (1992a). Comparative perspectives on dissemination and knowledge use policies: Supporting school improvement. *Knowledge, 13,* 287-304.

Louis, K. S. (1992b). Restructuring and the problem of teachers' work. In A. Lieberman (Ed.) *The changing contexts of teaching* (91st yearbook, pp. 138-156). Chicago: National Society for the Study of Education.

Louis, K. S. (1994, September 14). *Principal recruitment, preparation and development: This system is broken!* Invited address to the annual meeting of the Minnesota Association of Elementary School Principals, St. Cloud, MN.

Louis, K. S. (in press). Improving urban and disadvantaged schools: Dissemination and utilization perspectives. *Knowledge and Policy.*

Louis, K. S., & King, J. A. (1993). Professional cultures in reforming schools: Does the myth of Sisyphus apply? In J. Murphy (Ed.), *Restructuring schooling: Learning from ongoing efforts.* Newbury Park, CA: Corwin.

Louis, K. S., Marks, H., & Kruse, S. D. (1994, April). *Teachers' professional community in restructuring schools.* Paper presented at the annual meetings of the American Educational Research Association, New Orleans.

Louis, K. S., & Miles, M. (1990). *Improving the urban high school: What works and why.* New York: Teacher's College Press.

Louis, K. S., Rosenblum, S., & Molitor, J. (1981). *Strategies for knowledge use and school improvement.* Washington, DC: National Institute of Education.

Louis, K. S., & Smith, B. (1992). Student engagement and achievement in American secondary schools. In F. Newmann (Ed.), *Cultivating teacher engagement: Breaking the iron law of social class* (pp. 119-152). New York: Teachers College Press.

MacIntyre, A. (1981). *After virtue: A study in moral theory.* South Bend, IN: University of Notre Dame Press.

Malen, B., Ogawa, R. T., & Kranz, J. (1991). What do we know about school-based management? A case study of the literature—a call for research. In W. H. Clune & J. F. Witte (Eds.), *Choice and control in American education: Vol. 2. The practice of choice, decentralization and school restructuring* (pp. 289-342). New York: Falmer.

March, J., & Olsen, J. (1976). *Ambiguity and choice in organizations.* Oslo, Norway: Universitetsforlaget.

McDonnell, L., & Pascal, A. (1979). *Organized teachers in American schools.* Santa Monica, CA: RAND.

McGoldrick, M., & Carter, E. A. (1982). *The family life cycle. Normal family processes.* New York: Guilford Press.

McLaughlin, M. (in press). Strategic sites for teachers' professional development. In P. P. Grimmett, & J. P. Neufeld (Eds.), *The struggle for authenticity: Teacher development in a changing educational context.* New York: Teachers College Press.

McLaughlin, M. W. (1992). *What matters most in teachers' workplace context?* (CRC-P92-139). Washington, DC: Office of Educational Research and Improvement.

Meyer, J., & Rowan, B. (1983). The structure of educational organizations. In J. V. Baldridge & T. Deal (Eds.), *Dynamics of organizational change in education.* Berkeley, CA: McCutcheon.

Miles, M. B., & Huberman, A. M. (1984). *Qualitative data analysis: A sourcebook of new methods.* London: Sage.

Miller, G. (1985). Work, rituals structures, and the legitimation of alternative communities. *Work and Occupations, 12,* 3-22.

Minow, M. (1990). *Making all the difference: Inclusion, exclusion, and American law.* Ithaca: Cornell University Press.

Mitchell, T. R. (1993). Leadership, values and accountability. In M. M. Chemers & R. Ayman (Eds.), *Leadership theory and research: Perspectives and directions.* San Diego: Academic Press.

Mohrman, S., & Cummings, T. (1989). *Self-designing organizationa: Learning how to create high performance.* Reading, MA: Addison-Wesley.

Moore, D. R. (1992). *The case for parent and community involvement. Empowering teachers and parents: School restructuring through the eyes of anthropologists.* New York: Bergin & Garvey.

Moultrie, L. (1992). *The school reform left behind.* Unpublished master's thesis, University of Chicago.

Murphy, J. (1994). Transformational change and the evolving role of the principal. In J. Murphy & K. S. Louis (Eds.), *Reshaping the principalship: Insights for transformational reform efforts* (pp. 20-56). Thousand Oaks, CA: Corwin.

Murphy, J., & Louis, K. S. (Eds.). (1994). *Reshaping the principalship: Insights for transformational reform efforts.* Thousand Oaks, CA: Corwin.

Natriello, G., Pallas, A., & McDill, E. (1990). *Schooling disadvantaged children: Racing against catastrophe.* New York: Teachers College Press.

Newmann, F. M. (1991a). Linking restructuring to authentic student achievement. *Phi Delta Kappan, 72,* 458-463.

Newmann, F. M. (1991b). *What is a "restructured" school? A framework to clarify means and ends* (pp. 3-7+). Madison, WI: Center on Organization of Restructuring of Schools, Issues in Restructuring Schools.

Newmann, F. M., & Rutter, R. A. (1987). *Teachers' sense of efficacy and community as critical targets for school improvement.* Madison: University of Wisconsin Center for the Study of Effective Secondary Schools.

Noddings, N. (1984). *Caring: A feminine approach to ethics and moral education.* Berkeley: University of California Press.

Osterman, K. F. (1990). Reflective practice: A new agenda for education. *Education and Urban Society, 22,* 133-152.

Osterman, K. F. (1993). Reflective practice: Linking professional development and school reform. *Planning and Changing, 22,* 208-217.

Pallas, A., Natriello, G., & McDill, E. (1989, June-July). The changing nature of the disadvantaged population: Current dimensions and future trends. *Educational Researcher,* 16-22.

Perrow, C. (1972). *Complex organizations: A critical essay.* New York: Random House.

Peterson, P. (1985). *The politics of school reform: 1870–1940.* Chicago: University of Chicago Press.

Raywid, M. (1988). Community and schools: A prolegomenon. *Teachers College Record, 90,* 197-210.

Raywid, M. (1993). Finding time for collaboration. *Educational Leadership, 51,* 30-34.

Reese, W. (1986). *Power and the promise of school reform: Grassroots movements during the progressive era.* Boston: Routledge & Kegan Paul.

Rosenblum, S., & Louis, K. S. (1981). *Stability and change.* New York: Praeger.

Rosenblum, S., Louis, K. S., & Rossmiller, R. (1994). School leadership and teacher quality of work life in restructuring schools. In J. Murphy & K. S. Louis (Eds.), *Reshaping the principalship: Insights from transformational reform efforts.* Thousand Oaks, CA: Corwin.

Rosenholz, S. (1989). *Teachers' workplace: The social organization of schools.* New York: Longman.

Rowan, B. (1994). Comparing teachers' work with other occupations: Notes on the professional status of teaching. *Educational Researcher, 23,* 4-18.

Sandel, M. J. (1988, February 22). Democrats and community. *The New Republic,* pp. 20-23.

Sargent, J., & Miller, G. (1971). Some differences in certain behaviors of autocratic and democratic leaders. *Journal of Communication, 21,* 240-260.

Schein, E. H. (1985). *Organizational culture and leadership: A dynamic view.* San Francisco: Jossey-Bass.

Schön, D. A. (1982). *The reflective practitioner: How professionals think in action.* London: Temple Smith.

Sergiovanni, T. J. (1994). *Building community in schools.* San Francisco: Jossey-Bass.

Sirotnik, K. (1989). In T. Sergiovanni & J. H. Moore (Eds.), *Schooling for tomorrow: Directing reforms to issues that count* (pp. 89-113). Boston: Allyn & Bacon.

Siskin, L. (1991). Departments as different worlds: Subject subcultures in secondary schools. *Educational Administration Quarterly, 27,* 134-160.

Siskin, L. (in press). Is the school the unit of change?: Internal and external contexts of restructuring. In P. P. Grimett & J. P. Neufeld (Eds.), *The struggle for authenticity: Teacher development in a changing educational context.* New York: Teachers College Press.

Staessens, K. (1991, April). *The professional culture of innovating primary schools: Nine case studies.* Paper presented at the annual meetings of the American Educational Research Association, Chicago.

Strike, K. A. (1993). Professionalism, democracy, and discursive communities: Normative reflections on restructuring. *American Educational Research Journal, 30,* 255-275.

Talbert, J., McLaughlin, M., & Rowan, B. (in press). *Understanding context effects on secondary school teaching* New York: Teachers College Press.

Tomkins, A. (1895). *School management*. Boston: Ginn & Co.

Tönnies, F. (1957). *Gemeinschaft und gesellschaft* [Community and society] (C. P. Loomis, Ed. & Trans.). New York: HarperCollins. (Original work published 1887)

Vandenberghe, R., & Staessens, K. (1991, April). *Vision as a core component of school culture*. Paper presented at the annual meetings of the American Educational Research Association, Chicago.

Van Maanen, J., & Barley, S. R. (1984). Occupational communities: Culture and control in organizations. *Research in Organizational Behavior, 6,* 287-365.

Van Maanen, J., & Schein, E. H. (1979). Toward a theory of organizational socialization. In B. Staw (Ed.), *Research in organizational behavior.* Greenwich, CT: JAI Press.

Van Velzen, W. G., Miles, M. B., Ekholm, M., Hameyer, U., & Robin, D. (1985). *Making school improvement work: A conceptual guide to practice.* ACC Leuven: Amersfoort.

Wahlberg, H. (1989). District size and learning. *Education and Urban Society, 21,* 154-163.

Warren, D. (Ed.). (1989). *American teachers: History of a profession at work.* New York: Macmillan.

Wilson, W. J. (1987). *The truly disadvantaged: The inner city, the underclass, and public policy.* Chicago: University of Chicago Press.

Yin, R. (1984). *Case study research: Design and method.* Beverly Hills, CA: Sage.

Young, I. M. (1986). The ideal of community and the politics of difference. *Social Theory and Practice, 12,* 1-26.

Young, I. M. (1990). *Justice and the politics of difference.* Princeton, NJ: Princeton University Press.

Zald, M. (1970). *Occupations and organizations in American society.* Chicago: Markham.

Zeichner, K. M., & Tabachnick, B. R. (1991). Reflections on reflective teaching. In K. M. Zeichner & B. R. Tabachnick (Eds.), *Issues and practices in inquiry oriented teacher education* (pp. 1 -21). London: Falmer.

Additional Reading

Apple, M. (1991, February). The politics of curriculum and teaching. *NASSP Bulletin,* 39-50.

Arnet, R. C. (1986). *Communication and community.* Carbondale & Edwardsville: Southern Illinois University Press.

Ascher, C. (1989). School-college collaborations: A strategy for helping low-income minorities. *The Urban Review, 21,* 181-191.

Ball, S. J., & Goodson, I. F. (1985). *Teachers' lives and careers.* London: Falmer.

Bank, A., & Williams, R. C. (Eds.). (1987). *Information systems and school improvement: Inventing the future.* New York: Teachers College Press.

Bryk, A. S. (1992). *School reform Chicago style.* Paper presented at the annual meetings of the American Educational Research Association, San Francisco.

Carr, W., & Kemmis, S. (1986). *Becoming critical: Education, knowledge and action research.* London: Falmer.

Daft, R., & Huber, G. (1987). How organizations learn. In N. Di-Tomaso & S. Bacharach (Eds.), *Research in the sociology of organizations.* Greenwich, CT: JAI Press.

Darling-Hammond, L. (1990). Instructional policy into practice: The power of the bottom over the top. *Educational Evaluation and Policy Analysis, 12,* 233-241.

Devaney, K., & Sykes, G. (1988). Making the case for professionalism. In A. Lieberman (Ed.), *Building a professional culture in schools* (pp. 3-22). New York: Teachers College Press.

Firestone, W. A., & Bader, B. D. (1992). *Redesigning teaching: Professionalism or bureaucracy?* Albany: State University of New York Press.

Firestone, W. A., & Pennell, J .R. (1992). *Differential incentive policies, Working conditions, and teacher commitment* (OERI -R117G10007). Washington, DC: Office of Educational Research and Improvement.

Fullan, M. (1993). Innovation, reform, and restructuring strategies. In G. Cawelti (Ed.), *Challenges and achievements of American education: 1993 yearbook of the association for supervision and curriculum development* (pp. 116-133). Alexandria, VA: Association for Supervision and Curriculum Development.

Fullan, M., Miles, M., & Taylor, G. (1980). Organization development in schools: The state of the art. *Review of Educational Research, 50,* 121-183.

Gans, H. (1962). *The urban villagers.* New York: Free Press.

Goldring, E. (1990). The district context and principals' sentiments toward parents. *Urban Education, 24,* 391-403.

Hargreaves, A. (1988). Teaching quality: A sociological analysis. *Journal of Curriculum Studies, 20,* 211-231.

Hargreaves, A., & Macmillan, R. (1992). *Balkanized secondary schools and the malaise of modernity.* Paper presented at the annual meetings of the American Educational Research Association, San Francisco.

Harkavy, I., & Puckett, J. (1992). Universities and the inner cities. *Planning for Higher Education, 20,* 27-33.

Heydebrand, W. V. (1989). New organizational forms. *Work and Occupations, 16,* 323-357.

Huberman, M. (1990). Linkage between researchers and practitioners: A qualitative study. *American Educational Research Journal, 27,* 363-391.

Katz, J., & Gartner, W. B. (1988). Properties of emerging organizations. *Academy of Management Review, 13,* 429-440.

Klein, S. (1992). A framework for redesigning an R&D based national educational dissemination system in the United States. *Knowledge, 13,* 256-286.

Levitt, B., & March, J. G. (1988). Organizational learning. *Annual Review of Sociology, 14,* 319-340.

Lieberman, A., & McLaughlin, M. W. (1992). Networks for educational change: Powerful and problematic. *Phi Delta Kappan, 73,* 673-677.

Lieberman, A., & Miller, L. (1992). *Teachers their world and their work: Implications for school improvement.* New York: Teachers College Press.

Louis, K. S. (1994). Beyond managed change: Rethinking how schools change. *School Effectiveness and School Improvement, 5,* 2-24.

Louis, K. S., & Dentler, R. A. (1988). Knowledge use and school improvement. *Curriculum Inquiry, 18,* 32-62.

Lytle, J. (1990). Reforming urban education: A review of recent reports and legislation. *The Urban Review, 22,* 199-220.

Makay, J. J., & Brown, W. R. (1972). *The rhetorical dialogue.* Dubuque, IA: William C. Brown.

Mann, D. (1986). Authority and school improvement: An essay on little king leadership. *Teachers College Record, 88,* 41-52.

O'Conner, T. (1993). Looking back to forward. *Democracy and Education, 8,* 9-16.

Patton, M. Q. (1980). *Qualitative evaluation methods.* Beverly Hills, CA: Sage.

Patton, M. Q. (1988). Extension's future: Beyond technology transfer. *Knowledge, 9,* 476-491.

Petri, M., & Burkhardt, G. (1988). *CaMePe: An organizational and educational systems approach to secondary school development.* Andover: The Regional Laboratory for Educational Improvement of the Northeast and Islands in association with Algemeen Pedagogisch Studiecentrum.

Rogers, E. (1982). *Diffusion of innovations.* New York: Free Press.

Rollow, S. G., & Bryk, A. S. (1993). *Grounding a theory of school micropolitics: Lessons from Chicago school reform.* Madison: Center for the Organization and Restructuring of Schools, University of Wisconsin.

Rosenholz, S. (1985). Effective schools: Interpreting the evidence. *American Journal of Education, 93,* 352-388.

Rowan, B. (1991, April). *The shape of professional communities in schools.* Paper presented at the annual meetings of the American Educational Research Association, Chicago.

Ruffin, S. (1989, May). Improving urban communities and their schools: A national emergency. *NASSP Bulletin,* 61-70.

Schön, D. A. (1987). *Educating the reflective practitioner.* San Francisco: Jossey-Bass.

Smylie, M. A., & Denny, J. W. (1990). Teacher leadership: Tensions and ambiguities in organizational perspective. *Educational Administration Quarterly, 26,* 235-259.

Stevenson, R. B. (1993). Critically reflective inquiry and administrator preparation: Problems and possibilities. *Educational Policy, 7,* 96-113.

Sykes, G. (1991). In defense of teacher professionalism as a policy choice. *Educational Policy, 5,* 137-149.

Talbert, J. E. (1986). The staging of teachers' careers: An institutional perspective. *Work and Occupations, 13,* 421-443.

Talbert, J. E. (1991, April). *Boundaries of teachers' professional communities in U.S. high schools.* Paper presented at the annual meetings of the American Educational Research Association, Chicago.

Talbert, J. E., & McLaughlin, M. W. (1993, March). *Understanding teaching in context* (CRC-P92-142). Washington, DC: Office of Educational Research and Improvement, Center for Research on the Context of Secondary School Teaching.

Turner, P. (1993). *Toward establishing professional development schools: Faculty perceptions and colleges and schools of education in the Holmes Group.* Unpublished doctoral dissertation, University of Minnesota.

Wahlstrom, K., & Louis, K. S. (1993). Adoption revisited: Decision-making and school district policy. In S. Bachrach & R. Ogawa (Eds.), *Advances in research and theory of school management and educational policy* (Vol. 1, pp. 61-119). Greenwich, CT: JAI Press.

Wehlage, G. (1992). Restructuring urban schools: The new futures experiment. *American Educational Research Journal, 29,* 51-93.

Welker, R. (1992). *The teacher as expert: A theoretical and historical examination.* Albany: State University of New York Press.

Weick, K. (1978). Educational organizations as loosely coupled systems. *Administrative Science Quarterly, 21,* 1-19.

Weiss, C. (1993). *Structuring the field: Designing and teaching a course in knowledge use.* Paper presented at the annual meetings of the American Educational Research Association, Atlanta.

White, J., & Wehlage, G. (1994) *Community collaboration: If it is such a good idea, why is it so hard to do?* Madison: Center for the Organization and Restructuring of Schools, University of Wisconsin.

Wise, A. E., & Darling-Hammond, L. (1985). Teacher evaluation and teacher professionalism. *Educational Leadership, 42,* 28-33.

Author Index